BILL JOHNSON

LIVING IN THE
MIRACULOUS EVERY DAY

When
Heaven
— INVADES —
your
LIFE

A 365-DAY DEVOTIONAL

DESTINY IMAGE® PUBLISHERS, INC.
PO Box 310, Shippensburg, PA 17257-0310
"Publishing cutting-edge prophetic resources to supernaturally empower the body of Christ"

In cooperation with
Bethel Church, 933 College View Dr., Redding, California, 96003.
www.bethel.com

This book and all other Destiny Image and Destiny Image Fiction books are available at Christian bookstores and distributors worldwide.

For more information on foreign distributors, call 717-532-3040.
Or reach us on the Internet: www.destinyimage.com

ISBN 13 TP: 978-0-7684-7462-6
ISBN 13 EBook: 978-0-7684-7463-3
ISBN 13 HC: 978-0-7684-7464-0

For Worldwide Distribution.
1 2 3 4 5 6 / 26 25 24 23

MEDICAL DISCLAIMER

Disclaimer: This book contains information that is intended to help the readers be better informed in dealing with change and challenges in life. It is presented as general advice using the author's experience and best judgment but is in no way to be considered a substitute for necessary care provided by a physician or other medical professional.

Introduction

ETERNITY IS WRITTEN INTO our spiritual DNA. Living aware of that reality is both natural and necessary for those who are born again. The writer of Ecclesiastes says in chapter 3, verse 11 that He has put eternity in our hearts. This connection with the reality of heaven is at the very foundation of who we are as believers. We've been given access to God's Kingdom—more real than anything we see in front of us—through Jesus. That Kingdom is the present-tense reality of the King's domain, to be realized in the most broken conditions of humanity. He is the Person of heaven. Abiding in Christ is actually a foretaste of eternity, as there is nothing that exists in heaven that is separate from Him. Hosting Him is the great privilege of our lives.

We have been created, at our most fundamental level, to live aware of His presence. It's not something we have to strive for; it's the most natural thing in the world. He is the predominant feature of our lives, and His presence never grows stale. Christian routine, specific worship songs, or expressions of faith can all become familiar, but we can never outgrow the freshness of the presence of God. The main focus of the enemy is to do whatever he can—through manipulation, accusation, division—to distract us from the gift of His presence. He would love nothing more than to have us reduce our lives to religious routine and lose sight of God's true design for us.

Jesus said, *"If you abide in Me, and My words abide in you, you will ask what you desire, and it shall be done for you"* (John 15:7). He is telling us that if we live in the felt realization of His presence and we intentionally embrace what He has to say, treasuring His Word in our souls, we can ask for anything we desire, and it will be done for us. God isn't condoning self-centered Christianity. He isn't setting Himself up to be some sort of vending machine through which, if we read our Bibles and pray enough, we'll get what we want. He is telling us something vital, though. Jesus is inviting us to immerse ourselves into a journey where our hearts begin to beat so consistently with His that He can trust our dreams. And it is from that place, as a co-laborer, that we are called to impact the world, releasing heaven onto the earth.

The Gospel of John describes a moment when Jesus is standing with Nicodemus, attempting to describe heavenly realities that have no earthly correlation. He said, *"No one has ascended to heaven but He who came down from heaven, that is, the Son of Man who is in heaven"* (John 3:13). He is describing Himself. He is the One who came down from heaven and was ascending into heaven, while on earth. And He was, at that moment, in heaven. No wonder Nicodemus was confused! Jesus was portraying the ascended lifestyle that would be available to all believers. He lived acutely aware of His connection to eternity. Paul would later find language to describe this: We are seated "in heavenly places" (Ephesians 2:6).

If we think that our present reality is all there is, we've been deceived. We've been invited into the most vibrant, powerful relationship with the Father. We've been given all the authority needed to release the reality of His world into ours: on earth as it is in heaven. We cannot allow the magnitude of this truth to shrivel down to a doctrine without an experience. Living aware of God's presence, abiding in Him, means living from the place of absolute, triumphant victory. This is the normal Christian life.

Jesus was setting a standard for us in everything He did. He was and is eternally God, but He chose to live with human limitations, modeling a lifestyle we could actually follow. He taught His disciples about abiding in Him because it was the key to His ascended lifestyle. He stayed constantly aware of and connected to the Father, only saying what He was saying, and only doing what He was doing. Being seated in heavenly places does not mean whipping ourselves into an emotional frenzy so we can imagine heaven. Living from heaven to earth is all about a relationship with our heavenly Father through the Holy Spirit. Living conscious of His felt presence enables us to see the world through His eyes.

My wife, Beni, was so good at that. Brian and Jenn's first baby, Haley, was in very serious condition soon after she was born. Our whole family was gathered in the hospital waiting room when we got the troubling news, and Beni quickly separated herself to pray. She went off to the side and asked, "Father, what are we doing?" Fear was creeping in, and she knew that we all needed to anchor ourselves in God's perspective. She prayed, got a very clear word, and partnered with what the Lord was doing. Within a very short period of time, Haley had completely turned around and was a perfect, healthy baby.

Prayer was never meant to look like merely begging God to change a situation. Prayer is about joining with the Father, seeing His heart, and making the decrees necessary to bring about His will on the earth. I ache to see the realization of what Jesus taught. I long to see the world through His eyes. I want to look at my city and feel what He has in His heart. I want to become so united with Him that He can trust me to ask anything. I'm not interested in getting my way; that's terrifying. But I am interested in the felt realization of His presence released into the world. My desire is to host His presence and carry His Word in my heart to the extent that, when I speak, heaven will invade every situation. This is what we have been destined for—to live the reality of Christ on the earth.

My prayer, as you read through this devotional, is that you would encounter the living, transformative presence of God. May your hunger grow for the reality of eternity. May every aspect of your being—your physical senses, your intellectual capacity, your emotional perception—become more and more sensitive to His Spirit. May we all become more aware of heaven, how it functions, and what it means to live an ascended lifestyle. And may we release heaven on the earth through our relationship with the Father.

JANUARY

The Normal Christian Life

The miraculous is closer to the normal Christian life than what the Church normally experiences.

WE HAVE BEEN DESIGNED to see heaven invade every situation. A lack of miracles isn't because it is not in God's will for us. The problem exists between our ears. As a result, a transformation—a renewing of the mind—is needed, and it's only possible through a work of the Holy Spirit that typically comes upon desperate people.

We are ordinary people who serve an extravagant Father. Miracles are not dependent on us becoming spiritually powerful people; they're about Jesus. Our job is to simply make room for God, believing Him to be good 100 percent of the time. We are called to step out in faith and expectation, but God is the one who invades disease and destruction with His power to establish a testimony for His glory.

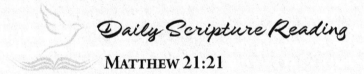

Daily Scripture Reading
MATTHEW 21:21

Prayer

Renew my mind, Holy Spirit. Help me to be consistently aware of Your goodness, expecting Your glory to invade every situation.

Our mandate is simple: Raise up a generation that can openly display the raw power of God.

JESUS COULD NOT HEAL the sick. Neither could He deliver the tormented from demons or raise the dead. To believe otherwise is to ignore what He said about Himself, and more importantly, to miss the purpose of His self-imposed restriction to live as a man.

Jesus Christ said of Himself, *"The Son can do nothing"* (John 5:19). In the Greek language that word nothing has a unique meaning—it means nothing, just like it does in English! He had no supernatural capabilities whatsoever! While He is 100 percent God, He chose to live with the same limitations that man would face once He was redeemed. He made that point over and over again. Jesus became the model for all who would embrace the invitation to invade the impossible in His name.

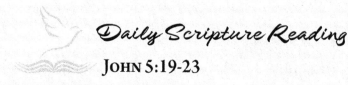

Daily Scripture Reading
JOHN 5:19-23

Prayer

Help me, Father, to see impossible situations through Your eyes. I want to view every area of need as an opportunity to see Your Kingdom come!

The gospel of the Kingdom is increasing.

JESUS PERFORMED MIRACLES, WONDERS, and signs, as a man in right relationship to God…not as God. If He performed miracles because He was God, then they would be unattainable for us. But if He did them as a man, we are responsible to pursue His lifestyle. Recapturing this simple truth changes everything. And, it makes possible a full restoration of the ministry of Jesus in His Church.

Jesus lived perfectly. He had no sin to separate Him from the Father. He was completely dependent on the power of the Holy Spirit working through Him. None of us have lived perfectly. We have all been marked by sin, but we have been cleansed by the blood of Jesus. Through His sacrifice, He has successfully dealt with the power and effect of sin for all who believe. Nothing now separates us from the Father. There remains only one unsettled issue: How dependent on the Holy Spirit are we willing to live?

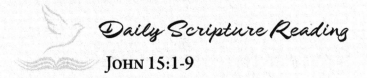

Daily Scripture Reading
JOHN 15:1-9

Prayer

Holy Spirit, I open my heart to You today. I want to live fully dependent on Your presence and power. Help me to live as Jesus did.

God's original design has always been for us to expand His Kingdom.

DISCOVERING GOD'S ORIGINAL COMMISSION and purpose for mankind can help to fortify our resolve to a life of history-changing significance. To find that truth we must go back to the beginning. Man was created in the image of God and placed into the Father's ultimate expression of beauty and peace: The Garden of Eden. Outside of that garden it was a different story. It was without the order and blessing contained within and was in great need of the touch of God's delegated one—Adam.

Adam and Eve were placed in the garden with a mission. God said, *"Be fruitful and multiply; fill the earth and subdue it"* (Genesis 1:28). It was God's intention that as they bore more children, who also lived under God's rule, they would be extending the boundaries of His garden (His government) through the simplicity of their devotion to Him. The greater the number of people in right relationship to God, the greater the impact of their leadership. This process was to continue until the entire earth was covered with the glorious rule of God through man.

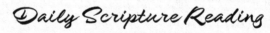

Daily Scripture Reading

GENESIS 1:26-31

Prayer

>*Show me, Father, an area of my life where You would have me increase and multiply. What area of my life are You breathing on today? I want to partner with Your expanding Kingdom.*

The backbone of Kingdom authority and power is found in the commission.

SATAN HAD REBELLED AND had been cast out of heaven, and with him a portion of the fallen angels took dominion of the earth. It's obvious why the rest of the planet needed to be subdued—it was under the influence of darkness (Genesis 1:2). God could have destroyed the devil and his host with a word, but instead He chose to defeat darkness through His delegated authority—those made in His image who were lovers of God by choice.

The Sovereign One placed us—Adam's children—in charge of planet Earth. *"The heaven, even the heavens, are the LORD'S; but the earth He has given to the children of men"* (Psalm 115:16). This highest of honors was chosen because love always chooses the best. That is the beginning of the romance of our creation…created in His image, for intimacy, that dominion might be expressed through love.

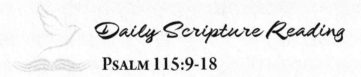

Daily Scripture Reading
PSALM 115:9-18

Prayer

You created me for intimacy with You, Father. Fill me with Your love so that I might pour it out to the world around me.

Satan is empowered through man's agreement.

IT IS FROM THE revelation of God's love for us that we are to learn to walk as His ambassadors, thus defeating the "Prince of this world." The stage was set for all of darkness to fall as man exercised His godly influence over creation. But instead, man fell.

Satan didn't come into the Garden of Eden violently and take possession of Adam and Eve. He couldn't! Why? He had no dominion there. Dominion empowers. And since man was given the keys of dominion over the planet, the devil would have to get his authority from them. The suggestion to eat the forbidden fruit was simply the devil's effort to get Adam and Eve to agree with him in opposition to God, thus empowering him. Through that agreement he is enabled to kill, steal, and destroy.

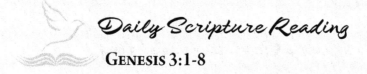

Daily Scripture Reading

GENESIS 3:1-8

Prayer

Holy Spirit, show me any area of my life where I have allowed discouragement, bitterness, or shame to empower the enemy in my life. I am a child of the King; I take back my God-given dominion today!

God's plan for man to rule never ceased.

MANKIND'S AUTHORITY TO RULE was forfeited when Adam ate the forbidden fruit. Paul said, *"You are that one's slaves whom you obey"* (Romans 6:16). In that one act mankind became the slave and possession of the Evil One. All that Adam owned, including the title deed to the planet with its corresponding position of rule, became part of the devil's spoil.

God's predetermined plan of redemption immediately kicked into play, *"I will put enmity between you and the woman, and between your seed and her Seed; He shall bruise your head, and you shall bruise His heel"* (Genesis 3:15). Jesus would come to reclaim all that was lost.

Jesus came to bear man's penalty for sin and recapture what had been lost. Luke 19:10 says that Jesus came *"to seek and to save that which was lost."* Not only was mankind lost to sin, his dominion over planet earth was also lost. Jesus came to recapture both.

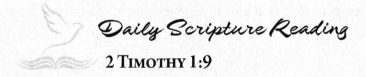

Daily Scripture Reading
2 TIMOTHY 1:9

Prayer

None of the missteps I've taken in my life could ever derail Your plan for redemption. Thank You, Lord, for being bigger than any of my mistakes.

We are on a quest for the King and His Kingdom.

SATAN TRIED TO RUIN God's plan for redemption at the end of Jesus' 40-day fast. The devil knew he wasn't worthy of Jesus' worship, but he also knew that Jesus had come to reclaim the authority that man had given away. Satan said to Him, *"All this authority I will give You, and their glory; for this has been delivered to me, and I give it to whomever I wish. Therefore, if You will worship before me, all will be Yours"* (Luke 4:6-7).

Notice the phrase *"for this has been delivered to me."* Satan could not steal it. It had been relinquished when Adam abandoned God's rule. It was as though satan was saying to Jesus, "I know what You came for. You know what I want. Worship me and I'll give You back the keys." In effect, satan offered Jesus a shortcut to His goal of recapturing the keys of authority that man lost through sin. Jesus said "no" to the shortcut and refused to give him any honor. (It was this same desire for worship that caused satan's fall from heaven in the first place.) (See Isaiah 14:12.) Jesus held His course, for He had come to die.

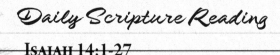

Daily Scripture Reading

ISAIAH 14:1-27

Prayer

I will give You all of my worship, God. I will give You all of my praise. Thank You for Your plan of redemption; thank You for sending Your Son to die in my place and reclaim the keys of authority.

In redeeming man, Jesus retrieved what man had given away.

THE FATHER WANTED SATAN defeated by man…one made in His image. Jesus, who would shed His blood to redeem mankind, emptied Himself of His rights as God and took upon Himself the limitations of man. Satan was defeated by a man—the Son of Man, who was rightly related to God.

Now, as people receive the work of Christ on the cross for salvation, they become grafted into that victory. Jesus defeated the devil with His sinless life, defeated him in His death by paying for our sins with His blood, and again, in the resurrection, rising triumphant with the keys of death and hell. We are no longer under the weight of sin and sickness. We are seated in heavenly places with Christ.

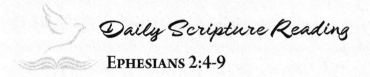

Daily Scripture Reading

EPHESIANS 2:4-9

Prayer

Thank You, Jesus, for Your unfathomable sacrifice. Thank You for all You did at the cross. Help me to live fully from the place of victory.

We will no longer make up excuses for powerlessness, because powerlessness is inexcusable.

FROM THE THRONE OF triumph Jesus declared, *"All authority has been given to Me in heaven and on earth. Go therefore…"* (Matthew 28:18-19). In other words: I got all of the authority back. Now go use it and reclaim mankind. In this passage Jesus fulfills the promise He made to the disciples when He said, *"I will give you the keys of the kingdom of heaven"* (Matthew 16:19).

The original plan was never aborted; it was fully realized once and for all in the resurrection and ascension of Jesus. We were then to be completely restored to His plan of ruling as a people made in His image. And as such we would learn how to enforce the victory obtained at Calvary: *"The God of peace will soon crush Satan under your feet"* (Romans 16:20 NIV).

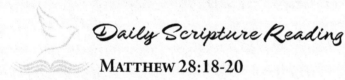

Daily Scripture Reading
MATTHEW 28:18-20

Prayer

I don't want to live as if You never came to earth, Jesus. I want to live with the awareness of my part in Your plan. I have been made in the image of God!

It is abnormal for a Christian not to have an appetite for the impossible.

WE WERE BORN TO rule—rule over creation, over darkness—to plunder hell and establish the rule of Jesus wherever we go by preaching the gospel of the Kingdom. Kingdom means: King's domain. In the original purpose of God, mankind ruled over creation.

Now that sin has entered the world, creation has been infected by darkness, namely: disease, sickness, afflicting spirits, poverty, natural disasters, demonic influence, etc. Our rule is still over creation, but now it is focused on exposing and undoing the works of the devil. We are to give what we have received to reach that end.

If I truly receive power from an encounter with the God of power, I am equipped to give it away. The invasion of God into impossible situations comes through a people who have received power from on high and learn to release it into the circumstances of life.

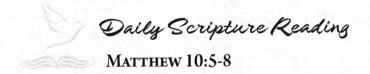

Daily Scripture Reading

MATTHEW 10:5-8

Prayer

God, I need You; I'm hungry for more of You. Fill me with Your presence so that I might overflow onto everyone around me.

It has been written into our spiritual DNA to invade the impossible in the name of Jesus.

THE GOSPEL OF SALVATION is to touch the whole man: spirit, soul, and body. John G. Lake called this a Triune Salvation. A study on the word *evil* confirms the intended reach of His redemption. That word is found in Matthew 6:13 (KJV), *"Deliver us from evil."* The word *evil* represents the entire curse of sin upon man. *Poneros*, the Greek word for *evil*, came from the word *ponos*, meaning "pain." And that word came from the root word *penes,* meaning "poor."

Look at it: evil-sin, pain-sickness, and poor-poverty. Jesus destroyed the power of sin, sickness, and poverty through His redemptive work on the cross. In Adam and Eve's commission to subdue the earth, they were without sickness, poverty, and sin. Now that we are restored to His original purpose, should we expect anything less? After all, this is called the better covenant!

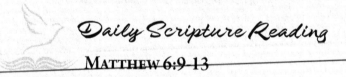

Daily Scripture Reading
MATTHEW 6:9-13

Prayer

I'm done putting limitations on the reach of Your redemption, Jesus. I come to You today filled with expectation for every impossibility in my life to bow to You name!

Let our lives reveal the King!

WE WERE GIVEN THE keys to the Kingdom (see Matthew 16:19)—which in part is the authority to trample over all the powers of hell. (See Luke 10:19.) There is a unique application of this principle found in the phrase "key of David" (see Isaiah 22:22; Revelation 3:7), which is mentioned in both Revelation and Isaiah.

Ungers' Bible Dictionary states, "The power of the keys consisted not only in the supervision of the royal chambers, but also in deciding who was and who was not to be received into the King's service." All that the Father has is ours through Christ. His entire treasure house of resources, His royal chambers, is at our disposal in order to fulfill His commission. But the more sobering part of this illustration is found in controlling who gets in to see the King. Isn't that what we do with this gospel?

When we declare it, we give opportunity for people to come to the King to be saved. When we are silent, we have chosen to keep those who would hear away from eternal life. Sobering indeed! It was a costly key for Him to purchase, and it's a costly key for us to use. But, it's even more costly to bury it and not obtain an increase for the coming King. That price will be felt throughout eternity.

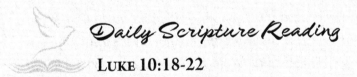

Daily Scripture Reading
LUKE 10:18-22

Prayer

You have given me the keys to Your boundless Kingdom, and I will not squander it, Lord. Help me to receive all of You that Your glory might radiate from my life to all who are searching for the Father.

It's time for a revolution in our vision.

WHEN PROPHETS TELL US, your vision is too small, many of us think the antidote is to increase whatever numbers we're expecting. For example: if we're expecting 10 new converts, let's change it to 100. If we were praying for cities, let's pray instead for nations.

With such responses, we're missing the sharp edge of the frequently repeated word. Increasing the numbers is not necessarily a sign of a larger vision from God's perspective. Vision starts with identity and purpose. Through a revolution in our identity, we can think with divine purpose. Such a change begins with a revelation of Him.

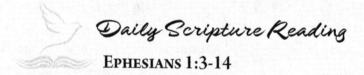

Daily Scripture Reading
EPHESIANS 1:3-14

Prayer

God, I lay my preconceived notions—all of the boxes I try to put You in —at Your feet. Show me any area of my life that is operating under a misunderstanding of who You are. I want to know You above all else.

God, give us courage, faith, and action to see Your will be done.

SO OFTEN, WE HOLD off receiving what God is trying to give us right now. There is a propensity to put off those things that require courage, faith, and action to another period of time. The mistaken idea is this: if it is good, it can't be for now.

A cornerstone in this theology is that the condition of the Church will always be getting worse and worse; therefore, tragedy in the Church is just another sign of these being the last days. In a perverted sense, the weakness of the Church confirms to many that they are on the right course. The worsening condition of the world and the Church becomes a sign to them that all is well. I have many problems with that kind of thinking, but only one I'll mention now—it requires no faith!

Daily Scripture Reading
1 CORINTHIANS 2:12-16

Prayer

I need a fresh revelation of Your faithfulness, God. I want to see this present moment as You see it. Holy Spirit, open my eyes and ears to see all that You're doing.

*We were never called to embrace
a worldview that requires no faith.*

WE CAN BECOME SO entrenched in unbelief that anything contrary to this worldview is thought to be of the devil. We can be so resistant to the idea of the Church having a dominating impact before Jesus returns. It's almost as though we want to defend the right to be small in number and make it by the skin of our teeth.

Embracing a belief system that requires no faith is dangerous. It is contrary to the nature of God and all that the Scriptures declare. Since He plans to do above all we could ask or think, according to Ephesians 3:20, His promises by nature challenge our intellect and expectations. "[Jerusalem] did not consider her destiny; therefore her collapse was awesome" (see Lamentations 1:9). The result of forgetting His promises is not one we can afford.

Daily Scripture Reading

LAMENTATIONS 1:1-9

Prayer

I will not hide, cowering from the world and waiting for heaven. I will take my place at Your side, Jesus, and release Your Kingdom here on earth.

The reality of the gospel must be made manifest in our daily lives.

IT DOESN'T TAKE GREAT faith to become convinced of our unworthiness, but that is not the final message of the gospel. We have been saved, washed clean, redeemed, seated in heavenly places. Now, we must operate from this new reality.

Too often, though, we are more convinced of our unworthiness than we are of His worth. Our inability takes on greater focus than does His ability. But the same One who called fearful Gideon a Valiant Warrior and unstable Peter a Rock has called us the Body of His beloved Son on earth. That has to count for something. We have been given an unimaginable gift to partner with Him to manifest His Kingdom, causing heaven to touch the earth.

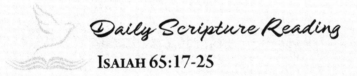

Daily Scripture Reading

ISAIAH 65:17-25

Prayer

You have called me by a new name. I am Your child, the recipient of Your Kingdom as an inheritance. Help me, Father, to live solely from this reality.

Most Christians repent enough to get forgiven, but not enough to see the Kingdom.

ISRAEL EXPECTED THEIR MESSIAH to come as the King who would rule over all other kings. And He did. But their misunderstanding of greatness in His Kingdom made it difficult for them to grasp how He could be born without earthly fanfare and become the servant of all.

They expected Him to rule with a rod of iron. In doing so they would finally have revenge on all those who had oppressed them throughout the ages. Little did they realize that His vengeance would not be aimed so much at the enemies of Israel as it would be toward the enemies of man: sin, the devil and his works, and the self-righteous attitudes fostered by religion.

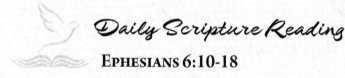

Daily Scripture Reading
EPHESIANS 6:10-18

Prayer

Holy Spirit, bring to mind any area of unforgiveness I've been harboring in my heart. I want to release those people from my human desire for vengeance. Help me to see the true battle clearly.

Repentance is the result of seeing God for who He truly is.

JESUS THE MESSIAH CAME … FULL of surprises. Only the contrite in heart could keep up with His constant coloring outside the lines and stay unoffended. His purpose was revealed in His primary message: *"Repent, for the kingdom of heaven is at hand"* (Matthew 4:17). Now there's something that caught them completely off guard; He brought His world with Him!

Repentance means much more than weeping over sin, or even turning from those sins to follow God. In fact, turning from sin to God is more the result of true repentance than it is the actual act. Repentance means you change your way of thinking. And it's only in changing the way we think that we can discover the focus of Jesus' ministry—the Kingdom.

This is not just a heavenly mandate to have happy thoughts. Obeying this command is possible only for those who surrender to the grace of God. The renewed mind is the result of a surrendered heart.

Daily Scripture Reading

GALATIANS 2:20-21

Prayer

Thank You, Father, that You haven't asked me to earn my salvation. When I see Your goodness, Your righteousness, and Your grace, I want nothing more than to be close to You. I surrender it all to You again and again.

Repentance is not complete until it envisions God's Kingdom.

REPENTANCE IS OFTEN DEFINED as doing an about-face. It implies that I was pursuing one direction in life and I change to pursue another. Scripture illustrates it like this, *"Repentance from dead works... faith toward God"* (Hebrews 6:1). Faith then is both the crown and the enabler of repentance.

This command has been preached strongly in recent years. The message is greatly needed. Hidden sin is the Achilles' heel of the Church in this hour. It has kept us from the purity that breeds boldness and great faith. But as noble as that target is, the message has fallen short. God wants to do more than just getting us out of the red. He wants to get us into the black! Repentance is not complete until it envisions His Kingdom.

The focus of repentance is to change our way of thinking until the presence of His Kingdom fills our consciousness. The enemy's attempt to anchor our affections to the things that are visible is easily resisted when our hearts are aware of the presence of His world. Such awareness aids us in the task of being co-laborers (see 1 Corinthians 3:9) with Christ—destroying the works of the devil. (See 1 John 3:8.)

Daily Scripture Reading

1 JOHN 3:1-8

Prayer

I want to turn from anything that does not fill me with Your life-giving presence, Lord. But, more than that, I want to be filled to overflowing with Your Kingdom. Help me to walk in both purity and power!

*God is in us to endear us
to a world we cannot see.*

IF THE KINGDOM IS here and now, then we must acknowledge it's in the invisible realm. Yet being at hand reminds us that it's also within reach. Paul said that the invisible realm is eternal, while that which is seen is only temporal. (See 2 Corinthians 4:18.)

Jesus told Nicodemus that he'd have to be born again to see the Kingdom. (See John 3:3.) That which is unseen can be realized only through repentance. It was as though He said, "If you don't change the way you perceive things, you'll live your whole life thinking that what you see in the natural is the superior reality. Without changing the way you think you'll never see the world that is right in front of you. It's My world, and it fulfills every dream you've ever had. And I brought it with Me." All that He did in life and ministry, He did by drawing from that superior reality.

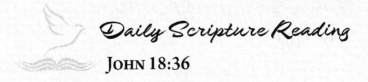

Daily Scripture Reading
JOHN 18:36

Prayer

I want to draw so close to You, Holy Spirit, that Your Kingdom becomes more real than my circumstances. Transform my mind, transform my heart, help me to see the world that's right in front of me.

Kingdom royalty are marked by their hunger for God.

"IT IS THE GLORY of God to conceal a matter, but the glory of kings is to search out a matter" (Proverb 25:2). Some things are only discovered by the desperate. That highly valued Kingdom attitude (see Matthew 5:6) is what marks the heart of true Kingdom royalty. (See Revelation 1:5.)

The God who put the gold in the rocks brought His Kingdom with Him, but left it unseen.

Paul dealt with this in his letter to the Colossians. There he informs us that God hid our abundant life in Christ. (See Colossians 3:3.) Where is He? Seated at the right hand of the Father, in heavenly places. (See Ephesians 1:20.) Our abundant life is hidden in the Kingdom realm. And only faith can make the withdrawals.

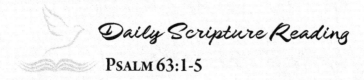

Daily Scripture Reading

PSALM 63:1-5

Prayer

Increase my hunger, God. I want to experience even more of Your Kingdom, to explore the mysteries You've hidden for me. I know that only You can satisfy.

We were born to rule—to plunder hell and establish heaven on earth.

LOOK AT THE WORD *Kingdom*—King-dom. It refers to the King's Domain, implying authority and lordship. Jesus came to offer the benefits of His world to all who surrender to His rule. The realm of God's dominion, that realm of all sufficiency, is the realm called the Kingdom. The benefits of His rule were illustrated through His works of forgiveness, deliverance, and healing.

The Christian life has been harnessed to this goal, verbalized in the Lord's Model Prayer: *"Your kingdom come. Your will be done on earth as it is in heaven"* (Matthew 6:10). His dominion is realized when what happens here is as it is in heaven.

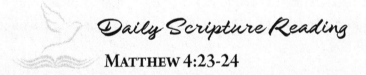

Daily Scripture Reading
MATTHEW 4:23-24

Prayer

I have been designed to see my family, my city, and my world change to look more and more like God's Kingdom. Help me, Holy Spirit, to see where You're inviting me to partner with You to see heaven come to earth.

When truth moves from concept to conviction, it affects behavior.

IN MATTHEW, CHAPTER 4, Jesus first declared the repentance message. People came from all over, bringing the sick and diseased, the tormented and handicapped. Jesus healed them all.

After the miracles He gave the most famous sermon of all time: the Sermon on the Mount. It is important to remember that this group of people just saw Jesus heal all kinds of sicknesses and perform mighty deliverances. Is it possible that instead of giving commands on the new way of thinking, Jesus was actually identifying for them the transformation of heart they had just experienced?

"Blessed are the poor in spirit, for theirs is the kingdom of heaven" (Matthew 5:3). How would you describe a people who left cities for days at a time, traveling great distances on foot, abandoning all that life involves, only to follow Jesus to some desolate place? And there He would do what they had thought impossible.

Daily Scripture Reading

PSALM 42:1-2

Prayer

I never want to lose my awareness of my hunger for You, Lord. I open my heart to You again, today. Shape me, transform every part of me until I look like You.

Spiritual hunger invites a response from the heart of God.

THE PEOPLE WHO HAD followed Jesus were filled with a spiritual hunger. And the hunger of their hearts pulled a reality from the heart of God that they didn't even know existed. Can their condition be found in the Beatitudes? I think so. I call them "poor in spirit." And Jesus gave them the promised manifestation of the Kingdom with healing and deliverance. He then followed the miracles with the Sermon, for it was common for Jesus to teach so He could explain what He had just done.

In this case, the actual Presence of the Spirit of God upon Jesus stirred up a hunger for God in the people. That hunger brought a change in their attitudes without their being told it should change. Their hunger for God, even before they could recognize it as such, had created a new perspective in them that even they were unaccustomed to. Without an effort to change, they had changed.

Daily Scripture Reading
PSALM 81:10

Prayer

Stir up my hunger for the things of Your Kingdom, Jesus. You promise that the hungry will be filled. I am hungry for more of You.

The Kingdom comes in the Presence of the Spirit of God.

IT WAS HIS PRESENCE those listening to Jesus give the Sermon on the Mount detected, and it was His Presence they longed for. For them it didn't matter if He was doing miracles or just giving another sermon, they just had to be where He was. Hunger humbles. Hunger for God brings about the ultimate humility. And He exalted them at the proper time (see 1 Peter 5:6) with a taste of His dominion.

The Sermon on the Mount is a treatise on the Kingdom. In it, Jesus reveals the attitudes that help His followers to access His unseen world. As citizens of heaven, these attitudes are formed in us that we might fully apprehend all that His Kingdom has available. The Beatitudes are actually the "lenses" that the Kingdom is seen through. Repentance involves taking on the mind of Christ revealed in these verses. He could have put it this way: This is how the repentant mind looks.

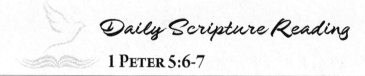

Daily Scripture Reading
1 PETER 5:6-7

Prayer

Thank You, Father, that I don't have to guess with You. You don't make it hard for me to be blessed. Soften my heart, Lord, fill me with humility. Give me Your Kingdom lenses through which to see the world.

You will show me the path of life; in Your presence is fullness of joy; at Your right hand are pleasures forevermore (Psalm 16:11).

IN HIS SERMON ON the Mount, Jesus describes the the joyful condition of the citizens of His world who are not yet in heaven! *Blessed* means "happy!" The following is a personal paraphrase:

> You are happy if you are poor in spirit, for yours is the kingdom of heaven.
> You are happy if you mourn, for you shall be comforted.
> You are happy if you are meek, for you shall inherit the earth.
> You are happy if you hunger and thirst for righteousness, for you shall be filled.
> You are happy if you are merciful, for you shall obtain mercy.
> You are happy if you are pure in heart, for you shall see God.
> You are happy if you are peacemakers, for you shall be called sons of God.
> You are happy if you are persecuted for righteousness' sake, for yours is the kingdom of heaven.
> You are happy if they revile and persecute you, and say all kinds of evil against you falsely for My sake.
> Rejoice and be exceedingly glad, for great is your reward in heaven, for so they persecuted the prophets who were before you.

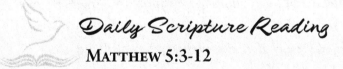

Daily Scripture Reading
MATTHEW 5:3-12

Prayer

Thank You, Jesus, that Your Kingdom is not somber and heavy. You long for us to live in your love and happiness! Highlight an attitude adjustment You would have me make today to increase the joy in my life.

Grace enables what it commands.

WHEN JESUS SHARES IN His Sermon on the Mount, He lays out a cause and effect of each mindset. Examine the promised result of each new attitude—receiving the Kingdom, being comforted, obtaining mercy, seeing God, etc.

Why is this important to recognize? Because many approach the teachings of Jesus as just another form of the Law. To most He just brought a new set of rules. Grace is different from the Law in that the favor comes before the obedience. Under grace the commandments of the Lord come fully equipped with the ability to perform them...to those who hear from the heart. (See James 1:21-25.) Grace enables what it commands.

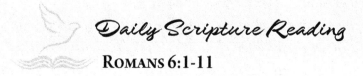

Daily Scripture Reading
ROMANS 6:1-11

Prayer

I'm so grateful that I don't have to transform my life with my own strength. You walk beside me, inviting me into further realms of Your freedom through the empowering nature of Your grace.

When light comes,
darkness must always flee.

THE UNSEEN WORLD HAS influence over the visible. If the people of God will not reach for the Kingdom at hand, the realm of darkness is ready to display its ability to influence. The good news is that *"His* [the Lord's] *kingdom rules over all"* (Psalm 103:19).

Jesus illustrated this reality in Matthew 12:28, saying, *"If I cast out demons by the Spirit of God, surely the kingdom of God has come upon you."* There are two things to notice here. First, Jesus worked only through the Spirit of God; and second, the Kingdom of God came upon someone in his deliverance. Jesus caused the collision between two worlds: the world of darkness and the world of light. Darkness always gives way to light! And in the same way, when the dominion of God was released through Jesus to that man, he became free.

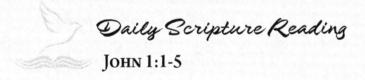

Daily Scripture Reading

JOHN 1:1-5

Prayer

There isn't darkness in this world that is any match for Your Light,
God. Help me to see the world through the truth of that statement.
You are not intimidated by evil; You are victorious.

We can become aware of a Kingdom that is more real than our circumstances.

THAT SAME COLLISION BETWEEN light and darkness happens when the sick are healed. Walter had experienced two strokes in the previous year, which left him without feeling on the entire right side of his body. He showed me a horrible burn on his arm that he had suffered, not knowing he was being burned.

Conviction, one of the words used to detect faith (see Hebrews 11:1 KJV), began to burn in my heart. While he was still talking I began to pray for him with my hand on his shoulder. I had to do so quickly. I had become aware of the Kingdom where no numbness existed. I didn't want to become more aware of how severe his problem was. My prayer went something like this: Father, this was Your idea. You commanded us to pray for things to be here as they are in heaven, and I know there is no numbness there, so there shouldn't be any here. So I command in the name of Jesus for the nerve endings to come to life. I command full restoration of feeling in this body.

Soon after I started to pray he told me that he felt my hand on his shoulder and could even feel the fabric of my shirt with his right hand. That world began to collide with the world of numbness. Numbness lost.

Daily Scripture Reading

HEBREWS 11:1-3

Prayer

There is no sickness, no suffering, no division in heaven. So, Father,
I lift up that circumstance that has been heavy on my heart to You.
Let Your Kingdom come.

Faith makes room for heaven's invasion.

FAITH IS THE KEY to discovering the superior nature of the invisible realm. It is the "gift of God" within to uncover. Faith is the mirror of the heart that reflects the realities of an unseen world—the actual substance of His Kingdom. Through the prayer of faith we are able to pull the reality of His world into this one. That is the function of faith.

Faith has its anchor in the unseen realm. It lives from the invisible toward the visible. Faith actualizes what it realizes. The Scriptures contrast the life of faith with the limitations of natural sight. (See 2 Corinthians 5:7.) Faith provides eyes for the heart.

Daily Scripture Reading
2 CORINTHIANS 5:1-8

Prayer

Open the eyes of my heart, Lord. I want to live a life filled with faith. Anchor me—spirit, soul, and body—in the reality of Your Kingdom.

FEBRUARY

Cultivating a Heart of Faith

Jesus expects people to see from the heart.

JESUS ONCE CALLED A group of religious leaders hypocrites because they could discern the weather but couldn't discern the times. It's obvious why Jesus would prefer people to recognize the times (spiritual climate and seasons) over natural weather conditions, but it's not quite so apparent why He would consider them hypocrites if they didn't.

Many of us have thought that the ability to see into the spiritual realm is more the result of a special gift than an unused potential of everyone. I remind you that Jesus addresses this charge to the Pharisees and Sadducees. The very fact that they, of all people, were required to see is evidence that everyone has been given this ability. They became blind to His dominion because of their own corrupted hearts and were judged for their unfulfilled potential.

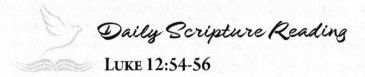

Daily Scripture Reading
LUKE 12:54-56

Prayer

Seeing into the spiritual realm is my birthright as a child of God. Open my eyes, Lord. Help me to see Your presence moving in my life.

A heart of faith is anchored in the unseen.

WHEN WE ARE BORN again, the landscape of our reality changes. God's grace empowers us to transform in ways that were impossible before. We are born again by grace through faith. (See Ephesians 2:8.) The born-again experience enables us to see from the heart. (See John 3:3.) A heart that doesn't see is a hard heart. (See Mark 8:17-18.)

Faith was never intended only to get us into the family. It isn't something we muster up by our own strength. Rather, it is the nature of life in this family. Faith sees. It brings His Kingdom into focus. All of the Father's resources, all of His benefits, are accessible through faith.

Daily Scripture Reading
MARK 8:17-18

Prayer

Soften my heart, Holy Spirit. I come to You in full surrender today. Fill me with faith; help me to bring Your Kingdom more clearly into view.

He only did what He saw His Father do.

To ENCOURAGE US IN our capacity to see, Jesus gave specific instruction, *"Seek first the kingdom of God..."* (Matthew 6:33). Paul taught us, *"Set your mind on things above, not on things on the earth"* (Colossians 3:2). He also stated, *"For the things which are seen are temporary, but the things which are not seen are eternal"* (2 Corinthians 4:18). The Bible instructs us to turn our attention toward the invisible. This theme is repeated enough in Scripture to make those of us bound by the logic of this Western culture quite nervous.

Herein lies the secret to the supernatural realm that we want restored to the Church. Jesus told us that He only did what He saw His Father do. Such an insight is vital for those who want more. The power of His actions, for instance, the mud in the eye of the blind, is rooted in His ability to see.

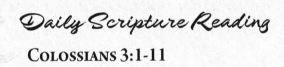

Daily Scripture Reading

COLOSSIANS 3:1-11

Prayer

My life can get so noisy, Father. There are so many things that compete for my attention. But my heart is Yours; I will focus on Your presence above all else.

Learning how to see into the spiritual realm is not the purpose for our worship, but it is a wonderful by-product.

THOSE WHO WORSHIP IN spirit and truth, as mentioned in John 4:23-24, learn to follow the Holy Spirit's lead. His realm is called the Kingdom of God. The throne of God, which becomes established upon the praises of His people (see Psalm 22:3), is the center of that Kingdom. It's in the environment of worship that we learn things that go way beyond what our intellect can grasp (see Ephesians 3:20)—and the greatest of these lessons is the value of His Presence.

David was so affected by this that all his other exploits pale in comparison to his abandoned heart for God. We know that he learned to see into God's realm because of statements like, *"I have set the Lord always before me; because He is at my right hand I shall not be moved"* (Psalm 16:8). The Presence of God affected his seeing. He would constantly practice recognizing the Presence of God. He saw God daily, not with the natural eyes, but with the eyes of faith. That priceless revelation was given to a worshiper.

Daily Scripture Reading

JOHN 4:23-24

Prayer

I abandon myself in worship before You, God. I lift up Your Holy Name in praise. My greatest purpose in life is to worship You.

Worship opens our eyes to the unseen.

GOD IS VERY COMMITTED to teaching us how to see the realities of His Kingdom. To make this possible He gave us the Holy Spirit as a tutor. The curriculum that the Holy Spirit uses is quite varied. But the one class we all qualify for is the greatest of all Christian privileges—worship.

It's in that wonderful ministry that we can learn to pay attention to this God-given gift: the ability to see with the heart. As we learn to worship with purity of heart, our eyes will continue to open. And we can expect to see what He wants us to see.

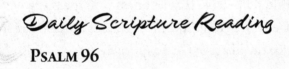

Daily Scripture Reading

PSALM 96

Prayer

I will spend my life ministering to Your heart in worship, Lord. You are worthy of all of my praise. Thank You that You have designed worship to change me, opening my eyes to Your Kingdom.

*Faith grows as we see
God for who He truly is.*

THE INVISIBLE REALM IS superior to the natural. The reality of that invisible world dominates the natural world we live in ... both positively and negatively. Because the invisible is superior to the natural, faith is anchored in the unseen.

Faith lives within the revealed will of God. When I have misconceptions of who He is and what He is like, my faith is restricted by those misconceptions. For example, if I believe that God allows sickness in order to build character, I'll not have confidence praying in most situations where healing is needed. But, if I believe that sickness is to the body what sin is to the soul, then no disease will intimidate me. Faith is much more free to develop when we truly see the heart of God as good.

Daily Scripture Reading

PSALM 145:8-10

Prayer

I need a fresh revelation of Your goodness, Father. I bring to You, today, every area of my heart that has experienced loss and disappointment. Show me who You are; increase my faith.

God is a good Father.

WHEN WE HAVE MISCONCEPTIONS of God's nature or His will, those misconceptions affect how we see the world, including our own circumstances. If we need faith for our own miracle, but we believe that God's mercy is inconsistent, doubt about God's will begins to corrode our faith.

At one point, a woman who needed a miracle in her body told me that she felt God had allowed her sickness for a purpose. I told her that if I treated my children that way I'd be arrested for child abuse. She agreed and eventually allowed me to pray for her. After truth came into her heart, her healing came minutes later.

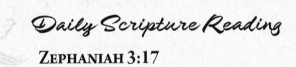

Daily Scripture Reading

ZEPHANIAH 3:17

Prayer

Forgive me, God, for any area of my life where I have adjusted my conception of You in order to explain away my circumstances. You are good all of the time.

For since the creation of the world God's invisible qualities— his eternal power and nature—have been clearly seen... (Romans 1:20).

UNBELIEF IS ANCHORED IN what is visible or reasonable apart from God. It honors the natural realm as superior to the invisible. The apostle Paul states that what you can see is temporal, and what you can't see is eternal. (See 2 Corinthians 4:18.) Unbelief is faith in the inferior.

The natural realm is the anchor of unbelief. But that realm is not to be considered as evil. Rather the humble of heart recognize the hand of God through what is seen. God has created all things to speak of Him—whether it is rivers and trees, or angels and heaven. The natural realm carries the witness of His greatness...for those with eyes to see and ears to hear.

Daily Scripture Reading

ROMANS 1:20-21

Prayer

Open my eyes, Holy Spirit, to the manifestation of God's nature that is all around me. I want to slow down and experience the wonder of Your creation.

Faith in the natural is unbelief.

MOST ALL OF THE people that I've known who are filled with unbelief have called themselves realists. This is an honest evaluation, but not one to be proud of. Those kinds of realists believe more in what is visible than they do in what they can't see. Put another way, they believe the material world rules over the spiritual world.

Materialism has been thought simply to be the accumulation of goods. Although it includes that, it is much more. I can own nothing and still be materialistic. I can want nothing and be materialistic because materialism is faith in the natural as the superior reality.

Daily Scripture Reading
MARK 9:23-25

Prayer

Jesus, help me. I want to be like the father of the child in Mark 9. I see the troubles in the natural before me, but I want to see You more. I believe; help my unbelief.

Faith doesn't deny a problem's existence; it denies a problem a place of influence.

WE ARE A SENSUAL society with a culture shaped by what is picked up through the senses. We're trained to believe only in what we see. Real faith is not living in denial of the natural realm. If the doctor says you have a tumor, it's silly to pretend that it's not there. That's not faith. However, faith is founded on a reality that is superior to that tumor. I can acknowledge the existence of a tumor and still have faith in the provision of His stripes for my healing.

I was provisionally healed 2,000 years ago. It is the product of the Kingdom of heaven—a superior reality. There are no tumors in heaven, and faith brings that reality into this one. Would satan like to inflict heaven with cancer? Of course he would. But he has no dominion there. He only has dominion here when and where man has come into agreement.

Daily Scripture Reading

EPHESIANS 3:16-17

Prayer

Thank You, Father, that I don't need to live in denial to be filled with faith. Troubles may surround me in the natural, but the greatest truth is that I am seated in heavenly places. I have been given full access to Your Kingdom, where darkness cannot survive.

God is jealous over our hearts.

FEAR OF APPEARING TO live in denial is what keeps many from living a life filled with faith. Why is what anyone thinks so important to you that you'd not be willing to risk all to trust God? The fear of man is very strongly associated with unbelief. Conversely, the fear of God and faith are very closely related.

People of faith are also realists. They just have their foundation in a superior reality. Unbelief is actually faith in something other than God. He is jealous over our hearts. The one whose primary trust is in another grieves the Holy Spirit.

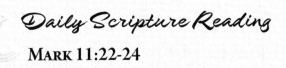

Daily Scripture Reading
MARK 11:22-24

Prayer

I will not withhold my trust from You, God, even when I don't understand what You're doing. I surrender my need for control and I embrace the mystery of walking with You.

Heart first, mind second.

FAITH IS BORN OF the Spirit in the hearts of mankind. Faith is neither intellectual nor anti-intellectual. It is superior to the intellect. The Bible does not say, with the mind man believes! It says, *"with the heart one believes unto righteousness"* (Romans 10:10). Through faith, man is able to come into agreement with the mind of God.

When we submit the things of God to the mind of man, unbelief and religion are the results. When we submit the mind of man to the things of God, we end up with faith and a renewed mind. The mind makes a wonderful servant, but a terrible master.

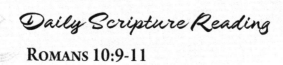

Daily Scripture Reading

ROMANS 10:9-11

Prayer

You are the Lord over my life, and I am Your surrendered child. Holy Spirit, show me if there are any areas where I have restricted the things of God to my own way of thinking. Help me to walk in true freedom and faith.

If you have a move of God that pleases everyone, it may not be a move of God.

MUCH OF THE OPPOSITION to revival comes from soul-driven Christians. The apostle Paul calls them carnal. They have not learned how to be led by the Spirit. Anything that doesn't make sense to their rational mind is automatically in conflict with Scripture. This way of thinking is accepted all throughout the Church in Western civilization, which should explain why our God so often looks just like us.

Most of the goals of the modern church can be accomplished without God. All we need is people, money, and a common objective. Determination can achieve great things. But success is not necessarily a sign that the goal was from God. Little exists in church life to ensure that we are being directed and empowered by the Holy Spirit. Returning to the ministry of Jesus is the only assurance we have of accomplishing such a goal.

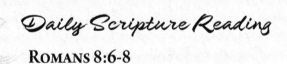

Daily Scripture Reading

ROMANS 8:6-8

Prayer

Thank You, God, that You love my mind. You love my curiosity and my questions. I submit my intellect to You. I do not want to do any part of this life independent of You.

Questions, in the context of trust, lead to revelation. Questions without trust lead to disbelief.

THE HOLY SPIRIT LIVES in my spirit. That is the place of communion with God. As we learn to receive from our spirits we learn how to be Spirit led. *"By faith, we understand"* (Hebrews 11:3). Faith is the foundation for all true intellectualism. When we learn to learn that way, we open ourselves up to grow in true faith because faith does not require understanding to function.

I'm sure that most of you have had this experience—you've been reading the Bible, and a verse jumps out at you. There is great excitement over this verse that seems to give so much life and encouragement to you. Yet initially you couldn't teach or explain that verse if your life depended on it. What happened is this: Your spirit received the life-giving power of the word from the Holy Spirit.

Daily Scripture Reading

1 JOHN 2:27

Prayer

You are the greatest gift of my life, Holy Spirit. Thank You that You are there to reveal the Father to me. I bring all of my questions to You with a heart of trust.

*Faith is the substance
of the unseen realm.*

THE HOLY SPIRIT IS our teacher and our guide as we learn to walk by faith. When we learn to receive from our spirit, our mind becomes the student and is therefore subject to the Holy Spirit. Through the process of revelation and experience our mind eventually obtains understanding. That is biblical learning—the spirit giving influence to the mind.

Faith is the mirror of the heart that reflects the realities of His world into ours. Now faith is the substance of things hoped for, the evidence of things not seen (Hebrews 11:1).

It is the substance of the unseen realm. This wonderful gift from God is the initial earthly manifestation of what exists in His Kingdom. It is a testimony of an invisible realm called the Kingdom of God. Through prayer we are able to pull that reality into this one—that is how faith functions.

Daily Scripture Reading
JOHN 14:26

Prayer

Teach me, Holy Spirit. I want to learn to engage with the unseen realm, surrendering my rational mind to Your greater truth. Help me to live from the place of trust in You.

God's Word verifies His heart for us.

IF I GO INTO the local pizza parlor and order a pizza, they will give me a number and a receipt. I am to place that number in a conspicuous place on the table. Someone may walk in off the street and come to my table and announce that they won't give me any pizza. I'll just point to the number and tell him, "When pizza number 52 is done, it's mine! "

That number is the substance of the pizza hoped for. If that guy tells me that my number isn't any good, I'll point to my receipt. It verifies the value of the number. When my pizza is done, the waiter will walk around looking for my number. How does the product of heaven know where to land? He looks for the substance…the number. If a question comes up over the validity of my number, my receipt, which is contained in the Bible, verifies my right to both the number and the pizza.

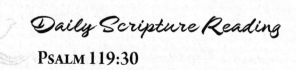

Daily Scripture Reading
PSALM 119:30

Prayer

I wait with eager expectation for Your hand to move in my life. I know what You've promised; I will not lose my faith in You.

Heaven is moved by faith.

HEAVEN IS NOT MOVED simply by the needs of man. It's not that God doesn't care. It was out of His great compassion that He sent Jesus. His Word commands and empowers us to care for the orphan, protect the widow, and provide for those in need. He is filled with compassion for our needs—body, soul, and spirit.

When God is moved by human need, He seldom fixes the problem outright; instead, He provides Kingdom principles that—when embraced—correct the problems. If God was moved solely by human need, countries like India and Haiti would become the wealthiest nations in the world. It doesn't work like that. Heaven is moved by faith. Faith is the currency of heaven.

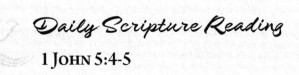

Daily Scripture Reading

1 JOHN 5:4-5

Prayer

Thank You, God, that You are my provider in so many ways. You give me my daily bread, but You are also aligning my heart with You so that I might—through faith—fully access Your Kingdom.

*Faith pulls God's
Kingdom into our world.*

THE ELEVENTH CHAPTER OF Hebrews is filled with the effects of faith. By faith—the elders obtained a testimony, we understand, Enoch was taken away having pleased God, Noah became an heir,

Abraham obeyed, and dwelled in a land of promise, Sarah received strength to conceive, and judged God as faithful who gave her the promise.

By faith—Abraham received promises, Isaac blessed his son, Joseph gave a prophecy of what would follow his death. By faith—Moses' parents preserved him, seeing he was special,

Moses refused to be aligned with the whole Egyptian system and chose instead to be rejected by people. By faith—the walls of Jericho fell, Rahab did not perish. By faith—they subdued kingdoms, worked righteousness, obtained promises, shut the mouths of lions, quenched the violence of fire, escaped the edge of the sword, were made strong, were made valiant in battle, turned to fight the enemies.

Daily Scripture Reading

HEBREWS 11:2-30

Prayer

I come to You, Jesus, hungry to live a life like those quoted in Hebrews. Give me the faith for the action Your dreams for me require.

Remain dependent on the living, current word of God.

"FAITH COMES BY HEARING…" (Romans 10:17). It does not say that it comes from having heard. It is the listening heart, in the present tense, that is ready for heaven's deposit of faith. The apostle Paul was driven by the command, *"Go into all the world and preach the gospel…"* (Mark 16:15). However, when he was ready to preach the gospel in Asia (see Acts 16), God said no.

What God had said appeared to be in conflict with what God was saying. Paul then prepared to go to Bithynia. Again, God said no. Following this, Paul had a dream of a man calling out to him from Macedonia. This was recognized as the will of God, and they went. Even though we may know the will of God from Scripture, we still need the Holy Spirit to help us with the interpretation, application, and empowerment to perform His will.

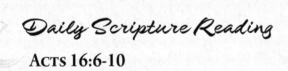

Daily Scripture Reading
ACTS 16:6-10

Prayer

I will quiet my soul today, God. I long to hear Your fresh word for My life. What do you want to say to me today?

Fear disconnects us from our awareness of God.

THE BIBLICAL COMMAND REPEATED most often is: Do not fear. Why? Fear attacks the foundation of our relationship with God…our faith. Our faith is rooted in love, in our connection to our perfectly good Father. We live from faith when we trust and rest in Him.

Fear corrodes resting place. It draws our attention from the abundant nature of the Father to whatever worry or lack we are facing. Fear is faith in the devil; it is also called unbelief. Jesus would ask His fearful disciples, "Why are you so faithless?" because fearfulness is the same as faithlessness. Fear and faith cannot coexist—they work against each other.

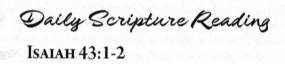

Daily Scripture Reading

ISAIAH 43:1-2

Prayer

I want to live fully connected to Your goodness, God. I bring You the fears that are plaguing my heart today. I lay them at Your feet. What do You have for me in exchange?

The enemy is attracted to decay of the heart.

THE DEVIL IS CALLED Beelzebub, which means, lord of the flies. He and his hosts are attracted to decay. We once had a freezer in a building detached from our house. One Sunday we came home from church only to be hit with a wall of smell that is unfortunately hard to forget. I realized in an instant what had happened. Our freezer had died. I thought the stench I had smelled for days was because my boys forgot to take all of the trash to the dump. Instead it was the ever-rotting meat and bear hide in the freezer.

From the front seat of my car I looked at the window of the shop about 40 feet away. It was black with flies … a number that is still hard to imagine these many years later. The freezer was filled with all sorts of meat. Flies found a happy breeding ground in spoiled flesh and were multiplying in unbelievable numbers. The enemy will always be attracted to any sign of decay—the result of disconnection from, Jesus, our life source.

Daily Scripture Reading
EPHESIANS 6:12

Prayer

I open my heart to You, Holy Spirit. Search me and highlight any areas of my heart that have become disconnected from You, any areas that are under the influence of a lie. Fill me with Your light and life!

Fear is a liar.

WE ARE CALLED TO watch over our hearts with diligence. Issues such as bitterness, jealousy, and hatred qualify as the decay of the heart that invites the devil to come and give influence—yes, even to Christians. Remember Paul's admonition to the church of Ephesus, *"Neither give place to the devil"* (Ephesians 4:27 KJV).

Fear is also a decay of the heart. It attracts the demonic in the same way as bitterness and hatred. How did the flies know where my broken freezer was? Through the scent of decaying meat. Fear gives off a similar scent. Like faith, fear is substance in the spiritual realm. Satan has no power except through our agreement. Fear becomes our heart's response when we come into agreement with his intimidating suggestions.

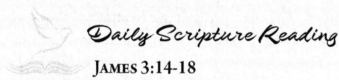

Daily Scripture Reading

JAMES 3:14-18

Prayer

I refuse to make myself or my life smaller because of the enemy's powerless threats. The devil has no place here with me! I am a child of the King.

Reaction to error usually produces error.

MANY WHO HAVE FEARED the excesses made by others in the name of faith have ironically embraced unbelief. Reaction to error usually produces error. Response to truth always wins out over those who react to error. Some people develop their belief systems solely in opposition to the error of others. As a result, those who strive for balance become anemic. The word *balance* has come to mean "middle of the road"—of no threat to people or the devil, with little risk, and above all … the best way to keep our nice image intact.

The Church warns its members about the great sin of presumption. God warns us of the sin of unbelief. Jesus didn't say, "When I return will I find people who are excessive and presumptuous?" He was concerned about finding people with faith, the kind He displayed. While we often huddle in groups of like-minded people, those with faith blaze a trail that threatens all of our comfort zones. Faith offends the stationary.

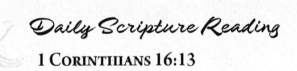

Daily Scripture Reading
1 CORINTHIANS 16:13

Prayer

Lord, forgive me for anywhere I've limited Your lordship over my life because of a fear of excess. I want to be filled with boldness. I want my life to be marked by radical faith.

Faith is risk.

PEOPLE OF GREAT FAITH are hard to live with. Their reasoning is other-worldly. My grandfather, a pastor, sat under the ministry of several great men and women of God of the early 1900s. He used to tell me how not everyone liked Smith Wigglesworth. His faith made other people feel uncomfortable. We either become like them or we avoid them. We find their lifestyle either contagious or offensive with little neutral ground. Smith is well loved today, but it's only because he's dead. Israel loved their dead prophets too.

There's something amazing about unbelief—it is able to fulfill its own expectations. Unbelief is safe because it takes no risk and almost always gets what it expects. Then, after a person gets the answer for their unbelief, they can say, I told you so.

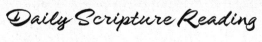

Daily Scripture Reading

ROMANS 1:17

Prayer

I refuse to live a safe life of unbelief. Give me the courage, Jesus, to follow Your guidance toward the risks You would have me take. Forgive me for any judgment I've harbored against other faith-filled radicals.

Faith is aggressive by nature.

MY FAITH IS NOT just an abiding faith; it is active. It is aggressive by nature. It has focus and purpose. Faith grabs hold of the reality of the Kingdom and forcefully and violently brings it into a collision with this natural one. An inferior kingdom cannot stand.

One of the more common things people tell me when I'm about to pray for their healing is, "I know God can do it." So does the devil. At best that is hope, not faith. Faith knows He will.

For one who has faith, there is nothing impossible. There are no impossibilities when there is faith … and there are no exceptions.

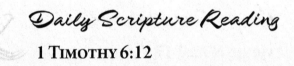

Daily Scripture Reading

1 TIMOTHY 6:12

Prayer

Holy Spirit, weed out any passivity in me when it comes to living out my faith. I want to step boldly toward impossibilities, knowing the heart and will of God.

God wants to speak to you.

"SO THEN FAITH COMES *by hearing, and hearing by the word of God*" (Romans 10:17). Notice it does not say, "faith comes from having heard." The whole nature of faith implies a relationship with God that is current. The emphasis is on hearing... in the now!

In Genesis, God told Abraham to sacrifice Isaac. As Abraham raised the knife to slay his son God spoke again. This time He told him not to slay his son, as he had passed the test of being willing to do anything for God. It's a good thing that Abraham's only connection with God was not just over what was said, but was based upon what He was saying!

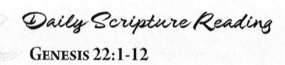

Daily Scripture Reading

GENESIS 22:1-12

Prayer

Thank You, Father, that You want to speak to me today. Thank You that You are not distant or cold; You are engaged and pursuing me constantly. I open my heart to hear what You're saying right now.

Obedience comes from faith.

WHAT THIS WORLD NEEDS is for the Church to return to a show and tell message on the Kingdom of God. They need an anchor that is greater than everything they can see. The world system has no answers to the world's increasing problems—every solution is only temporary.

Faith is not the absence of doubt; it's the presence of belief. I may not always feel that I have great faith. But I can always obey, laying my hands on someone and praying. It's a mistake for me to ever examine my faith. I seldom find it. It's better for me to obey quickly. After it's over I can look back and see that my obedience came from faith.

Daily Scripture Reading
GALATIANS 3:26-27

Prayer

Holy Spirit, I give up trying to gauge my level of faith. I hand that job over to You. I will choose obedience, instead.

In His presence, there is healing.

WHEN THE CORPORATE LEVEL of faith grows, it has what I call a cluster bomb effect, where innocent bystanders get touched by the miracle-working power of God. Frances is a woman who had esophagus cancer. One Sunday morning during worship she leaned over to her husband and said, "I was just healed!" She felt the fire of God touch her hands and concluded that it represented God's healing touch.

When she went to the doctor, she told him of her experience. His response was, "This kind does not go away." After examining her he stated, "Not only do you not have cancer, you have a new esophagus!" Corporate faith, a congregation of surrendered worshipers gathered together, pulls on heaven in marvelous ways. His world becomes manifest all around us.

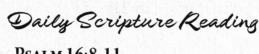

Daily Scripture Reading
PSALM 16:8-11

Prayer

Thank You, Jesus, for Your Body. I will unite with my brothers and sisters, openhearted and surrendered to You, to worship You. We welcome Your presence.

MARCH

Aligning with His Presence

Exponential power is the product of unity of faith.

SHARON HAD SUFFERED AN accident many years ago in which she had destroyed a tendon that ran down her leg. It left her with restricted movement and partial numbness in her foot. I was giving an altar call for people to get right with God during one of our Saturday night meetings. She began to make all kinds of noise. I stopped the altar call and asked her what happened. She told us of the tingling feeling that ran down her leg and the subsequent restoration of all movement and feeling to her foot. A creative miracle happened without anyone praying.

The crowd at this particular meeting was quite small. But power is not in the number of people in attendance. It's the number of people in agreement. Exponential power (see Deuteronomy 32:30) is the product of the unity of faith. It's easy to mistake enthusiasm for faith. In that setting I emphasize the use of testimonies to stir people's hearts to believe for the impossible so He might invade.

Daily Scripture Reading
DEUTERONOMY 32:30

Prayer

Open my heart, Lord, to the present power of these testimonies. Stir up my heart to believe for the impossible. Invade every area of my life with Your presence and power.

Sometimes faith looks like quiet trust.

JUST AS FEAR IS a tangible element in the spirit world, so faith is tangible there. In the natural a loud voice may intimidate another man. But devils know the difference between the one who is truly bold and aggressive because of their faith, and the one who is simply covering his fears with aggressive behavior.

Christians often use this tactic when casting out devils. Many of us have yelled threats, called on angels for help, promised to make it harder on the demons on Judgment Day, and other foolish things only to try and cover immaturity and fear. Real faith is anchored in the invisible realm and is connected to the authority given in the name of the Lord Jesus Christ.

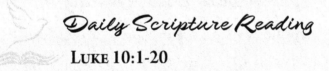

Daily Scripture Reading
LUKE 10:1-20

Prayer

I don't have to be loud and aggressive to prove my faith in You, God. My authority comes from You. You have already given it to me. Give me the strength to act from that place of quiet confidence.

Authority is found in rest.

THE AUTHORITY TO CAST out demons is found in rest. Rest is the climate that faith grows in. (See Hebrews 3:11-4:11.) It comes out of the peace of God. And it is the Prince of Peace who will soon crush satan underneath our feet! (See Romans 16:20.) What is restful for us is violent to the powers of hell. That is the violent nature of faith.

This is not to be a soulish attempt at self-confidence or self-determination. Instead it is a moving of the heart into a place of surrender...a place of rest. A surrendered heart is a heart of faith. And faith must be present to please God.

Daily Scripture Reading

HEBREWS 3:11-4:11

Prayer

Today, I intentionally rest in Your promises, Father. Every area of my heart that can slip into striving, I open up to Your grace. Help me to experience Your true rest. I surrender it all into Your hands.

*Until now the kingdom of heaven
suffers violence, and the violent
take it by force (Matthew 11:12).*

TWO BLIND MEN (SEE Matthew 9:27) who sat by the road called out to Jesus. People told them to be quiet. That only hardened their determination. They became more desperate and cried out all the louder. He called them forth and healed them saying, *"The kingdom has come near you."* He attributed their miracle to their faith.

A woman (see Matthew 9:20-22) who had hemorrhaged for 12 years pressed through a crowd. When she was finally able to touch the garment of Jesus, she was healed. He attributed it to her faith.

The stories of this kind are many, all with similar endings—they were healed or delivered because of their faith. Faith may quietly press in, or it may cry out very loudly, but it is always violent in the spirit world. It grabs hold of an invisible reality and won't let go. Taking the Kingdom by faith is the violent act that is necessary to come into what God has made available.

Daily Scripture Reading
MATTHEW 9:18-26

Prayer

Anchor me in the supremacy of Your Kingdom, Lord. Establish such an assurance of Your goodness in my heart that I can co-labor with You to bring heaven to earth.

Prayer connects us with God's heart.

AN AUTOMOBILE MAY HAVE several hundred horsepower. But the car will go nowhere until the clutch is released, connecting the power contained in the running motor and transferring that power to the wheels. So it is with faith. We have all the power of heaven behind us. But it is our faith that connects what is available to the circumstances at hand. Faith takes what is available and makes it actual.

It's not illegal to try to grow in faith. It's not wrong to seek for signs and the increase of miracles. Those are all within the rights of the believer. But learning how to pray is the task at hand. It is the only thing the disciples asked Jesus to teach them. His model for prayer gives us insights into His view of prayer and the release of His dominion.

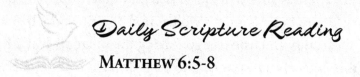

Daily Scripture Reading

MATTHEW 6:5-8

Prayer

I don't want to walk through life never accessing all that is available to me. Jesus, teach me how to connect with Your heart so that Your dominion might be released through my connection with You.

*Hands, surrendered to God,
can release the power of heaven.*

ONE YEAR, AT OUR town's carnival, a fortune-teller pitched her tent and laid out her tarot cards, crystal ball, and other psychic paraphernalia. As I walked around her tent I began to declare, "You don't exist in heaven; you are not to exist here. This is my town. You are here illegally. I forbid you to establish roots here! God has declared that wherever the soles of my feet tread, God has given it to me. I bind you to the word of God that declares that I have authority over you. Be gone!" I continued to walk around the tent like Israel walked around Jericho. Nothing fell in the natural.

I did not speak these things to the woman. I didn't even do it loud enough to draw her attention. She was not my enemy, nor was she my problem. The kingdom of darkness that empowered her was my target. Even though the fair went on for many more days, she left town the next morning. The power that influenced her had been broken. She couldn't leave fast enough. It was as though the hornets of Exodus drove her out of town. (See Exodus 23:28.)

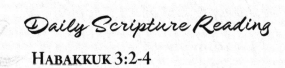

Daily Scripture Reading
HABAKKUK 3:2-4

Prayer

> *Holy Spirit, is there any area where I've turned a person into the enemy rather than focusing on the powers of darkness? Forgive me. Refocus my attention; give me Your words to pray, so that I might release the power of heaven.*

Biblical prayer is always accompanied by radical obedience.

THE LORD'S MODEL PRAYER provides the clearest instruction on how we bring the reality of His world into this one. The generals of revival speak to us from ages past saying, "If you pray, He will come!" Biblical prayer is always accompanied by radical obedience. God's response to prayer with obedience always releases the nature of heaven into our impaired circumstances.

Jesus' model reveals the only two real priorities of prayer: First, intimacy with God that is expressed in worship—holy is Your name. And second, to bring His Kingdom to earth, establishing His dominion over the needs of mankind—Your Kingdom come.

As disciples, we are both citizens and ambassadors of another world. This world is our assignment, but not our home. Our purpose is eternal. The resources needed to complete the assignment are unlimited. The only restrictions are those between our ears.

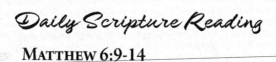

Daily Scripture Reading

MATTHEW 6:9-14

Prayer

> Shift my thinking, Holy Spirit. I want to see the world as You do. I want to know Your heart so clearly that I can partner with You to see this world transformed.

*Our Father in heaven,
hallowed be Your name.*

THE TITLE FATHER IS a title of honor and a call to relationship. What He did to make it possible for us to call Him "our Father" is all one needs to see to begin to become a true worshiper. *Hallowed* means respected or revered. This too is an expression of praise.

In the Book of Revelation, which is actually entitled The Revelation of Jesus Christ (not the antichrist! See Revelation 1:1.), it is obvious that praise and worship are the primary activities of heaven. And so it is to be for the believer here on earth. The more we live as citizens of heaven, the more heaven's activities infect our lifestyles.

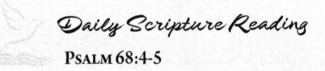

Daily Scripture Reading

PSALM 68:4-5

Prayer

How great You are, God! You are my faithful Father. There is no one like You. I praise Your holy name.

Worship is our primary calling.

WORSHIP IS OUR NUMBER one priority in ministry. Everything else we do is to be affected by our devotion to this call. He inhabits our praise. One translation puts it this way, "But You are holy, enthroned in the praises of Israel. God responds with a literal invasion of heaven to earth through the worship of the believer" (see Psalm 22:3).

One of my sons is a worship leader. He took a friend, along with his guitar to the mall, to worship God. They stopped after three hours of singing and dancing before the Lord. An unsuspecting man walked through the same area where they had been worshiping God. He stopped, reached into his pocket, pulled out illegal drugs, and dropped them onto the ground. No one said anything to him about his sin. How did it happen? Heaven touched earth, and there are no illegal drugs in heaven.

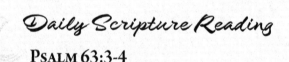

Daily Scripture Reading
PSALM 63:3-4

Prayer

Thank You, God, that as I align my heart with Yours in worship, I will be transformed into Your likeness more and more. I long to release Your presence through worship everywhere I go today.

Never underestimate the effect of God's presence.

SOMETIMES THE MIRACULOUS HAPPENS in the worship environment. As His presence becomes manifest upon a worshiping people even unbelievers are brought into an encounter with God. My son and daughter have ministered to the Lord on troubled streets in San Francisco. As people walked by we saw many who manifested demons while others broke out in joyful laughter as they came into the presence of the Lord.

These things shouldn't surprise us. Healing and deliverance is the norm in the presence of God. Look at how God responds to the praises of His people as mentioned in Isaiah 42:13: *"The Lord shall go forth like a mighty man; He shall stir up His zeal like a man of war. He shall cry out, yes, shout aloud; He shall prevail against His enemies."*

Daily Scripture Reading

ISAIAH 12:4

Prayer

You are worthy of all of my praise, God. Your presence is all that I am seeking after. And yet, You pour out Yourself so generously in response to the praises of Your people. I am filled with wonder.

Your kingdom come. Your will be done on earth as it is in heaven.

THIS IS THE PRIMARY focus for all prayer: If it exists in heaven, it is to be loosed on earth. It's the praying Christian who looses heaven's expression here. When the believer prays according to the revealed will of God, faith is specific and focused. Faith grabs hold of that reality. Enduring faith doesn't let go. Such an invasion causes the circumstances here to line up with heaven.

The critics of this view sarcastically say, "So I guess we're supposed to pray for streets of gold." No! But our streets should be known for the same purity and blessing as heaven—*"Let our cattle bear without mishap and without loss, let there be no outcry in our streets!"* (Psalm 144:14 NASB). Everything that happens here is supposed to be a shadow of heaven. In turn, every revelation that God gives us of heaven is to equip us with a prayer focus.

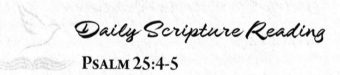

Daily Scripture Reading
PSALM 25:4-5

Prayer

> I won't stop pressing in for more of You, Lord, until what I see on earth reflects perfectly Your heavenly Kingdom. I won't compromise; I want to see Your will be done in my family, in my city, and in my nation as it is in heaven.

Let nothing become larger than our awareness of God's presence in our lives.

How much of heaven has God purposed to become manifest here on earth? No one knows for sure. But we do know through Church history that it's more than we have now. And we know through the Scripture that it's even more than has ever entered our minds. (See 1 Corinthians 2:9-10 and Ephesians 3:20-21.)

The will of God is seen in the ruling presence of God, for *"where the Spirit of the Lord is, there is liberty"* (2 Corinthians 3:17). Wherever the Spirit of the Lord is demonstrating the Lordship of Jesus, liberty is the result. Yet another way to say it is that when the King of kings manifests His dominion, the fruit of that dominion is LIBERTY. That is the realm called The Kingdom of God. God, in response to our cries, brings His world into ours.

Daily Scripture Reading
1 Corinthians 2:9-10

Prayer

God, I surrender every area of my life to Your lordship. I invite Your healing, transforming presence into my life. I want to walk in all of the freedom You have for me.

If it doesn't exist in heaven, it's not supposed to exist here. If it does exist there, it's supposed to be here.

JUST AS WE ARE called to loose the things of heaven here on earth, we are also called to bind those elements of darkness that try to infiltrate our world. If it is not free to exist in heaven, it must be bound here. Again, through prayer we are to exercise the authority given to us. *"I will give you the keys of the kingdom of heaven; and whatever you bind on earth **shall have been bound** in heaven, and whatever you loose on earth **shall have been loosed** in heaven"* (Matthew 16:19 NASB, emphasis mine). Notice the phrase shall have been. The implication is that we can only bind or loose here what has already been bound or loosed there. Once again, heaven is our model.

Daily Scripture Reading
MATTHEW 16:19-20

Prayer

Today, I take the authority given to me by the death and resurrection of Christ Jesus. I bind every spirit of darkness that has tried to coexist with my family, that has tried to influence my community. I say enough! Be gone, in the name of Jesus.

Give us this day our daily bread.

IS ANYONE STARVING IN heaven? Of course not. This request is a practical application of how His dominion should be seen here on earth—abundant supply. The abuses of a few in the area of prosperity does not excuse the abandonment of the promises of God to provide abundantly for His children. It is His good pleasure to do so. Because there is complete and perfect provision in heaven, there must be the same here.

Heaven sets the standard for a Christian's material world—enough to satisfy the desires born of God and enough *"for every good work"* (2 Corinthians 9:8). Our legal basis for provision comes from the heavenly model given to us in Christ Jesus: *"And my God shall supply all your need according to His riches in glory by Christ Jesus"* (Philippians 4:19). According to what? His riches. Where? In glory. Heaven's resources are to affect us here and now.

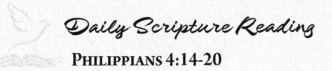

Daily Scripture Reading
PHILIPPIANS 4:14-20

Prayer

I'm so grateful, Jesus, that I am not limited to my own resources in the natural. You will supply my needs according to the great abundance of Your Kingdom. Open my mind to the vast storehouses of heaven.

And forgive us our debts,
as we forgive our debtors.

IS THERE ANY UNFORGIVENESS in heaven? No! Heaven provides the model for our relationships here on earth. *"And be kind to one another, tender-hearted, forgiving one another, even as God in Christ forgave you. Therefore be imitators of God as dear children"* (Ephesians 4:32-5:1). These verses make it quite clear that our model is Jesus Christ...the One ascended to the right hand of the Father...the One whose Kingdom we seek. Once again, the Lord's Prayer illustrates a practical way to pray for heaven's reality to bring an effect on planet earth.

Daily Scripture Reading

MICAH 7:18-19

Prayer

Search my heart, Holy Spirit. Show me any unforgiveness in me. I open my heart to You. I want to release any bitterness or judgment I've been holding onto today.

And do not lead us into temptation,
but deliver us from the evil one.

THERE IS NO TEMPTATION or sin in heaven. Neither is there any presence of evil. Keeping separate from evil is a practical evidence of our coming under our King's rule. This prayer does not imply that God wants to tempt us. We know from James 1:13 that it is impossible for God to entice us to sin.

Praying this portion of the Lord's Prayer is important because it requires us to face our need for grace. It helps us to align our heart with heaven—one of absolute dependency on God. God's Kingdom gives us the model for the issues of the heart. This prayer is actually a request for God not to promote us beyond what our character can handle. Sometimes our anointing and gift are ready for an increase of responsibility, but our character isn't. When promotion comes too soon, the impact of our gift brings a notoriety that becomes the catalyst of our downfall.

Daily Scripture Reading
JAMES 1:12-15

Prayer

God, I need Your grace every day. Develop my character, God, so that it can withstand the destiny You have called me to. I am fully dependent on You.

The devil will flee from you.

THE PHRASE DELIVER US from evil, as it is traditionally rendered, actually means, "deliver us from the evil one." A heart modeled after heaven has great success in spiritual warfare. That's why it says, *"Submit to God. Resist the devil and he will flee from you"* (James 4:7).

When we submit our hearts completely to God, we have authority over the evil one. Jesus was able to say, "Satan has nothing in Me." The believer is to be completely free from all satanic influence and attachments. That is the cry voiced in this prayer.

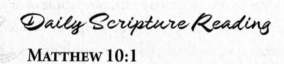

Daily Scripture Reading

MATTHEW 10:1

Prayer

Jesus, shape and mold my heart. I invite You to adjust my attitude anywhere I am straying from Your example. I want my heart to be completely free from the influence of evil.

For Yours is the kingdom and the power and the glory forever. Amen.

THE KINGDOM OF GOD is His possession, which is why He alone can give it to us. When we declare that reality we move into declarations of praise! All through the Scriptures we hear the declarations of praise similar to this one contained in His model prayer declaring that all glory and power belong to Him.

One of the most important teachings that I have ever received came from Derek Prince about thirty years ago. It was a wonderful message on praise. In it he suggested that if we only have ten minutes to pray we should spend about eight praising God. It's amazing how much we can pray for with the two minutes we have left. That illustration helped me to reinforce the priority of worship that I was learning from my pastor…my dad.

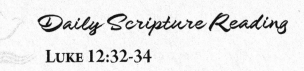

Daily Scripture Reading
LUKE 12:32-34

Prayer

I never want to forget my primary calling—to minister to You, God, through worship. You are worthy of all of my praise. All the power and all the glory are Yours.

Seek first the kingdom of God and His righteousness, and all these things shall be added to you (Matthew 6:33).

THIS VERSE IS NOT in the Lord's Prayer modeled by Jesus, but it is in the context of His overall message of the Kingdom in the Sermon on the Mount. In it He establishes the priority that encompasses all Christian values and objectives. Seek His Kingdom first!

Understanding this prayer helps us to realize the intended goal of all prayer—that the Lordship of Jesus would be seen in all circumstances of life. As the Kingdom of God confronts sin, forgiveness is given and change comes to the nature that had only known how to sin. When His rule collides with disease, people are healed. When it runs into the demonized, they are set free. The Kingdom message's nature provides salvation for the whole man—spirit, soul, and body. That is the gospel of Jesus Christ.

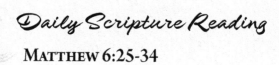

Daily Scripture Reading

MATTHEW 6:25-34

Prayer

I will run after Your presence, making the pursuit of Your Kingdom my highest priority. Your presence changes everything; help me to remember that every good thing starts with You.

His Kingdom comes fully equipped for all of our needs.

IT HAS ALWAYS SEEMED to me that the phrase *"and all these things shall be added to you"* meant that if my priorities were correct He'd make sure I got what I needed. After understanding the model prayer better, I'm not so sure that was His intent. He was saying that if we seek His Kingdom first, we'll find His Kingdom comes fully equipped. It brings with it His answer to our material and relational needs, and our fight against evil.

God wants every person to come to Him and believe, but that's not all. His vision for us does not end with salvation. He longs for us to be filled with the fullness of God, releasing His Kingdom onto the earth. He wants to pour out all things of His Kingdom onto His children.

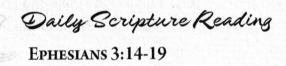

Daily Scripture Reading
EPHESIANS 3:14-19

Prayer

Thank You, Father, that every solution for my life can be found in You. I turn to You today for the needs I'm aware of and those that I'm not. Prepare my heart to receive everything You want to pour out.

Your Kingdom come.

SUPPOSE I OWNED A very successful restaurant and you wanted to purchase the right to a franchise. By purchasing a franchise of my restaurant, you would be investing your money to obtain its name and all that goes with it—menus, unique design, management program, and the quality of training for workers. You would be required to follow the prescribed standards established at the flagship restaurant. The color scheme would be the same, as would be the type of furnishings and menu items. The policy manual for employees and the management style would be copied from the main campus. In essence, I would superimpose the main restaurant over each new location until all the locations looked alike.

When we pray for His Kingdom to come, we are asking Him to superimpose the rules, order, and benefits of His world over this one until this one looks like His. That's what happens when the sick are healed or the demonized are set free. His world collides with the world of darkness, and His world always wins. Our battle is always a battle for dominion—a conflict of kingdoms.

Daily Scripture Reading
MATTHEW 25:34

Prayer

I want to align every aspect of my life to Your Kingdom, God. Align my heart to Yours, align my thinking to Yours. I want to say "yes" to all that You're saying "yes" to. I want to say "no" to anything that is not of You.

Royalty is our identity. Servanthood is our assignment. Intimacy with God is our life source.

WE WERE CREATED FOR intimacy. From that intimacy comes our commission to rule. Keep in mind that He views ruling differently than most of us. We rule through service. Many have made the mistake of thinking that Christians are to be the heads of all corporations, governments, and departments. As good as that may sound, it's actually a fruit of the true goal. Christ-likeness—excellence with humility is the real goal. Promotion comes from the Lord. If we spent more time developing a Kingdom heart, we'd have more people in key places of leadership.

Daily Scripture Reading

PHILIPPIANS 2:1-11

Prayer

Teach me, Holy Spirit, how to walk as Christ did. Purify my heart. I want to serve from a place of true connection and intimacy with God. I want to lay down my life because I am a child of the King.

God's inviting us into a relationship where our requests can move His heart.

PRAYER IS THE SIMPLEST activity of the believer—child to Father, lover to lover. It is a constant conversation that is sometimes spoken. Prayer is also one of the more complicated issues for us. Formulas don't work in this Kingdom relationship.

The honor that we have in being able to pray is beyond all comprehension. We are His representation on earth—ambassadors of His world. Our cries, all of them, touch His heart.

Daily Scripture Reading

1 SAMUEL 1:1-20

Prayer

You're not a remote God, sitting far off in judgment. You are so near, closer than my own breath, and You've given me direct access to affect Your heart. I'm amazed by who You are.

The world is longing to see an authentic Heavenly Father interacting with His sons and daughters.

INTIMACY IS THE MAIN purpose of prayer. And it's through relationship that God entrusts to us the secrets of His heart, that we might express them in prayer. That's what He did with Simeon and Anna as He stirred their hearts to pray for the coming of the Messiah long before He was born. Even the return of the Lord will be preceded by the declaration of the bride: *"The Spirit and the bride say, 'Come'"* (Revelation 22:17 NASB).

If these things were going to happen anyway, what would be the purpose of prayer? God has apparently given Himself a self-imposed restriction—to act in the affairs of man in response to prayer. God has chosen to work through us. We are His delegated authority on planet Earth, and prayer is the vehicle that gives occasion for His invasion. Those who don't pray allow darkness to continue ruling. The enemy's greatest efforts at deceiving the Church are centered on the purpose and effect of prayer.

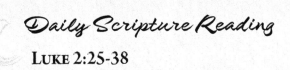

Daily Scripture Reading

LUKE 2:25-38

Prayer

Give me a hunger for prayer, Jesus. I never want to forget the privilege I have of communing with You through prayer. Let my prayers invite Your invasion into every realm of my life.

Our lives are meant to reflect the nature of God.

"FOR OUR CITIZENSHIP IS in heaven, from which we also eagerly wait for the Savior, the Lord Jesus Christ" (Philippians 3:20). Paul spoke these words to the church at Philippi, a Roman city in the country of Macedonia. It enjoyed a Roman culture and the rule and protection of the Roman government, all while living in Macedonia.

Philippians understood very well Paul's charge about being citizens of another world. Paul spoke, not about going to heaven some day, but about living as citizens of heaven today... specifically from heaven toward earth. We have the privilege of representing heaven in this world, so that we might bring a manifestation of heaven to this world.

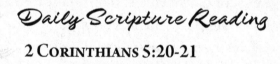

Daily Scripture Reading
2 CORINTHIANS 5:20-21

Prayer

Instill in me my true identity, Lord, as a citizen of heaven. I want to know Your heart so well that I can represent it to my family, at work, and online. Help me to see the great privilege I carry.

Our resources are based on the economy of heaven.

AS AMBASSADORS WE LIVE in one world while representing another. An embassy is the headquarters of an ambassador and his or her staff. It is actually considered a part of the nation it represents. So it is with the believer/ambassador. The Bible promises: *"Every place that the sole of your foot will tread upon I have given you"* (Joshua 1:3).

Just as ambassadors of the United States have an income based on the standard of living of this nation regardless of what nation they serve in, so also ambassadors of the Kingdom of God live according to the economy of heaven, though they are still on earth. All of our King's resources are at our disposal to carry out His will. That is how Jesus could speak of the carefree life—consider the sparrow. (See Matthew 6:26.)

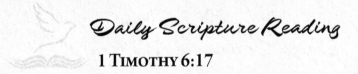

Daily Scripture Reading

1 TIMOTHY 6:17

Prayer

Expand my mind, God. I don't want to limit Your plans for my life based on my limited perspective. You are so much bigger than my capacity to gather resources. All that I have is Yours.

If You have someone as large as Jesus living inside of you, it must show.

As AN AMBASSADOR, THE military of the Kingdom I represent is at my disposal to help me carry out the King's orders. If as a representative of a nation my life is threatened, all of my government's military might is prepared to do whatever necessary to protect and deliver me. So it is with the heaven's angelic host. They render service for those who would inherit salvation. (See Hebrews 1:14.)

This ambassador mentality is one I first picked up from Winkey Pratney. When he boards a plane, he reminds himself that while others may represent IBM and XEROX, he is there representing another world. I have followed his example and practiced this principle for close to thirty years. It has helped me to keep a clear perspective on the eternal purpose of every outing.

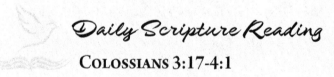

Daily Scripture Reading

COLOSSIANS 3:17-4:1

Prayer

Holy Spirit, remind me, whenever I wake up in the morning, I am representing another world to those around me. Enlarge my vision for each action throughout my day accordingly.

Partnering with God in prayer is an occasion for joy.

ONE OF THE BEST reasons to not pray comes from watching some who do. Many who call themselves intercessors live depressed lives. I don't want to minimize the genuine effect of the burden of the Lord that comes upon us when we are praying effectively. It is real and necessary. But an unstable lifestyle has been promoted by those who claim to be intercessors but have not learned to release things in prayer. The burden of the Lord takes us somewhere! I learned this the hard way.

Sometimes the situation is bigger than we can handle in one prayer session. Obviously we are to continue sowing into that prayer need. But it does no one any good to do it under the "cloud" of our unbelief.

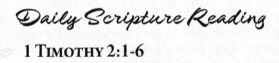

Daily Scripture Reading

1 TIMOTHY 2:1-6

Prayer

You hold the entire world in Your hands, God. I want to partner with You to see heaven touch the world, but I know that You don't need me to take on the weight of responsibility for the miraculous. You are mighty and all-powerful. It is my joy to partner with You in prayer.

*Prayer is a time to focus on
the goodness of God.*

I WAS TAUGHT EARLY in life about the importance of prayer. My youth pastor, Chip Worthington, kept me on track with his teachings, as well as the many books he gave me to read. I spent a great deal of time praying, and I carried that priority into early adulthood. But my focus in prayer often turned to my own spirituality... or should I say, the lack of it.

I would rise early and pray late into the night. God honored the sacrifice I made, but my personal victories did not coincide with my elaborate prayer times. Instead, they seemed more linked to my acts of faith. Because my focus was still on me, there was little victory I actually could trace back to my prayers.

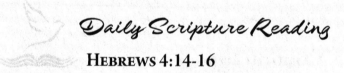

Daily Scripture Reading

HEBREWS 4:14-16

Prayer

Thank You, Jesus, that You know exactly what I am going through. You see my struggles with such compassion and love. Thank You that my job is to draw near to Your throne of grace; You will supply the grace to help my need.

Pray until there's a breakthrough

TRAVAILING IN PRAYER IS not always a sign of true intercession. Many are not yet able to distinguish the difference between the burden of their own unbelief and the burden of the Lord. I now pray until I come into a place of faith for that situation. When that happens, my perspective on the problem changes. I begin to see it from heaven's view.

My role also changes. Instead of asking God to invade my circumstances, I begin to command the mountains to be removed in His name. It is from this place of faith (or rest) that I discover my role as the pray-er. Pray until there's a breakthrough. Then exercise the authority given to execute His will over the circumstances at hand.

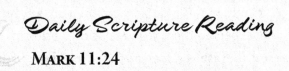

Daily Scripture Reading
MARK 11:24

Prayer

Lord, I bring to You that thing which is heaviest on my heart today. Help me to see things as You do. I will stand in my authority, commanding the obstacles to breakthrough be removed in Your name.

*You have authority over
any storm you can sleep in.*

JESUS WAS SLEEPING IN the middle of a life-threatening storm. The disciples woke Him because they were afraid of dying. He exercised authority and released peace over the storm. It was the peace of heaven that enabled Him to sleep. And it was that same peace that subdued the storm. You only have authority over the storm you can sleep in.

If I am filled with anxiety in any given situation, it becomes hard for me to release peace—because I can only give what I have. Authority functions from heaven's peace.

Even after the disciples got their answer to prayer, a stilled storm, Jesus asked them about their unbelief. For most of us an answer to prayer is the reward for our great faith. In this case they got their answer but were said to be small in faith. He expected them to exercise the authority He had given them to quiet the seas themselves. Instead they asked Him to do it. We often pray in the place of risky obedience.

Daily Scripture Reading

MATTHEW 8:23-34

Prayer

I don't want to lose my focus on Your goodness when the storms of life come. I want to exercise the authority You've given me to bring peace to chaos. Help me to function from heaven's peace.

APRIL

Surrendered to Jesus, Filled with the Spirit

The Spirit of Him who raised Jesus from the dead dwells in you... (Romans 8:11).

CORRECT THEOLOGY ALONE HAS not enabled us to complete the assignment Jesus gave us 2,000 years ago. The Great Commission hasn't been accomplished through our vast resources of money or personnel. We aren't called to spread His Kingdom through our own might, ability, or charisma.

To see the kinds of breakthroughs that Jesus had, we must embrace what Jesus embraced: the Holy Spirit. The gift of the Spirit is unlike any other. The realm of the Spirit is the realm of God's Kingdom. And that realm now lives inside of every believer.

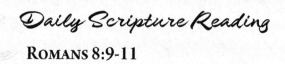

Daily Scripture Reading

ROMANS 8:9-11

Prayer

There is nothing I long for more than communion with You, Holy Spirit. I cherish Your presence. Show me what it means to develop intimacy with You. I want to know You more fully.

*Our greatness is measured
by our dependence on Jesus.*

JOHN THE BAPTIST WAS the high-water mark for all under the Old Covenant. But the least in this new era were born to surpass him through their relationship with the Holy Spirit. Jesus sets a standard with this statement—John the Baptist was the greatest of all Old Testament Prophets.

He didn't do any miracles that we know of. His ministry was gloriously necessary, but not one we'd normally compare to some of the more spectacular prophets like Elijah or Daniel. Yet the One who knows all says he's the greatest. There is a truth contained in this passage that helps us to see our potential from heaven's perspective. It is such a wonderful truth that all of hell has made a priority of trying to keep us from its simplicity. John knew that he needed Jesus.

Daily Scripture Reading
MATTHEW 11:7-11

Prayer

Jesus, I need You. I am not ashamed to admit my need for Your presence, Your love, and Your lordship over my life. Help me to keep things that simple.

The lifestyle of Jesus is available to each one of us, through the baptism of the Holy Spirit.

WITH THAT IN MIND, a more startling bit of news comes next—he who is least in the Kingdom of heaven is greater than John the Baptist. Jesus wasn't saying that the people in heaven were greater than John. There's no purpose for such a statement. He was talking about a realm of living that was soon to become available to every believer. John prophesied of Christ's coming, and went so far as to confess his personal need of Jesus' baptism.

Not one of the Old Testament prophets, not even John, had what was about to be offered to the least of all saints. It is the baptism in the Holy Spirit that became God's goal for mankind.

The baptism in the Holy Spirit makes a lifestyle available to us to which not even John had access. Jesus whetted our appetite for this lifestyle through His example, then He gave us the promise of its availability.

Daily Scripture Reading
MATTHEW 3:11-14

Prayer

I am so amazed by the gift of Your Spirit, Jesus. That I would be given something that Abraham, Moses, and John the Baptist never had is humbling beyond comprehension. Fill me with Your presence, Holy Spirit; baptize me again.

God wants us to be filled with the Holy Spirit.

THERE IS A DIFFERENCE between immediate and ultimate goals. Success with an immediate goal makes it possible to reach an ultimate goal. But failure in the immediate prevents us from reaching our final goal.

Bowlers know this. Each lane not only has ten pins at the far end, it also has markers on the lane itself. A good bowler knows how his or her ball rotates as it is released from a hand. Bowlers will aim at a marker in the lane as an initial target. Yet they receive no points for hitting it. Points are only given when the ultimate target is hit—the pins at the end of the lane.

Likewise, salvation was not the ultimate goal of Christ's coming. It was the immediate target…the marker in the lane. Without accomplishing redemption, there was no hope for the ultimate goal—which was to fill each born again person with the Holy Spirit.

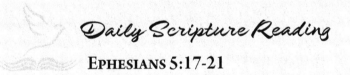

Daily Scripture Reading
EPHESIANS 5:17-21

Prayer

I don't want to settle for less than You would have for me, God. Be it unto me according to Your will—fill me with the Holy Spirit until I am overflowing!

*We cannot exhaust what
we know of God's goodness.*

GOD'S DESIRE IS FOR the believer to overflow with Himself, that we might "... *be filled with all the fullness of God*" (Ephesians 3:19). The resulting fullness of the Spirit was different than anyone had ever before experienced. For that reason, John the Baptist—the greatest of all Old Testament prophets—could confess: *"I need to be baptized by you,"* meaning, "I need your baptism...the one I was assigned to announce!"

The baptism in the Holy Spirit makes a lifestyle available to us that not even John had access to. Consider this: we could travel off of this planet in any direction at the speed of light, 186,000 miles a second, for billions of years, and never begin to exhaust what we already know to exist. All of that rests in the palm of His hand. And it's this God who wants to fill us with His fullness. That ought to make a difference!

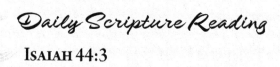

Daily Scripture Reading

ISAIAH 44:3

Prayer

I will never come to the end of knowing Your heart, Lord. Your goodness, Your power, Your faithfulness all stretch before me as an invitation to an encounter with You. I need to be filled with Your Spirit.

We are not called merely to leave behind the enslaving death of sin; we are called to step fully into our Promised Land.

ISRAEL LEFT EGYPT WHEN the blood of a lamb was shed and applied to the doorposts of their homes. In the same way, we were set free from sin when the blood of Jesus was applied to our lives. The Israelites soon arrived at the Red Sea. Going through that body of water is referred to as the baptism of Moses.

Similarly, we face the waters of baptism after our conversion. When the Jews finally entered the Promised Land, they entered through a river—another baptism. This second baptism was not a departure from sin. Such was illustrated when they left Egypt. This new baptism would take them into a different way of life.

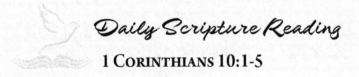

Daily Scripture Reading

1 CORINTHIANS 10:1-5

Prayer

You have taken me out of the slavery of sin, rescuing me from the bondage of my own control. But I want more, Holy Spirit. I want to see the Promised Land.

He'll give us His baptism of fire if we'll give Him something worth burning.

AS THE NEWLY-FREED ISRAELITES journeyed through the wilderness, they fought wars and won. But once they crossed the Jordan River into the Promised Land, wars were fought differently. Before, they fought like warriors. Now, they would march around a city in silence for days, finally raising up a shout and watching the walls fall.

Later, the Israelites would experience the challenge of sending a choir into battle first. (See 2 Chronicles 20:21.) And then there was the time God intentionally sent over 30,000 soldiers back home so He could fight a war with 300 torch-wielding trumpet blowers. He makes the Promised Land possible, and we pay the price to live there. He'll give us His baptism of fire if we'll give Him something worth burning.

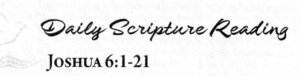

Daily Scripture Reading

JOSHUA 6:1-21

Prayer

Holy Spirit, teach me what it looks like to fight like a worshiper. I want to grow in my trust of You; I want to be a part of Your confounding victories. I give my life into Your hands daily.

Fill us with a holy dissatisfaction, God!

THIS BAPTISM IN THE Holy Spirit is the fulfillment of the Old Testament picture of entering the Promised Land. Suppose the children of Israel had chosen to cross the Jordan but became content to live on the banks of the river. They would have missed the purpose for crossing the river in the first place. There were nations to destroy and cities to possess. Contentment short of God's purposes would mean having to learn to live with the enemy.

That is what it is like when a believer is baptized in the Holy Spirit but never goes beyond speaking in tongues. When we become satisfied apart from God's ultimate purpose of dominion, we learn to tolerate the devil in some area of our life. As glorious as the gift of tongues is, it is an entrance point to a lifestyle of power. That power has been given to us that we might dispossess the strongholds of hell and take possession for the glory of God.

Daily Scripture Reading
ACTS 2:38-45

Prayer

I don't want to live a comfortable life devoid of Your presence, God. I was born to take ground for Your Kingdom. Let me not be satisfied with anything less.

We will be clothed in power from on high.

"*THERE ARE SOME OF you standing here who will not taste of death until you see the kingdom come with power*" (Mark 9:1). Each time this is mentioned in the Gospels it is followed by the incident on the Mount of Transfiguration. Some have considered this to mean that what happened to Jesus on that mountain was the Kingdom coming in power.

However, if that were so then why would Jesus need to emphasize that some there would not die until they saw the Kingdom come with power? Jesus was speaking of a much grander event. He spoke of the coming promise of the Father. He was describing the event that would clothe us with power from on high—the baptism in the Holy Spirit.

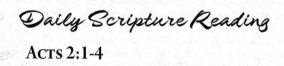

Daily Scripture Reading
ACTS 2:1-4

Prayer

Increase my expectation, Jesus. It's a lie to think that Your supernatural interventions ended with the first disciples. You are here. You have poured out Your Spirit. You want to fill me with Your empowering presence.

We are not limited to one encounter with the Holy Spirit; we need to be refilled regularly.

SOMEHOW, I ALWAYS THOUGHT that the baptism in the Holy Spirit was a one-time event; I received my prayer language and that was it. The Bible teaches differently. In Acts 2, we find 120 being baptized in the Spirit in the upper room. Yet, in Acts 4 we find some of the same crowd being refilled. Some have put it this way: one baptism, many fillings. Why? We leak.

Only two chapters later, Peter and John had been arrested for preaching the gospel. Once freed, instead of hiding away, they went back to the group and prayed for even more boldness to do the very thing that had landed them in prison. They knew they needed more of God, and God responded by shaking the place where they gathered. They were all filled again with the Holy Spirit, receiving the boldness they had cried out for.

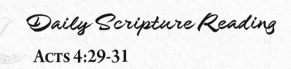

Daily Scripture Reading

ACTS 4:29-31

Prayer

Help me to see every setback, like Peter and John, as an opportunity to lean into You. I need a fresh filling of You, Holy Spirit.

*Freely you have received,
freely give (Matthew 10:8).*

OVER THE PAST DECADE, revival fire has been carried by Rodney How-ard-Browne, and it has found a home in Toronto and Pensacola. People travel from around the world to these different watering holes because of an instinctive hunger for more. In some places they stand in lines, waiting for prayer. In others they crowd around the front of a sanctuary waiting for someone to be used by God to lay hands on them and bless them.

Critics have called this activity a "bless me club." Personally, because of my passion for the blessing of God I have little problem with those who return time after time to receive another blessing. I need His blessing. The problem is not in receiving more of the blessing of God. It's the refusal to give it away to others once we have received it ourselves. The time spent receiving prayer has become a tool God has used to fill His people with more of Himself. It has become a method for this wonderful time of impartation.

Daily Scripture Reading
NUMBER 6:24-26

Prayer

> I will never grow tired of Your blessing, God. Help me to remember
> to pour out onto others all that You have so generously given to me.

The Holy Spirit encompasses the Kingdom.

"BUT IF I CAST out demons by the Spirit of God, surely the kingdom of God has come upon you" (Matthew 12:28). Look at this phrase, "by the Spirit of God... the kingdom." The Holy Spirit encompasses the Kingdom. While they are not the same, they are inseparable. The Holy Spirit enforces the lordship of Jesus, marking His territory with liberty (see 2 Corinthians 3:17). The king's domain becomes evident through His work.

The second part of this verse reveals the nature of ministry. Anointed ministry causes the collision of two worlds—the world of darkness with the world of light. This passage shows the nature of deliverance. When the Kingdom of God comes upon someone, powers of darkness are forced to leave.

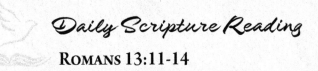

Daily Scripture Reading
ROMANS 13:11-14

Prayer

Thank You, Father, that Your Kingdom brings light into every dark place. Thank You that there is no darkness that can remain in the presence of Your light. In Your presence, all powers of darkness are forced to flee.

Jesus is Lord, period.

WHEN A LIGHT IS turned on, darkness doesn't resist. There is no debate. It doesn't stay dark for a few minutes until light finally wins. On the contrary, light is so superior to darkness that its triumph is immediate.

The Holy Spirit has no battle wounds. He bears no teeth marks from the demonic realm fighting for preeminence. Jesus is Lord, period. Those who learn how to work with the Holy Spirit actually cause the reality of His world (His dominion) to collide with the powers of darkness that have influence over a person or situation. The greater the manifestation of His Presence, the quicker the victory.

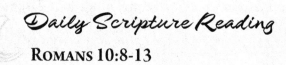

Daily Scripture Reading

ROMANS 10:8-13

Prayer

I won't be intimidated by the weak attempts of the enemy. The powers of darkness will not distract me from my assignment. I will focus on You, God, and You alone.

It's impossible to adequately demonstrate the love of God apart from power.

BY FAR THE GREATEST gift ever received by us is the Holy Spirit Himself. Those who discover the value of His presence enter realms of intimacy with God never previously considered possible. Out of this vital relationship arises a ministry of power that formerly was only a dream. The incomprehensible becomes possible because He is with us.

God doesn't have to try to do supernatural things. He is supernatural. He would have to try to not be. If He is invited to a situation, we should expect nothing but supernatural invasion.

Daily Scripture Reading
JEREMIAH 32:27

Prayer

Increase my anticipation for Your supernatural intervention, Lord. I will no longer be satisfied with less than Your love demonstrated through Your miraculous power in every area of my life.

The Holy Spirit is in me for my sake, but He rests upon me for yours.

I WILL BE WITH you is a promise made by God to all His servants. Moses heard it when he faced the challenge of delivering Israel from Egypt. (See Exodus 3:12.) Joshua received this promise when he led Israel into the Promised Land. (See Joshua 1:9.) When Gideon received the call of God to be a deliverer for Israel, God sealed it with the same promise.

In the New Testament, this promise came to all believers through the Great Commission. (See Matthew 28:19.) It comes when God has required something of us that is humanly impossible. It's important to see this. It's the Presence of God that links us to the impossible. I tell our folks, He is in me for my sake, but He's upon me for yours. His presence makes anything possible!

Daily Scripture Reading

JUDGES 6:11-16

Prayer

I was born to face impossible situations with Your presence, Holy Spirit. I will not shy away from things that seem too large for me. I have the most powerful force in the universe living inside of me.

We cannot be salt and light to a world we are not a part of.

PART OF THE PRIVILEGE of ministry is learning how to release the Holy Spirit in a location. When I pastored in Weaverville, California, our church offices were downtown, located directly across from one bar and right next to another. This downtown area was the commercial center for the entire county—a perfect place for a church office!

It's not good when Christians try to do business only with other Christians. We are salt and light. We shine best in dark places! I love business and business people and have genuine interest in their success. Before entering a store, I often pray for the Holy Spirit to be released through me. If I need something on one side of the store, I'll enter on the opposite end in order to walk through the entire store. Many opportunities for ministry have developed as I've learned how to release His presence in the marketplace.

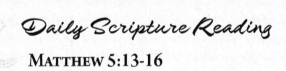

Daily Scripture Reading
MATTHEW 5:13-16

Prayer

Open my eyes, Lord, to the daily ministry opportunities You have placed in my path. I am not scared to interact with the world; give me Your heart for every person I encounter today.

Our shadows will always release whatever overshadows us.

PEOPLE LAID THE SICK in the streets hoping that Peter's shadow would fall on them and they'd be healed. (See Acts 5:15.) Nevertheless, it wasn't Peter's shadow that brought healing. There is no substance to a shadow. Peter was overshadowed by the Holy Spirit, and it was that presence that brought the miracles.

The anointing is an expression of the person of the Holy Spirit. He is tangible. There were times in Jesus' ministry when everyone who touched Christ's clothing was healed or delivered. (See Mark 6:56.) The anointing is substance. It is the actual presence of the Holy Spirit, and He can be released into our surroundings.

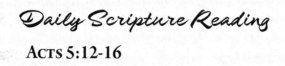

Daily Scripture Reading

ACTS 5:12-16

Prayer

I want to be so saturated by You, Holy Spirit, that my presence emanates Your presence. Thank You for these stories in the Bible that stretch my imagination for what is possible with You.

Faith and compassion are never self-centered.

A BOTTLE IS NOT completely full until it overflows. So it is with the Holy Spirit. Fullness is measured in overflow. When we get introspective, we restrict the flow of the Holy Spirit. We become like the Dead Sea; water flows in, but nothing flows out, and nothing can live in its stagnant waters.

Too often, well-meaning believers expend large amounts of energy in self-analysis and self-criticism. The problem is that, instead of focusing on the transformative grace poured out on us, we can fall into the downward spiral of focusing on ourselves. The Holy Spirit is released through faith and compassion, and faith and compassion are never self-centered.

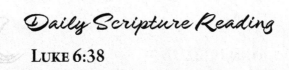

Daily Scripture Reading
LUKE 6:38

Prayer

I give up trying to fix myself, Holy Spirit. I give up digging up problems or analyzing my motivations. Instead, I open my heart to You. Search me, know me, correct me. I want to walk in faith and compassion.

We owe God the absolute abandonment of our yes.

HISTORY PROVIDES US WITH a lesson from a great military leader. Alexander the Great led his armies in victory after victory, and his desire for ever greater conquest finally brought him to the foot of the Himalayas. He wanted to go beyond these intimidating mountains. Yet, no one knew what was on the other side. Senior officers were troubled by his new vision. Why? They had gone to the edge of their map—there was no map for the new territory that Alexander wanted to possess. These officers had a decision to make: would they be willing to follow their leader off the map, or would they be content to live within its boundaries? They chose to follow Alexander.

Daily Scripture Reading

JOHN 12:22-26

Prayer

Forgive me, Father, for any time I have put my trust in a map—that which I can hold onto with a semblance of control—instead of Your will. I give that up today. I will follow You off the map.

The Holy Spirit is very comfortable contradicting our understanding of Scripture.

FOLLOWING THE LEADING OF the Holy Spirit will eventually present us all with a choice to make: Will we trust in Him even when we don't understand? While He never contradicts His Word, He is very comfortable contradicting our understanding of it. Those who feel safe because of their intellectual grasp of Scriptures enjoy a false sense of security.

None of us has a full grasp of Scripture, but we all have the Holy Spirit. He is our common denominator who will always lead us into truth. But to follow Him, we must be willing to follow off the map—to go beyond what we know. To do so successfully we must recognize His presence above all.

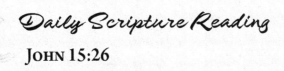

Daily Scripture Reading
JOHN 15:26

Prayer

I will not cling to that which I think I know. I will not hold my own understanding above Your presence, Holy Spirit. I surrender it all to You.

Following the Holy Spirit off of the map will bear fruit for the King.

THERE IS A GREAT difference between the way Jesus did ministry and the way it typically is done today. He was completely dependent on what the Father was doing and saying. He illustrated this lifestyle after His Holy Spirit baptism. He followed the Holy Spirit's leading, even when it seemed unreasonable, which it often did.

The Church has all too often lived according to an intellectual approach to the Scriptures, void of the Holy Spirit's influence. We have programs and institutions that in no way require the Spirit of God to survive. In fact, much of what we call ministry has no safeguard in it to ensure that He is even present. When our focus is not the presence of God, we end up doing the best we can for God. Our intentions may be noble, but they are powerless in effect.

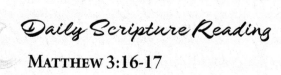

Daily Scripture Reading

MATTHEW 3:16-17

Prayer

Strip away any ministry or programming I've built that is devoid of Your presence. My focus is on nothing but You. I will follow You off of the map, wherever You lead.

You can't love God without loving people.

JESUS OFTEN HEALED AFTER being moved with compassion. His love for others was like a magnet, pulling Him toward those in need of supernatural breakthrough. When we are filled with God's love for one another, we create the kind of atmosphere that attracts miracles.

I frequently detect the leading of the Holy Spirit by recognizing His affection for someone else. Being drawn to a person through compassion usually means that there will be some realm of supernatural ministry to them—either with a word of encouragement or a miracle of healing or deliverance. Loving people is Christ's agenda, and surrender of my own agenda makes me available for His.

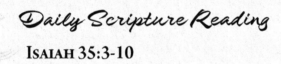

Daily Scripture Reading
ISAIAH 35:3-10

Prayer

Fill me with Your compassion, Jesus. I want my heart to be tender toward those in need, to see the hurting people around me with Your compassionate gaze. Fill me with Your heart for others.

Like Jesus, we must be anointed with the Holy Spirit.

CHRIST IS NOT JESUS' last name. The word *Christ* means "Anointed One "or Messiah. It is a title that points to an experience. It was not sufficient that Jesus be sent from heaven to earth with a title. He had to receive the anointing in an experience to accomplish what the Father desired.

The word *anointing* means "to smear." The Holy Spirit is the oil of God that was smeared all over Jesus at His water baptism. (See Luke 3:21-22.) The name Jesus Christ implies that Jesus is the One smeared with the Holy Spirit.

But there is another spirit that works to ambush the Church in every age. This power was identified by the apostle John when he said, *"Even now many antichrists have come"* (1 John 2:18). The nature of the antichrist spirit is found in its name: anti, "against"; Christ, "Anointed One."

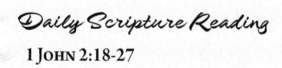

Daily Scripture Reading

1 JOHN 2:18-27

Prayer

Jesus, You are more than a good teacher or a wonderful role model. You are the Anointed One. You lived Your life on earth covered by the Holy Spirit; let me be the same.

Jesus lived His earthly life with human limitations.

JESUS LIVED HIS EARTHLY life with human limitations. He laid his divinity aside as He sought to fulfill the assignment given to Him by the Father: to live life as a man without sin, and then die in the place of mankind for sin. This would be essential in His plan to redeem mankind. The sacrifice that could atone for sin had to be a lamb, (powerless), and had to be spotless, (without sin).

Jesus showed us what was possible for us. Refusing the do anything He didn't see the Father do, or say anything He hadn't first heard the Father say, He lived a perfect life for us to follow.

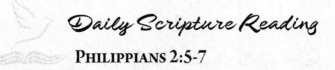

Daily Scripture Reading

PHILIPPIANS 2:5-7

Prayer

> Jesus, You are the perfect model for My life. Thank You for showing me what was possible for one life, completely surrendered to God. Help me to learn Your way.

Heaven is within arm's reach.

THE ANOINTING JESUS RECEIVED was the equipment necessary, given by the Father to make it possible for Him to live beyond human limitations. For He was not only to redeem man, He was to reveal the Father. In doing so, He was to unveil the Father's realm called heaven. That would include doing supernatural things.

The anointing is what linked Jesus, the man, to the divine, enabling Him to destroy the works of the devil. These miraculous ways helped to set something in motion that mankind could inherit once we were redeemed. Heaven—that supernatural realm—was to become mankind's daily bread. Its "present tense" existence was explained in Jesus' statement, "The kingdom of heaven is at hand." That means heaven is not just our eternal destination, but also is a present reality, and it's within arm's reach.

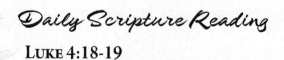

Daily Scripture Reading
LUKE 4:18-19

Prayer

Holy Spirit, I need You. I want to experience the heavenly realm as within arm's reach, and I know it's possible because Jesus did it. My communion with You changes everything.

The Holy Spirit revealed the Father to Jesus.

To FULFILL HIS MISSION, Jesus needed the Holy Spirit; and that mission, with all its objectives, was to finish the Father's work. (See John 4:34.) If the Son of God was that reliant upon the anointing, His behavior should clarify our need for the Holy Spirit's presence upon us to do what the Father has assigned.

It's vital to understand that we must be clothed with the Holy Spirit for supernatural ministry. In the Old Testament, it was the anointing that qualified a priest for ministry. According to Jesus' example, New Testament ministry is the same—anointing brings supernatural results. This anointing is what enabled Jesus to do only what He saw His Father do, and to say only what He heard His Father say. It was the Holy Spirit that revealed the Father to Jesus.

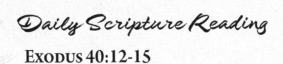

Daily Scripture Reading

EXODUS 40:12-15

Prayer

If Jesus needed You, Holy Spirit, how much more am I dependent on Your presence. Show me the heart of the Father.

God anointed Jesus of Nazareth with the Holy Spirit and with power (Acts 10:38).

IT WOULD SEEM THAT with all the significance attached to the name *Jesus,* anyone desiring to undermine His work of redemption might be referred to as *Anti-Jesus,* not *Anti-Christ.* Even religious cults recognize and value Jesus, the man. At the very least, cults consider Him to be a teacher or a prophet and possibly "a" son of God.

The horrendous error of minimizing who the Son of God was provides us with an understanding of why antichrist was the name given to this spirit of opposition. The spirits of hell are at war against the anointing, for without the anointing mankind is no threat to their dominion.

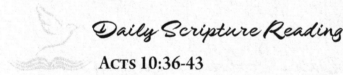

Daily Scripture Reading

ACTS 10:36-43

Prayer

May I never minimize who Jesus was and who He has called me to be. He was anointed with the Holy Spirit and with power, and I have been given the same.

The anointing releases the supernatural.

JESUS' CONCERN FOR MANKIND was applauded. His humility was revered, but it was the anointing that released the supernatural. And it was the supernatural invasion of God Himself that was rejected by the religious leaders. Most people seem to be comfortable with Jesus the teacher, but He is Jesus Christ, the anointed One, the miracle-working Son of God.

This anointing is actually the person of the Holy Spirit upon someone to equip them for supernatural endeavors. So revered is the Holy Spirit in the Godhead, that Jesus said, *"Anyone who speaks a word against the Son of Man, it will be forgiven him; but whoever speaks against the Holy Spirit, it will not be forgiven him, either in this age or in the age to come"* (Matthew 12:32).

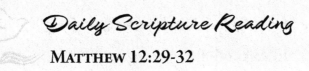

Daily Scripture Reading
MATTHEW 12:29-32

Prayer

Holy Spirit, I open my life to Your presence. Come, have Your way;- show me how You would have me live. I love You and invite You into every area of my life.

The presence of the Holy Spirit exposes the condition of our hearts.

IT WAS HOLY SPIRIT-EMPOWERED ministry that caused people to forsake all to follow Jesus. They were drawn by the supernatural in word and in deed. His words cut deep into the heart of mankind, while His deeds revealed the heart of the Father. The anointing of the Holy Spirit forever changed the lives of the humble.

But it was also Holy Spirit-empowered ministry that caused great offense to the proud and brought about His crucifixion. The same sun that melts the ice hardens the clay. Similarly, a work of God can bring about two completely different responses, depending on the condition of the hearts of people.

Daily Scripture Reading

JOHN 6:66-69

Prayer

Search my heart, God. Cut away any part of me that has harbored offense or doubt. I come to You in loving humility.

The antichrist spirit works to reduce the gospel to a mere intellectual message, rather than a supernatural God encounter.

GOD IS OUR FATHER, and we inherit His genetic code. Every believer has written into his or her spiritual DNA the desire for the supernatural. It is our predetermined sense of destiny. This God-born passion dissipates when it has been taught and reasoned away, when it's not been exercised, or when it's been buried under disappointment.

The spirit of the antichrist is at work today, attempting to influence believers to reject everything that has to do with the Holy Spirit's anointing. This rejection takes on many religious forms, but basically it boils down to this: we reject what we can't control. That spirit tolerates the mention of power if it's in the past. Occasionally it considers that power is appropriate for people in faraway places. But, never does this spirit expect the anointing of God's power to be available in the here and now.

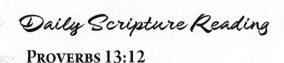

Daily Scripture Reading

PROVERBS 13:12

Prayer

I refuse to fall for the lie that the King of Kings, the Lord of Lords, is no longer operating with power on the earth. You are mighty and sovereign, Lord. I long to see You invade my life with Your supernatural power.

MAY

Saved, Healed, Transformed

God is not looking to make
us more intelligent, but to
make us more transformed.

THE SPIRIT OF CONTROL works against one of God's favorite elements in man: faith. Trust is misplaced as it becomes anchored in man's ability to reason. A religious spirit is a demonic presence that works to get us to substitute being led by our intellect instead of the Spirit of God. Being led by the Holy Spirit is an ongoing God encounter. Religion idolizes concepts and avoids personal experience. It works to get us to worship past accomplishments at the expense of any present activity of God in our life.

That spirit often feeds on the residue of past revivals. Its favorite tactic is to cast in stone an ideology learned from previous moves of the Holy Spirit. For example: it values tears and despises laughter. Sounds like idolatry, doesn't it? Anything that will take the place of dependence upon the Holy Spirit and His empowering work can be traced back to this spirit of opposition.

Daily Scripture Reading

1 CORINTHIANS 1:27-31

Prayer

Bypass my mind, Holy Spirit, and invade my heart. I give up the right to understand and control Your presence. I fully trust in You.

Our number one priority is His presence.

FOLLOWING THE ANOINTING, THE presence of the Holy Spirit, is very similar to Israel following the cloud of the Lord's presence in the wilderness. The Israelites had no control over Him. He led, and the people followed. Wherever He went, supernatural activities took place. If they departed from the cloud, the miracles that sustained them would be gone.

Can you imagine what would have happened if our fear-oriented theologians had been there? They would have created new doctrines explaining why the supernatural ministry that brought them out of Egypt was no longer necessary to bring them into the Promised Land. After all, now they had the tablets of stone. Then, as today, the real issue is the priority we place upon His presence. When that's intact, the supernatural abounds, but without it we have to make up new doctrines for why we're OK as we are.

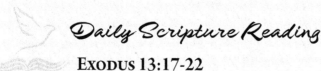

Daily Scripture Reading

EXODUS 13:17-22

Prayer

I never want to explain away the absence of Your presence, God. I don't want to move forward without Your guiding Spirit. I won't depart from You.

*It is reasonable for us to live
beyond reason as we follow Him.*

IN NEW TESTAMENT TERMS, being a people focused on God's presence means that we are willing to live beyond reason. Not impulsively or foolishly, for these are poor imitations for real faith. The realm beyond reason is the world of obedience to God. Obedience is the expression of faith, and faith is our claim ticket to the God realm.

Strangely, this focus on His presence causes us to become like wind, which is also the nature of the Holy Spirit. (See John 3:8.) His nature is powerful and righteous, but His ways cannot be controlled. He is unpredictable. As church leaders, this hits us at our weakest point. For most churches, very little of what we do is dependent upon the Holy Spirit. If He were not to show up, most churches would never miss Him.

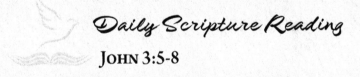

Daily Scripture Reading

JOHN 3:5-8

Prayer

God, I don't want to be confined by the limits of my own logic. I want to live with the reason of Your Kingdom. I will not control Your presence.

It's God Himself we long for.

BILLY GRAHAM IS CREDITED with saying, "Ninety-five percent of today's church activities would continue if the Holy Spirit were removed from us. In the early Church, ninety-five percent of all her activities would have stopped if the Holy Spirit were removed." I agree. We plan our services, and call it diligence. We plan our year, and call it vision.

I'll never forget the Sunday that the Lord informed me that it wasn't my service, and I couldn't do as I pleased. (Planning is biblical. But our diligence and vision must never include usurping the authority of the Holy Spirit. The Lordship of Jesus is seen in our willingness to follow the Holy Spirit's leading. He wants His Church back!) But how can we follow Him if we don't recognize His presence?

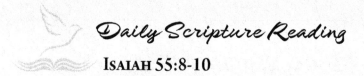

Daily Scripture Reading

ISAIAH 55:8-10

Prayer

Holy Spirit, sometimes I am so intoxicated by my own plans for my life. Forgive me. It's You that I want. It's Your path I want to walk down.

We must train ourselves to recognize the Holy Spirit.

IT'S DIFFICULT FOR MOST to follow the leading of the Holy Spirit because we are so limited in our experience with Him. Most know Him only as the One who convicts of sin or gives comfort when we're troubled. The bottom line is we are not accustomed to recognizing the Holy Spirit's actual presence. We are acquainted with a small list of acceptable manifestations that sometimes happen when He shows up, such as tears, or perhaps a sense of peace when our favorite song is sung. But few recognize just Him alone.

To make matters worse, many unknowingly reject Him because He either shows up in a way that they are unaccustomed to, or He failed to come as He has in the past. It's a kind of arrogance to automatically reject everything that we don't understand or have never recognized the Scriptures to say. It implies that if God hasn't done it or shown it to us first, He wouldn't possibly do it to someone else.

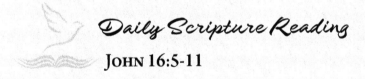

Daily Scripture Reading

JOHN 16:5-11

Prayer

Sensitize me, God, train me to recognize the presence of Your Spirit. Open my spiritual eyes so that I might see how You move. Heighten my senses to Your nearness.

We must adjust ourselves to His presence, not the other way around.

WHILE FEW WOULD ADMIT it, the attitude of the Church in recent days has been, "If I'm uncomfortable with something, it must not be from God." This attitude has given rise to many self-appointed watchdogs who poison the Church with their own fears. Hunger for God then gives way to fear of deception.

How could I know all that the Lord is doing on the earth? What do I trust most, my ability to be deceived or His ability to keep me? And why do you think He gave us the Comforter? He knew His ways would make us uncomfortable first.

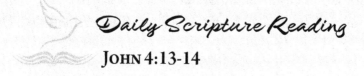

Daily Scripture Reading
JOHN 4:13-14

Prayer

Holy Spirit, I invite you to make me uncomfortable with Your presence! Move freely in and through my life. I will not restrict You with my fear and control.

Fear is a thief.

FEAR OF DECEPTION HAS opened the door for a tragic movement among believers. It states that because we have the Bible we are emotionally unbalanced and in danger of deception if we seek for an actual "felt" experience with God. Such fears cause believers to become polarized—fear separates and alienates.

This is the picture that many believers paint: In one corner, we have balanced-looking people who value the Bible as the Word of God, and in the other we have emotionally unbalanced people who seek after esoteric, spiritual experiences with God. Is that an accurate biblical picture? Jesus made a frightening statement regarding those who hold to Bible study vs. experience, *"You search the Scriptures, for in them you think you have eternal life; and these are they which testify of Me"* (John 5:39).

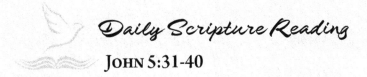

Daily Scripture Reading
JOHN 5:31-40

Prayer

Thank You, Holy Spirit, that I don't need to have anxiety about being deceived. Thank You that You are with me—guiding and teaching me. I trust in You completely.

The word of God is living and powerful....(Hebrews 4:12).

IF OUR STUDY OF the Bible doesn't lead us to a deeper relationship—an encounter— with God, then it simply is adding to our tendency toward spiritual pride. We increase our knowledge of the Bible to feel good about our standing with God, and to better equip us to argue with those who disagree with us. Any group wanting to defend a doctrine is prone to this temptation without a God encounter.

Consider the potential implications of this thought: Those who first appear to be under control may, in fact, be out of control—His control! And many of those accused of being members of an emotional "bless me club" can give actual testimony of God's touch that has changed their lives forever. They become the more biblical picture of balance.

Daily Scripture Reading
HEBREWS 4:12-13

Prayer

Jesus, the Bible says that You are the Word. I cannot separate Scriptures from Your living, powerful presence. I love the Bible, and I want to encounter You daily as I read.

God's voice will always be confirmed by Scripture.

JESUS DID NOT SAY, "My sheep will know my book." It is His voice that we are to know. Why the distinction? Because anyone can know the Bible as a book—the devil himself knows and quotes the Scriptures. But only those whose lives are dependent on the person of the Holy Spirit will consistently recognize His voice.

This is not to say that the Bible has little or no importance. Quite the opposite is true. The Bible is the Word of God, and His voice will always be confirmed by scripture. That voice gives impact to what is in print. We must diligently study the Scriptures, remembering that it is in knowing Him that the greatest truths of Scripture will be understood.

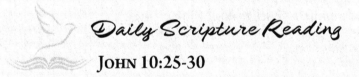

Daily Scripture Reading

JOHN 10:25-30

Prayer

Thank You, Father, for giving us the precious gift of Your Word. I cherish the Scriptures, immersing myself in them daily to know You. As I read the Bible, train my heart to know Your voice.

His voice is what releases life.

IN THIS PRESENT OUTPOURING, we are being saturated with His presence in order that we might learn His voice. As He opens up His Word to us, we become more dependent upon Him. People are once again turning their focus on the greatest gift ever received—God Himself. While the anointing is often referred to as an it, it is more accurately Him.

As the Holy Spirit receives back the reins over His people, He works to reset a more biblical parameter for the Christian life. This frightening change is for the better. We can and must know the God of the Bible by experience. The apostle Paul put it this way, *"To know the love of Christ which passes knowledge; that you may be filled with all the fullness of God"* (Ephesians 3:19). Do you know what surpasses knowledge? It is His promise. Consider the result: *"That you may be filled with all the fullness of God."* What a reward! Jesus puts it this way, *"And he who loves Me will be loved by My Father, and I will love him and manifest Myself to him"* (John 14:21).

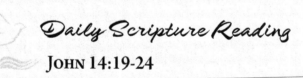

Daily Scripture Reading

JOHN 14:19-24

Prayer

I'm so grateful for You, God. I'm so grateful that I can know You more and more each day by experiencing Your presence. Open Your Word to me that I might know You even more.

Avoid a form of godliness without power.

THE ANTICHRIST SPIRIT HAS a goal for the Church—embrace Jesus apart from the anointing. Without the anointing, He becomes a safe religious figure who is sure not to challenge or offend us. Paul described this deceptive possibility as, *"having a form of godliness but denying its power. And from such people turn away!"* (2 Timothy 3:5).

How can people who love God be offended by the anointing of the Holy Spirit? He moves like wind—apart from our control. (See John 3:8.) His thoughts are very different from ours. The scripture states that our logic and His are not just different, they are opposed to each other. (See Romans 8:7 and Isaiah 55:8-9.) Let's be honest…they are worlds apart! The Holy Spirit also refuses to be restricted by our understanding of His Word.

Every time we follow the leading of the Holy Spirit, we fly in the face of the antichrist spirit. While the foolishness of some who claim to be Spirit-led have made this adventure more difficult, we nevertheless are assured of succeeding if it is truly our passionate desire. He'll not give a stone to anyone who asks for bread.

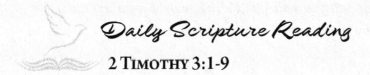

Daily Scripture Reading
2 TIMOTHY 3:1-9

Prayer

The idea of being in control can be so intoxicating, but it leads me so quickly astray. Holy Spirit, I will hand over control to You daily. I trust Your ways even more than my own.

Jesus modeled the gift of teaching.

IF THE HOLY SPIRIT is the power behind the teaching gift, what should it look like? What kind of model did Jesus provide for this particular ministry? Any revelation from God's Word that does not lead us to an encounter with God only serves to make us more religious. The Church cannot afford "form without power," for it creates Christians without purpose.

Jesus, the model teacher, never separated teaching from doing. He is the pattern for this gift. God's revealed Word, declared through the lips of an anointed teacher, ought to lead to demonstrations of power.

Daily Scripture Reading

1 CORINTHIANS 2:1-5

Prayer

I won't be satisfied with good ideas, Jesus. I want my life to be marked by Your wisdom, purity, and power.

Kingdom teaching includes both understanding and action.

NICODEMUS SAID TO JESUS, *"Rabbi, we know that You are a teacher come from God; for no one can do these signs that You do unless God is with him"* (John 3:2). It was understood that God's kind of teachers don't just talk—they do. And the doing that is referred to in John's Gospel is the performing of signs and wonders.

Jesus established the ultimate example in ministry by combining the proclamation of the gospel with signs and wonders. Matthew records this phenomenon this way: *"And Jesus went about all Galilee, teaching in their synagogues, preaching the gospel of the kingdom, and healing all kinds of sickness and all kinds of disease among the people"* (Matthew 4:23). And again, *"Then Jesus went about all the cities and villages, teaching in their synagogues, preaching the gospel of the kingdom, and healing every sickness and every disease among the people"* (Matthew 9:35).

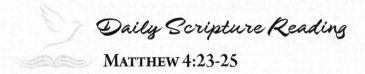

Daily Scripture Reading
MATTHEW 4:23-25

Prayer

God, I know that Your Kingdom came in transformative, miraculous power. I don't want to settle for anything less. Show me what You would have me do to reveal Your gospel today.

The gospel is incomplete without the power of God.

JESUS ALSO COMMANDED HIS disciples to minister with the same focus on signs and wonders—the twelve were sent out with, *"And as you go, preach, saying, 'The kingdom of heaven is at hand.' Heal the sick, cleanse the lepers, raise the dead, cast out demons. Freely you have received, freely give"* (Matthew 10:7-8). He commissioned the seventy by saying, *"And heal the sick there, and say to them, 'The kingdom of God has come near to you'"* (Luke 10:9).

The Gospel of John records how this combination of words and supernatural works takes place, *"The words that I speak to you I do not speak on My own authority; but the Father who dwells in Me does the works."* (John 14:10). It's apparent that we speak the word, and the Father does the works—miracles!

Daily Scripture Reading
ROMANS 1:16

Prayer

Forgive me, Holy Spirit, for any time that my fear of being disappointed has led me to express a small version of the gospel. I will not be ashamed of the full gospel of Jesus Christ, filled with the power to transform.

We must require of ourselves doing, with power!

AS MEN AND WOMEN of God who teach, we must require from ourselves doing, with power! And this doing must include a breaking into the impossible—through signs and wonders.

Bible teachers are to instruct in order to explain what they just did or are about to do. Those who restrict themselves to mere words limit their gift, and may unintentionally lead believers to pride by increasing knowledge without an increased awareness of God's presence and power.

It's in the trenches of Christlike ministry that we learn to become totally dependent upon God. Moving in the impossible through relying on God short-circuits the development of pride.

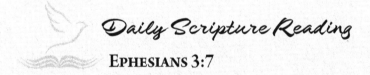

Daily Scripture Reading

EPHESIANS 3:7

Prayer

I was made to face impossible situations with You, God. I am not alone. You're not dependent on my might or intellect to change the world. The same power that raised Christ from the dead lives within me. I get to partner with You.

*We were designed to
bear supernatural fruit.*

IN 1987 I ATTENDED one of John Wimber's conferences on signs and wonders in Anaheim, California. I left discouraged. Everything that was taught, including many of the illustrations, I had taught. The reason for my discouragement was the fact that they had fruit for what they believed. All I had was good doctrine.

There comes a time when simply knowing truth will no longer satisfy. If it does not change circumstances for good, what good is it? A serious reexamination of personal priorities began. It was apparent that I could no longer expect good things to happen simply because I believed they could…or even should. There was a risk factor I had failed to enter into—Wimber called it faith. Teaching MUST be followed with action that makes room for God to move.

Daily Scripture Reading
1 THESSALONIANS 1:5

Prayer

> *I want to take risks with You, Lord. It's not enough for me to simply sit back and believe in Your goodness. I want to see Your goodness revealed to a hungry and hurting world. How would You have me step out in faith today?*

The Holy Spirit is worth our absolute focus.

AS SOON AS WE began to take risks, combining our faith with our actions, things changed. We prayed for people and saw miracles. It was glorious, but it didn't take long to discover that there were many also that weren't healed. Discouragement set in, and the pursuit with risks decreased.

On my first trip to Toronto in March of 1995, I promised God if He would touch me again, I would never back off. I would never again change the subject. My promise meant that I would make the outpouring of the Holy Spirit, with the full manifestations of His gifts—the sole purpose for my existence. And I would never stray from that call—no matter what! He touched me, and I have pursued without fail.

Daily Scripture Reading
PSALM 77:11-15

Prayer

You are the God of wonders! I will never take my eyes off of You. I will never change the subject. I will pursue the fullness of Your presence in every area of my life.

God is inviting us to experience His power.

OUR CULTURE HAS CASTRATED the role of the teacher. It is possible to attend college, get a business degree, and never have received any teaching by someone who ever owned a business. We value concepts and ideas above experience with results.

I wish that pertained only to secular schools—but the culture, which values ideas above experience, has shaped most of our Bible schools, seminaries, and denominations. Many present-day movements have made a virtue out of staying the course without a God experience. Jesus modeled a completely different way of teaching, though. And He told us that we would do the same, and even greater works than He did.

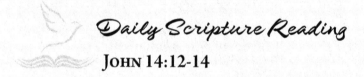

Daily Scripture Reading

JOHN 14:12-14

Prayer

Show me the areas of my life where I have valued concepts above encountering Your presence, God. I want to raise my expectations; I want to anticipate experiencing Your supernatural interventions daily.

Anyone who doesn't have an experience with God, doesn't know God. —Randy Clark

EVEN WORSE THAN REMOVING power from our teaching, those who speak subjectively of an experience with God are often considered suspect, and even dangerous. But God cannot be known apart from experience.

Randy Clark, the man God used to initiate the fires of revival in Toronto in 1994, puts it this way: "Anyone who doesn't have an experience with God, doesn't know God." He is a person, not a philosophy or a concept. It's time for those who have encountered God to stop pandering to fear by watering down their story. We must whet the appetites of the people of God for more of the supernatural.

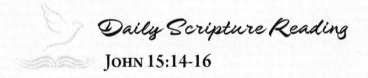

Daily Scripture Reading
JOHN 15:14-16

Prayer

I want a fresh encounter with You, God. I want to know You in a new way today. Open my eyes to see more of who You truly are.

Testimony has the ability to stir up hunger.

AS OUR MINISTRY TEAMS travel around the world, we have come to expect the miraculous. Healing, deliverance, and conversions are the fruits of our labors. While healing is seldom the subject we teach on, it is one of the most common results. As we proclaim the message of the Kingdom of God, people get well. The Father seems to say, "Amen!" to His own message by confirming the word with power.

Peter knew this when he prayed for boldness in his preaching, expecting that God would respond by *"extending His hand to heal, and signs and wonders would be done in the name of His holy servant Jesus"* (Acts 4:29-30 NASB). God has promised to back up our message with power if our message is the gospel of His Kingdom.

Daily Scripture Reading

MARK 16:14-20

Prayer

Thank You, Jesus, for Your example of living with boldness and complete surrender to the Father. Help me to step out with the same kind of faith.

It is time for us to gather around fathers.

THE PROBLEMS WE FACE today are not new. The apostle Paul had great concern for the Corinthian church, for they were being enticed by a gospel without power:

> I do not write these things to shame you, but as my beloved children I warn you. For though you might have ten thousand instructors in Christ, yet you do not have many fathers… But I will come to you shortly, if the Lord wills, and I will know, not the word of those who are puffed up, but the power. For the kingdom of God is not in word but in power (1 Corinthians 4:14-20).

Paul begins by contrasting teachers and fathers. Those who taught without power gathered around ideas, whereas fathers led in all areas of their life. Paul contrasts pride (puffed up) with humility, mere words with power, and a focus on thoughts rather than a complete Kingdom focus. The teachers mentioned were different from the kind that Jesus intended the Church to have.

Daily Scripture Reading
1 CORINTHIANS 4:14-20

Prayer

> Lord, keep me humble before Your presence. Show me the fathers in my own life, the ones who are leading with their lifestyle. Let me be one who others can follow as I follow You.

Let God's apostolic order be restored.

IN THIS POST-DENOMINATIONAL ERA, we are seeing an unprecedented movement of believers gathering around spiritual fathers (not gender specific). In times past, we gathered around certain truths, which led to the formation of denominations. The strength of such a gathering is the obvious agreement in doctrine, and usually practice. The weakness is it doesn't allow for much variety or change.

At the turn of the twentieth century, the people who received the baptism in the Holy Spirit with speaking in tongues were no longer welcome in many of these churches, because most denominations held statements of faith cast in stone. But now this gravitational pull toward fathers is happening even within denominations. Such a gathering of believers allows for differences in nonessential doctrines without causing division. Many consider this movement to be a restoration of the apostolic order of God.

Daily Scripture Reading

1 THESSALONIANS 2:11-12

Prayer

Forgive me, Holy Spirit, for any time that I've chosen division over Your unity. I want to help build a healthy spiritual family with You.

An encounter with the God of power
is worth more than any great sermon.

PAUL ADDRESSED A CONCERN to the Corinthian church about the puffed-up condition of his spiritual children. To make his point, Paul contrasts faithfulness and pride, which he defined as being puffed up. (See 1 Corinthians 4:14-20.) Paul was very concerned that they would be tricked by the theories of good public speakers. Personal charisma is often valued more by the Church than either anointing or truth. People of little character can often have positions of leadership in the Church if they have personality. Paul found this particularly troubling.

He had worked hard to bring the Corinthians into the faith. He had chosen not to wow them with what he knew. In fact, he led them to an encounter with the God of all power who would become the anchor of their faith. (See 1 Corinthians 2:1-5.) But now the sermonizers had come on the scene. Paul's answer was to send them someone just like himself—Timothy. They needed a reminder of what their spiritual father was like. This would help them to recalibrate their value system to imitate people of substance, who are also people of power!

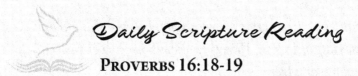

Daily Scripture Reading
PROVERBS 16:18-19

Prayer

I open my heart to You, Holy Spirit. Search me for areas of pride.
I never want to give the world only my skills or charisma when I
could give them a taste of Your goodness instead.

The Kingdom of God is in dunamis power.

PAUL MAKES A STUNNING statement clarifying the priorities of God's Kingdom. He said, *"The kingdom of God is not in word but in power"* (1 Corinthians 4:20). The original language puts it like this—"The Kingdom of God is not in *logos* but in *dunamis.*"

Apparently, they had a lot of teachers who were good at speaking many words, but displayed little power. They did not follow the pattern that Jesus set for them. *Dunamis* is "the power of God displayed and imparted in a Holy Spirit outpouring." That is the Kingdom!

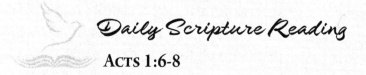

Daily Scripture Reading

ACTS 1:6-8

Prayer

Fill me with Your presence and power, God. I do not want to limit my representation of You. I want to show Your power for restoration, healing, and transformation.

...in demonstration of the Spirit and of power...(1 Corinthians 2:4).

PAUL LAID OUT HIS ministry priority as bringing the people of Corinth to a place of faith in God's power *(dunamis)*. (See 1 Cornthians 2:5.) He reminded them that he had purposefully not used his skill as an orator to convince them about the testimony of God. He had focused on the demonstrations of the Spirit and of power. Without placing their faith in God's power, he explained, they were set up to fail if things didn't change.

Any time the people of God become preoccupied with concepts and ideologies instead of a Christlike expression of life and power, they are set up to fail, no matter how good those ideas are. Christianity is not a philosophy; it is a relationship. It's the God encounter that makes the concepts powerful. We must require this of ourselves. How? We must seek until we find.

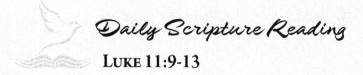

Daily Scripture Reading
LUKE 11:9-13

Prayer

I'm so grateful for my ongoing relationship with You, God. Thank You for making Yourself available to me. Thank You for the ways You love me with compassion and power. I will pursue more of You forever.

You are wrong because you know neither the Scriptures nor God's power (Matthew 22:29 NLT).

IN THE PASSAGE ABOVE, Jesus rebukes the Pharisees for their ignorance of the Scriptures and God's power. His rebuke comes within the context of marriage and resurrection, but is aimed at the ignorance infecting every area of their lives.

What was the cause? They didn't allow the Scriptures to lead them to God. They didn't know…not really understand. The word *know* in this passage speaks of "personal experience." They tried to learn apart from such an experience. They were the champions of those who spent time studying God's Word. But their study didn't lead them to an encounter with God. It became an end in itself.

Daily Scripture Reading

DEUTERONOMY 4:29-31

Prayer

How can I ever forget how available You have made Yourself to me, Father? I will open Your Word, today, expecting to personally encounter You on every page.

*It is illegitimate to allow fear
to keep us from pursuing a
deeper experience with God.*

THE HOLY SPIRIT IS the *dunamis* of heaven. An encounter with God is often a power encounter. Such encounters vary from person to person according to God's design. And it's the lack of power encounters that lead to a misunderstanding of God and His Word. Experience is necessary in building a true knowledge of the Word.

Many people fear experience because it might lead away from Scripture. The mistakes of some have led many to fear experiential pursuit. But it is illegitimate to allow fear to keep us from pursuing a deeper experience with God! Embracing such fear causes a failure to the other extreme, which is culturally more acceptable, but significantly worse in eternity.

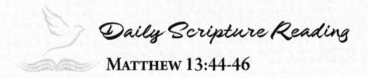

Daily Scripture Reading
MATTHEW 13:44-46

Prayer

I surrender myself to You, Lord, and ask You to lead me. I don't want to turn away from more of You just because I'm scared of the unknown. I trust You; I love You; I want more of You at any cost.

Truth is held in tension.

GOD DOES AS HE pleases. While true to His Word, He does not avoid acting outside of our understanding of it. For example, He's a loving God who hates Esau. (See Malachi 1:2-3.) He's the One who has been respectfully called a gentleman, yet who knocked Saul off of his donkey (see Acts 9:4) and picked Ezekiel up off the ground by his hair (see Ezekial 8:3). He's the bright and morning star (see Revelation 22:16) who veils Himself in darkness (see Psalm 97:2). He hates divorce (see Malachi 2:16), yet is Himself divorced (see Jeremiah 3:8).

This list of seemingly conflicting ideas could go on for much longer than any of us could bear. Yet this uncomfortable tension is designed to keep us honest and truly dependent on the Holy Spirit for understanding who God is and what He is saying to us through His book. God is so foreign to our natural ways of thinking that we only truly see what He shows us—and we can only understand Him through relationship.

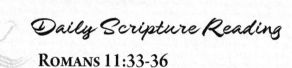

Daily Scripture Reading
ROMANS 11:33-36

Prayer

You are bigger than my understanding, God. I will trust You in the mystery of all that doesn't make sense to me now. I will lean on Your Spirit to show me the way forward.

*Trust is birthed in
the realm of mystery.*

THE BIBLE IS THE absolute Word of God. It reveals God; the obvious, the unexplainable, the mysterious, and sometimes offensive. It all reveals the greatness of our God. Yet it does not contain Him. God is bigger than His book.

Revival is mixed with many such dilemmas—God doing what we've never seen Him do before, all to confirm that He is who He said in His Word. We have the inward conflict of following the One who changes not, yet promises to do a new thing in us. This becomes even more confusing when we try to fit that new thing into the mold made by our past successful experiences.

Not everyone handles this challenge well. Many hide their need to be in control behind the banner of "staying anchored to the Word of God." By rejecting those who differ from them, they successfully protect themselves from discomfort, and from the change for which they've been praying.

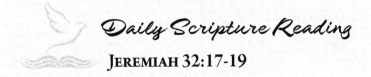

Daily Scripture Reading

JEREMIAH 32:17-19

Prayer

Strip me of control, Holy Spirit. I want to move beyond my own self-protective instincts and into the realm of absolute trust in You.

*The Holy Spirit is
the Spirit of truth.*

WITHOUT THE GUIDANCE OF the Holy Spirit, studying Scripture puts the power of revelation into the hands of anyone who can afford a Strong's Concordance and a few other miscellaneous study materials. Put in the time, and you can learn some wonderful things. I don't want to discount a regular disciplined approach to study, or certainly those wonderful study tools, as it is God who gives us the hunger to learn.

But in reality, the Bible is a closed book. Anything I can get from the Word without God will not change my life. It is closed to ensure that I remain dependent on the Holy Spirit. It is that desperate approach to Scripture that delights the heart of God. *"It is the glory of God to conceal a matter, but the glory of kings is to search out a matter"* (Proverb 25:2). He loves to feed those who are truly hungry.

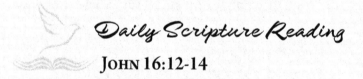

Daily Scripture Reading
JOHN 16:12-14

Prayer

I come hungry to Your Word, Father. Open up each verse to me. Transform my heart through Your Spirit. Lead me into all truth.

Grace gives me a tour guide, not a road map.

BIBLE STUDY IS OFTEN promoted so that we will get formulas for living. Certainly, there are scriptural principles that can be laid in an A to Z fashion. But too often that approach makes the Bible a road map. When I treat the Bible as a road map I live as though I can find my way through my own understanding of His book.

I believe this perspective of scriptures actually describes living under the law, not living under grace. Living under the law is the tendency to desire a list of preset boundaries, and not a relationship. While both the Law and Grace have commandments, Grace comes with an inbuilt ability to obey what was commanded. Under Grace I don't get a road map…I get a tour guide—the Holy Spirit. He directs, reveals, and empowers me to be and do what the Word says.

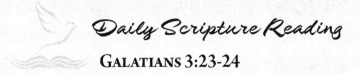

Daily Scripture Reading

GALATIANS 3:23-24

Prayer

I want a deep, thriving relationship with You, Holy Spirit. I am so grateful for Your nearness as I follow Your lead. As I engage with the Word, direct me, reveal the truth to me, and empower me to be and do what it says.

JUNE

We Owe the World an Encounter with God

*Revelation that doesn't lead us
to an encounter with God only
serves to make us more religious.*

THERE ARE MANY CONCEPTS that the Church has held dear desiring to maintain a devotion to Scripture. But some of these actually work against the true value of God's Word. For example: many who reject the move of the Holy Spirit have claimed that the Church doesn't need signs and wonders because we have the Bible. Yet, that teaching contradicts the very Word it tries to exalt.

If you assign ten new believers the task of studying the Bible to find God's heart for this generation, not one of them would conclude that spiritual gifts are not for today. You have to be taught that stuff! The doctrine stating signs and wonders are no longer needed because we have the Bible was created by people who hadn't seen God's power and needed an explanation to justify their own powerless churches.

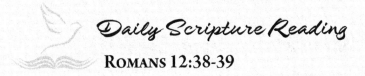

Daily Scripture Reading
ROMANS 12:38-39

Prayer

You came to reveal the Father, Jesus. You stretched the imaginations of all of those who saw Your signs and wonders. I want to be like the disciples—following Your lead in everything. I never want to choose a concept over my relationship with You.

Unless Scripture leads me to Him, I only become better equipped to debate with those who disagree with my way of thinking.

"KNOWLEDGE PUFFS UP" (1 Corinthians 8:1). Notice Paul didn't say unbiblical knowledge, or carnal knowledge. Knowledge, including that which comes from Scripture, has the potential to make me proud. So how can I protect myself from the pride that comes from knowledge, even when it's from the Bible? I must be certain that it takes me to Jesus!

The pride that comes from mere Bible knowledge is divisive. It creates an appetite for one's own opinion. *"He who speaks from himself seeks his own glory; but He who seeks the glory of the One who sent Him is true, and no unrighteousness is in Him"* (John 7:18). Those trained without a revelation that takes us to Him are trained to speak from themselves, for their own glory. This drive for knowledge without an encounter with God wars against true righteousness.

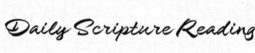

Daily Scripture Reading

JOHN 7:16-18

Prayer

Sometimes I forget that I know so little. I feel safe and protected behind the walls of my own understanding, but I can easily shut out Your voice. Forgive me for any time I've sought my own glory; I only want to seek after Your ways.

The fear of the Lord is the beginning of knowledge...(Proverbs 1:7).

WHEN WE RUN AFTER our own glory, not only does righteousness suffer, so does our faith. *"How can you believe, who receive honor from one another, and do not seek the honor that comes from the only God?"* (John 5:44). That desire for glory from man somehow displaces faith. The heart that fears God only—the one that seeks first His Kingdom and desires God to receive all honor and glory—that heart is the heart where faith is born.

The mission of heaven is to infiltrate earth with its realities. All teaching is to lead us to that end, for training in the Kingdom is not without purpose. We are being trained to run the family business.

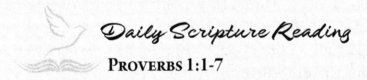

Daily Scripture Reading
PROVERBS 1:1-7

Prayer

Strip away any fear of man, any area of my heart where I care more about what other people think of me than how You see me. I want my life to bring Your glory. I want to be filled with Your presence.

Unless I do the works of the Father, do not believe me (John 10:37 NKJV).

FOR HUNDREDS OF YEARS the prophets spoke of the Messiah's coming. They gave over 300 specific details describing Him. Jesus fulfilled them all! The angels also gave witness to His divinity when they came with a message for the shepherds: *"For there is born to you this day… a Savior, who is Christ the Lord"* (Luke 2:11). Nature itself testified to the arrival of the Messiah with the star that led the wise men. (See Matthew 2:1.)

Yet with this one statement, *"Unless I do the works of the Father, do not believe me"* (John 10:37). Jesus put the credibility of all these messengers on the line. Their ministries would have been in vain without one more ingredient to confirm who He really was. That ingredient was miracles.

Jesus gave people the right to disbelieve it all if there was no demonstration of power upon His ministry. I hunger for the day when the Church will make the same statement to the world: If we're not doing the miracles that Jesus did, you don't have to believe us.

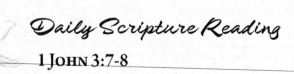

Daily Scripture Reading
1 JOHN 3:7-8

Prayer

Jesus, I want to place the same priority on the miraculous as You do. I never want to let what You've highlighted take a back seat. Help me to know the Father more, that I might walk in the same confidence You did.

Obedience is far better than sacrifice (1 Samuel 15:22).

THERE ARE MULTIPLE VERSES in the Bible that help to clarify the purpose of Christ's coming—doing the works of the Father and destroying the works of the devil. These two things are inseparable. Jesus was driven by one overwhelming passion: pleasing His heavenly Father.

The unveiling of His priorities started long before His ministry began. He was only twelve. The realization that Jesus was missing came after Mary and Joseph had traveled several days from Jerusalem. They returned to search for their twelve-year-old son. We can only imagine what might have been going through their minds during their three days of separation. He was their miracle child…the promised One. Did they lose Him through carelessness? Was their job of raising Him finished? Had they failed?

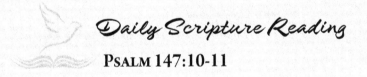

Daily Scripture Reading
PSALM 147:10-11

Prayer

May my desire to please You, Lord, be the anchor for my life. I will follow You in obedience, surrendering to You, worshiping You, and learning what pleases Your heart.

Obeying the Father is to be our whole ambition.

WHEN JOSEPH AND MARY finally tracked down their young son after losing Him, Jesus didn't seem the least bit concerned about their anxiety. In fact, He seems a little surprised that they didn't know where He'd be. We hear no apology; we find no explanations, just a statement about His priorities: *"Did you not know that I must be about My Father's business?"* (Luke 2:49). Here the revelation of purpose began. Even at a young age, He seemed to show no concern for the probability that He caused an offense in His attempt to obey His heavenly Father.

Think about it—any fear of what people might think of Him was nonexistent at the age of 12. He refused to allow the possibility of misunderstanding and conflict to keep Him from the Father's purposes. The first and only recorded words of Jesus in His youth were all about His purpose. Obeying the Father was His whole ambition. Those words were sufficient. Later in adulthood He confessed that obeying the Father remained His priority. It actually brought Him nourishment—*"My food is to do the will of Him who sent me"* (John 4:34).

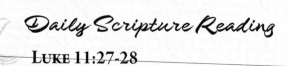

Daily Scripture Reading
LUKE 11:27-28

Prayer

Purify my vision, Holy Spirit. I want to be so focused on You and following Your leading that I am as unbothered as Jesus was to be found in the temple. Doing Your will brings me nourishment— mind, body, and spirit.

We must be willing to be misunderstood as we follow Christ.

DID JESUS FORGET TO tell Mary and Joseph where He would be when He stayed behind in Jerusalem? Or, did He do what He did realizing that it would affect others the way it did? I believe the latter: He was willing to risk being misunderstood. The Father's business often requires such a risk. Remember, He had not yet gained the credibility He had later in life; as yet there hadn't been any moving sermons, healings, water turned into wine, raising of the dead, or casting out of demons. He was simply a 12-year-old with priorities that were different from everyone else.

Eighteen years later, at the beginning of His ministry, Jesus is found teaching His disciples what He tried to teach Mom and Dad: the priority of the Father's business. Statements such as, *"I can of Myself do nothing"* (John 5:19), *"I do not seek My own will but the will of the Father"* (John 5:30), and *"I always do those things that please Him"* (John 8:29), all testify of His utter dependence on the Father, and His one passion to please Him alone.

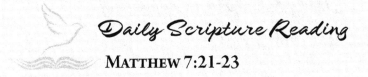

Daily Scripture Reading
MATTHEW 7:21-23

Prayer

I want to be known as one who follows You no matter what the cost. I lay down my need to be right, my need to be understood, and my own personal dignity. My eyes are on You alone, God.

This is My beloved Son, in whom I am well pleased (Matthew 3:17).

IT WAS THE CUSTOM of a Jewish father to take his son to the city square when he had reached manhood. He would announce to the city that his son was equal to himself in all business affairs, meaning when they dealt with the son they were dealing with the father. In doing so, he would announce to the whole city, *"This is my beloved son, in whom I am well pleased."*

At the water baptism of Jesus, when He was 30 years old, the prophet John the Baptist pronounced that Jesus was *"The Lamb of God who takes away the sin of the world"* (John 1:29). The Holy Spirit came upon Him, clothing Him in power, enabling Him to carry out His purpose. Then the Father spoke from heaven, *"This is My beloved Son, in whom I am well pleased"* (Matthew 3:17). In that moment, both the Father and the Holy Spirit affirmed the primary purpose embraced by the Son of God was to reveal and carry on the Father's business.

Daily Scripture Reading
MATTHEW 3:13-17

Prayer

I want people to see clear evidence of the Father when they look at my life. I want to represent You to the world like Jesus did. Help me, Holy Spirit.

God came to redeem us— spirit, soul, and body.

JESUS DECLARED THE SPECIFICS of that role in His first sermon,

> *The Spirit of the Lord is upon Me, because He has anointed Me to preach the gospel to the poor; He has sent Me to heal the broken-hearted, to proclaim liberty to the captives and recovery of sight to the blind, to set at liberty those who are oppressed; to proclaim the acceptable year of the Lord.* (Luke 4:18-19).

Jesus' life illustrated what that pronouncement was all about—bringing salvation to the spirit, soul, and body of man, thus destroying the works of the devil. (See 1 John 3:8.) This was an expression of a Kingdom that is ever increasing, and continually unfolding.

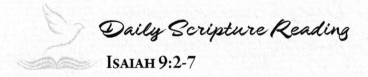

Daily Scripture Reading
ISAIAH 9:2-7

Prayer

> *Thank You, Father, that Your plan of redemption is for my complete being. I will walk in health, peace, and freedom! I want to partner with You as You bring restoration to the world.*

We can't overemphasize the fact that everything good in us is by God's grace.

THE SECRET OF THE ministry of Jesus is seen in His statements: *"The Son can do nothing of Himself, but what He sees the Father do… the Son also does in like manner"* (John 5:19) and *"I speak to the world those things which I heard from Him"* (John 8:26). Jesus revealed the truth about our relationship with the Father: Everything is rooted in the Father who has enabled and empowered us to do that which is humanly impossible.

His obedience put the bounty of heaven on a collision course with the desperate condition of mankind on earth. It was His dependence on the Father that brought forth the reality of the Kingdom into this world. It's what enabled Him to say, *"The Kingdom of Heaven is at hand!"*

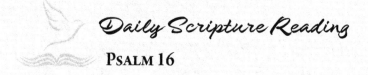

Daily Scripture Reading
PSALM 16

Prayer

God, Your goodness overwhelms me. Your grace has transformed me and continues to empower me to follow You. I would be lost without You.

Our relationship with God starts with, Follow Me.

JESUS DISPLAYED THE FATHER'S heart. All His actions were earthly expressions of His Father in heaven. The Book of Hebrews calls Jesus the exact representation of His Father's nature. Jesus said, *"If you've seen me you've seen my Father"* (John 14:9). The life of Jesus is a revelation of the Father and His business. It is the heart of that business to give life to mankind (see John 10:10) and destroy all the works of the destroyer. (See 1 John 3:8.)

Jesus continues to point the way to the Father. It has now become our job, by means of the Holy Spirit, to discover and display the Father's heart: giving life and destroying the works of the devil.

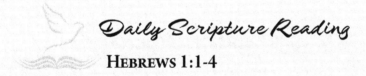

Daily Scripture Reading
HEBREWS 1:1-4

Prayer

Are there any areas in my heart, Holy Spirit, where I've become preoccupied with my own desires? Show me, and I will adjust. It is my joy to die to myself so that I might live in You.

Jesus, break into our comfort zones!

MOST OF THE PHARISEES spent their lives serving God without ever discovering the Father's heart! Jesus offended these religious leaders most because He demonstrated what the Father wanted. While the Pharisees thought God was concerned about the Sabbath, Jesus worked to help the ones the Sabbath was created for.

These leaders were accustomed to the miracles of the Scriptures remaining in the past. But Jesus broke into their comfort zones by ushering the supernatural into their cities. With every miracle He showed the entire religious community the Father's business. For them to adapt, everything would have to be overhauled. It was easier to brand Him a liar, declaring His works to be of the devil and eventually killing this One who reminded them of what had to be changed.

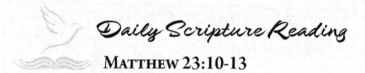

Daily Scripture Reading

MATTHEW 23:10-13

Prayer

Break into any comfort zone I have, Jesus! I invite You to bring Your holy disruption into any area of my life. I lay down my need for control; I welcome Your mystery.

Every miracle is an invitation to know our good, good Father.

UNDERSTANDING THAT THE FATHER'S business has to do with signs and wonders is no guarantee that we will truly fulfill God's purpose for our lives. It is much more than doing miracles, or even getting conversions. The supernatural interventions of God were done to reveal the extravagant heart of the Father for people. Every miracle is a revelation of His nature. And in that revelation is embedded an invitation for relationship.

The Pharisee's error is a very easy one for us to repeat. They had no understanding of the Father's heart. And much Christian activity exists that has no relationship to that supreme value. In this present hour we need much more than to learn how to identify our personal gifts or discover ways to be more successful in ministry. We need the Father Himself. We need His presence—His alone. The gospel is the story of the Father wooing the hearts of mankind through His love. All the other stuff we do overflows from that discovery.

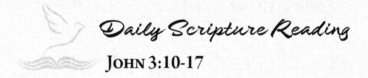

Daily Scripture Reading
JOHN 3:10-17

Prayer

God, let me never forget that everything You did was from Your infinite, encompassing love for us. Will You give me a glimpse, today, of how You feel about me? Fill me with Your love so that I can overflow onto everyone around me.

Love never fails.

WE CAN TRAVEL THE globe and preach the gospel, but without a personal revelation of the Father's heart we're carrying around secondhand news—a story without a relationship. It might save people because it is truth, but there is so much more. Jesus, at the age of 12, taught us that lesson: we must be about our Father's business. And the Father's business flows from His heart. When we discover this, we find both the joy and the power of all ministry—we will find His presence. His presence always reveals His heart.

In the same way that Jesus revealed the Father's heart to Israel, so the Church is to be a manifestation of the Father's heart to the world. We are the carriers of His presence, doers of His will. Giving what we have received releases Him into situations previously held in the grip of darkness. That is our responsibility and privilege.

Daily Scripture Reading

1 CORINTHIANS 13:1-7

Prayer

I sit with You today, Lord, in awe of all that You've given me. I am so grateful for the ways that You've loved me. I will never stop praising Your name.

Love looks like something.

EVERYONE WE COME ACROSS, every single human, is a target for God's love. There are no exceptions. Testimonies of God's radical transformation come from every sector of society and every conceivable place—school, work, home, the malls and stores, and even the parks, streets, and homeless camps. Why?

There is a growing company of people who have the Father's business in mind. They consciously take Him wherever they go. No one has been left out of God's plan for redemption, and when we release the Kingdom, we see His love in action. That is the Father's business, and every believer has a part to play in carrying out this privileged assignment.

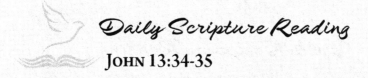

Daily Scripture Reading
JOHN 13:34-35

Prayer

Father, too often I keep Your love in the realm of the theoretical. I want to be a part of Your business. Show me who You would have me love today.

Pursue Him in prayer.

WE HAVE THE PRIVILEGE of rediscovering God's original purpose for His people. We who long for this must pursue Him with reckless abandon. But, what does it look like to pursue Him in this way? Practically, we can begin with prayer.

Be specific, be relentless in praying for miracles in every part of your life. Bring the promises of God before Him in your pursuit. He hasn't forgotten what He has said and does not need our reminder. However, He enjoys seeing us standing on His covenant when we pray. Prayer with fasting is to be an integral part of this quest, as He revealed this to be an important way to get a breakthrough (see Mark 9:29). I even pray for specific diseases for which I'm not seeing a breakthrough.

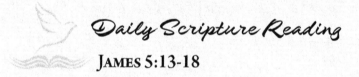

Daily Scripture Reading

JAMES 5:13-18

Prayer

Stir up my hunger for prayer, God. I want to spend time interceding on behalf of those around me, partnering with You to see Your Kingdom come.

Pursue Him in our studies.

ANOTHER PRACTICAL WAY TO pursue God's miraculous presence is through the study of His Word. Spend months reading and rereading the Gospels. Look for models to follow. Look especially at all references to the Kingdom, and ask God to open the mysteries of the Kingdom to you. (See Matthew 13:11.) The right to understand such things belongs to the saints who are willing to obey.

Another great place for study is to find all references to "reformation," those periods of transformation that Israel went through under different leaders (revivalist) in the scriptures. Good places to begin are with David, Hezekiah, Ezra, and Nehemiah. Their lives become prophetic messages for us. All true study is driven by hunger. If you don't have questions, you won't recognize the answers.

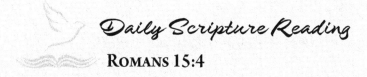

Daily Scripture Reading
ROMANS 15:4

Prayer

I refuse to be complacent when it comes to engaging with Your Word. Where would You have me start my studies, God? Plant in me a dissatisfaction with the way things are; I want to be filled with pursuit of You.

Pursue Him through our reading of history.

WE CAN STIR UP a hunger within ourselves for more of God by reading about great moves of God in history. Find the books that have been written by the generals of God's army—those who truly do the stuff. There is a great storehouse of information for those willing to pursue. Don't forget the leaders of the great healing revival of the 1950s. *God's Generals*, by Roberts Liardon, is a great place to start.

If you're afraid of reading about those who later fell into sin and deception (some of these people ended in disaster), stay away from Gideon, Samson, Solomon's Proverbs, and the Song of Solomon. The author of those books also ended in tragedy. We must learn to eat the meat and throw out the bones.

Daily Scripture Reading

JOSHUA 4:19-24

Prayer

God, thank You that the testimonies of Your faithfulness and Your miraculous power never depreciate. I will read the stories of Your incredible goodness throughout history. Let them stir up my spirit for what is possible with You!

Pursue Him through the laying on of hands.

PURSUE THE MEN AND women of God who carry an anointing in their lives for the miraculous. Such an anointing can be transferred to others through the laying on of hands. (See 2 Timothy 1:6.) Of course, having an anointing for the miraculous does not mean that person is perfect, but it does mean that the Lord has given them a gift that is available to others. He is no respecter of persons. (See Acts 10:34.)

Occasionally there are ministry times when such an individual is willing to pray for those who desire an increase of anointing. And, most of the time, pursuing this type of prayer means leaving the comfort of our homes—in humility—to receive. I have traveled extensively in pursuit of more.

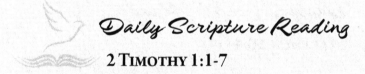

Daily Scripture Reading
2 TIMOTHY 1:1-7

Prayer

I want more of You, God. I want more of Your presence. I will go wherever You call me to go. I lay down any pride or fear of pursuing Your anointing.

Pursue Him through the people we choose to associate with.

KING DAVID WAS KNOWN for killing Goliath in His youth. Yet there are at least four other giants killed in Scripture—all killed by the men who followed David, the giant killer. If you want to kill giants, hang around a giant killer. It rubs off.

Grace is that which enables us to live in the Kingdom, and in part it is received by how we respond to the gifts of Christ: apostles, prophets, evangelists, pastors, and teachers. We actually receive the grace to function from these gifts. If you hang around an evangelist, you will think evangelistically. The same happens when we associate with those who regularly experience signs and wonders in their lives.

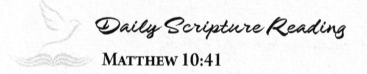

Daily Scripture Reading
MATTHEW 10:41

Prayer

Highlight the individuals in my life who are running after You, Holy Spirit. I want to surround myself with hungry people.

Pursue Him through obedience.

NO MATTER HOW MUCH preparation is done to increase the anointing for miracles in a life, it never comes to fruition without radical obedience. I must look for the sick and tormented in order to pray for them. And if they are healed, I give God the praise. If they aren't, I still give God the praise, and continue to look for people to pray for.

I learned a long time ago that more people are healed when you pray for more people! Until we act on what we know, our knowledge is nothing more than a theory. Real learning comes through doing. Jesus said, *"As the Father sent me, I also send you."* He did the works of the Father, and then passed the baton on to us.

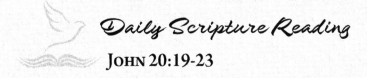

Daily Scripture Reading
JOHN 20:19-23

Prayer

I won't sit back and wait for breakthrough to come. I will lean into Your voice, Lord, and act boldly in line with my beliefs. I will search for opportunities to see Your Kingdom come.

The world doesn't need more polite Christians; it needs an encounter with power of the living God.

I'M NOT IMPRESSED WITH anyone's life unless they have integrity. But I'm not happy with their life until they are dangerous. As much as I have the ability to do so, I'll not let those around me get away with just being nice people!

Many believers have made it their primary goal in life to be well-respected citizens of their communities. Good character enables us to be solid contributors to society, but most of what is recognized as a Christian lifestyle can be accomplished by people who don't even know God. Every believer should be highly respected and more. It's the "and more" part that we're often lacking.

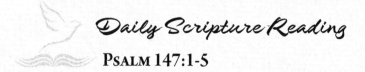

Daily Scripture Reading

PSALM 147:1-5

Prayer

I won't be satisfied with an anemic version of Christianity. I want my life to reveal You fully, Father, in Your mercy and Your power. I need more of You.

We will walk in both purity and power.

WHILE CHARACTER MUST BE at the heart of our ministries, power revolutionizes the world around us. Until the Church returns to Jesus' model for true revolutionaries, we will continue to be recognized by the world merely as nice people—while it is overcome with disease and torment, on its way to hell.

Some Christians actually have considered it to be more noble to choose character over power. But we must not separate the two. It is an unjustifiable, illegitimate choice. Together they bring us to the only real issue—obedience.

Daily Scripture Reading

1 CHRONICLES 29:10-12

Prayer

Yours is the greatness, the power, and the glory, God. My life belongs to You. I will not stop pursuing the full manifestation of Your presence in my life.

Loving God looks like keeping His commandments.

ONCE, WHILE TEACHING A group of students about the importance of signs and wonders in the ministry of the gospel, a young man spoke up saying, "I'll pursue signs and wonders when I know I have more of the character of Christ in me." As good as that may sound, it comes from a religious mindset, not a heart abandoned to the gospel of Jesus Christ.

In response to this student's comment, I opened to the Gospel of Matthew and read the Lord's charge: *"Go therefore and make disciples of all nations... teaching them to observe all things that I have commanded you"* (Matthew 28:19). I then asked him, "Who gave you the right to determine when you are ready to obey His command?"

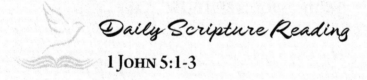

Daily Scripture Reading

1 JOHN 5:1-3

Prayer

I may not feel ready to be used by You, God, but I lay down that faulty thinking. I surrender myself fully to You, trusting that You will shape my heart—developing my character—as I follow You.

The standard of Jesus Christ remains the standard for us today.

DOES ANYONE THINK THAT God is impressed with us when we tell Him, "I'll obey You when I have more character?" Character is shaped through obedience. Jesus commanded His disciples to go, and in going they were to teach all that they had been taught. And part of what they were taught was specific training on how to live and operate in the miraculous (see Matthew 10:1,5-8,17).

They were commanded to *"heal the sick, cleanse the lepers, raise the dead, and cast out demons"* (Matthew 10:8). And now they were responsible to teach this requirement as the lifestyle for all who were to become followers of Jesus Christ. In this way, His standard could remain the standard—the norm for all who call upon the name of the Lord for salvation.

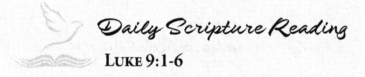

Daily Scripture Reading

LUKE 9:1-6

Prayer

It's pride to think I could evaluate myself better than You can, Lord. I cannot disqualify myself from something that You have commanded me to do. I will follow You.

But we all, with unveiled face, beholding as in a mirror the glory of the Lord, are being transformed into the same image from glory to glory... (2 Corinthians 3:18).

MANY CONSIDER THEMSELVES UNWORTHY of God using them in the miraculous, and therefore never pursue that realm. Isn't it ironic that Christians will disobey God by not diligently seeking after spiritual gifts—they won't lay hands on the sick or seek to deliver the demonized—because they realize their need for more character? In none of the commissions of Jesus to His disciples did He deal specifically with character.

Is it possible the reason there are so few miracles in North America is because too many before us thought they had to become better Christians before God could use them? Yes, I believe it is.

Daily Scripture Reading
2 CORINTHIANS 3:15-18

Prayer

I cannot transform myself, God. I will follow You, beholding Your glory and obeying Your commands. My transformation is dependent on following You.

Transformation comes through a power-encounter with Him.

THE SINGLE LIE, THAT we can't be used by God until we're perfect, has kept us in perpetual immaturity because it protects us from the power encounter that transforms us. The result is we have converts trained and overtrained until they have no life, vision, or ingenuity left. This next generation of converts must be handled differently. We must help them by giving them their identity as world changers, provide them with a model for character, passion, and power, and open up opportunities to serve.

Mario Murillo describes this next generation of believers this way: "When he picks up a Bible, his focus will not be on emotional healing or self-esteem. He'll ask you where the trigger is and how you fire it. When he reads the Word, he will want to apply it to the taking over of neighborhoods for God!"

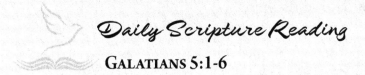

Daily Scripture Reading

GALATIANS 5:1-6

Prayer

Strip away any restrictive thinking I have, Jesus. You have made me free, and I will not become entangled with religious thinking that keeps me from living fully alive in You.

The anointing transforms the vessel it flows through.

CHRISTLIKE CHARACTER CAN NEVER be fully developed without serving under the anointing. Anointed ministry brings us into contact with the power needed for personal transformation. Both the Old and New Testaments are filled with great examples of empowering for supernatural endeavors.

An important principle is found in the story of King Saul. God spoke saying that the Spirit of the Lord would come upon him and turn him into another man (see 1 Samuel 10:6). The anointing transforms the vessel it flows through. Two key phrases follow this promise:

1. *"God gave him another heart."*

2. *"Then the Spirit of the Lord came upon him, and He prophesied among them* [the prophets]" (1 Samuel 10:9-10).

Saul was given an opportunity to become all that Israel needed him to be (a king with a new heart) and learn to do all he needed to do (hear from God and declare His words—prophesy).

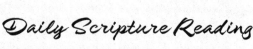

Daily Scripture Reading

1 SAMUEL 10:1-10

Prayer

Flow through me, Holy Spirit. I need to encounter Your transforming grace. I cannot fulfill the call on my life—to release God's presence through supernatural encounters—without You.

Our exposure to God's presence establishes our victory.

I HAVE A DEAR friend who had a huge character flaw that spiritually crippled him and his family for a season. Yet during this time, he still had a very strong prophetic anointing. He was not the first person to think that his successful ministry was a sign of God's approval of his private life. Many have fallen victim to that error through the years. When I confronted him about his secret sin, he wept with deep sorrow.

Because of his place of influence in the church, I felt a keen responsibility to bring him under discipline. Part of my restriction for him was to keep him from giving prophetic words for a season. He accepted this direction as necessary.

After several months of this restriction, I became increasingly troubled. I realized if I didn't allow him to minister (under the anointing), I'd be limiting his exposure to the very thing that would seal and establish his victory. When I released him to prophesy again, there was a new purity and power in his voice. It was his personal encounter with the anointing in ministry that changed him.

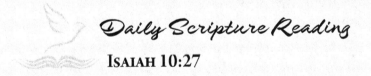

Daily Scripture Reading
ISAIAH 10:27

Prayer

Thank You, Holy Spirit, that my character weaknesses do not disqualify me from relationship with You. I run to You. I bring all of my flaws into the transforming light of Your presence.

The devil only tries to counterfeit that which has great potential for the Kingdom.

A COUNTERFEIT ONE-HUNDRED-DOLLAR BILL does not nullify the value of the real thing. Likewise, a counterfeit, abused, or abandoned gift does not invalidate our need for the Holy Spirit's power to live as Jesus did.

Pennies are not counterfeited because they're not worth the effort. In the same way, the devil only works to copy or distort those things in the Christian life that have the greatest potential effect. When I see others who have pursued great things in God but have failed, I get motivated to pick up where they left off. It tells me there's a treasure in that field, and I'm ready to look for it with reckless abandon. The abuses of one person never justify the neglect of another.

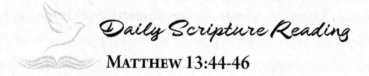

Daily Scripture Reading

MATTHEW 13:44-46

Prayer

I release to You, Jesus, any offense I've carried against Your Body. I don't want anything to get in the way of my pursuit of all that You have for me. Just because something has been executed imperfectly doesn't mean You're not in it. Open my eyes to what You're doing, Lord.

JULY

Nothing Is Impossible with God

Nevertheless, when the Son of man comes, will He really find faith on the earth?(Luke 18:8).

MANY OF THOSE WHO are embarrassed over the abuses of power, and the subsequent blemishes upon the Church, are seldom offended over the absence of signs and wonders. The eyes of the critics quickly move to the ones who tried and failed, overlooking the countless millions who confess salvation in Jesus, but never pursue the gifts as commanded.

But the eyes of Jesus quickly look to see if there is faith on the earth— "When I return will I find faith on earth?" (See Luke 18:8.) For every charlatan there are a thousand good citizens who accomplish little or nothing for the Kingdom.

Daily Scripture Reading
LUKE 18:1-8

Prayer

I want to be the persistent widow, God. I want to keep asking, keep pursuing Your supernatural interventions, and keep believing that Your will will be done on the earth. I will not be dissuaded from following You by those who abuse their power.

*The battle against sin
has been fought and won.*

MANY BELIEVE GOD'S POWER exists only to help us overcome sin. This understanding stops very short of the Father's intent for us to become witnesses of another world. Doesn't it seem strange that our whole Christian life should be focused on overcoming something that has already been defeated?

Sin and its nature have been yanked out by the roots. Many constantly call out to God for more power to live in victory. What more can He do for us? If His death wasn't enough, what else is there? That battle has already been fought and won! Is it possible that the process of constantly bringing up issues dealt with by the blood is what has actually given life to those issues?

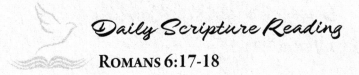

Daily Scripture Reading

ROMANS 6:17-18

Prayer

I am free from the anchor of sin in my life. I no longer am bound to living in the destructive patterns that lead to death. You defeated sin, Jesus. I am now bound to righteousness.

Our minds need to catch up with our changed reality—we are dead to sin, but alive in Christ.

MANY IN THE CHURCH are camped on the wrong side of the Cross. The apostle Paul spoke to this issue when he said, *"Likewise you also, reckon yourselves to be dead indeed to sin, but alive to God in Christ Jesus our Lord"* (Romans 6:11). We are no longer sinners, but have been crucified with Christ!

The word *reckon* points to our need to change our minds. We need to shift our thinking to align with our changed reality. I don't need power to overcome something if I'm dead to it. But I do need power for boldness (see Acts 4:28-29) for the miraculous and for the impossible.

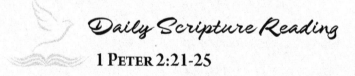

Daily Scripture Reading
1 PETER 2:21-25

Prayer

Transform my mind, Holy Spirit, to align with my new identity. I am not a sinner, so I don't need to operate defensively. I have been set free, I am alive in Christ, and I am on the offense. Fill me with power to invade the impossible.

Because nothing is impossible with God, we are required to take risks.

PART OF OUR PROBLEM is this: we are accustomed only to doing things for God that are not impossible. If God doesn't show up and help us, we can still succeed. There must be an aspect of the Christian life that is impossible without divine intervention. That keeps us on the edge and puts us in contact with our true calling.

Make no mistake, character is a supreme issue with God. But His approach is much different than ours. His righteousness/character is not built into us by our own efforts. It is developed when we quit striving and learn to abandon ourselves completely to His will.

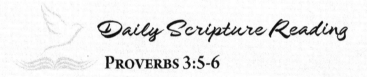

Daily Scripture Reading

PROVERBS 3:5-6

Prayer

> *I abandon myself all over again to Your will, God. I surrender my plan to Yours. Fill me with Your vision for my community. What impossibility would You have me engage with today?*

We must be clothed with power from on high.

SO GREAT WAS THE disciples' need for power to become witnesses that they were not to leave Jerusalem until they had it. That word *power, dunamis,* speaks of the miracle realm. It comes from *dunamai,* which means "ability." Think about it—we get to be clothed with God's ability!

The remaining eleven disciples were already the most trained people in signs and wonders in all of history. No one had seen or done more, except Jesus. And it was those eleven who had to stay until they were clothed with power from on high. When they got it, they knew it. This power came through an encounter with God.

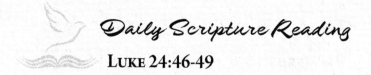

Daily Scripture Reading
LUKE 24:46-49

Prayer

I can't do what You have called me to do without Your power and Your presence, Father. My ability will never be enough. I need a fresh encounter with You!

For everyone who has, more will be given, and he will have abundance...(Matthew 25:29).

SOME PEOPLE, BECAUSE OF their fear of error, have said it's improper to seek for an experience with God. After all, many deceived groups have come from those who based their beliefs on experiences in conflict with Scripture. Under the guidance of such attitudes, fear becomes our teacher.

But why aren't those same individuals afraid of belonging to the doctrinally stable camps that are powerless? Is this deception any less dangerous than that of the power abuser? Will you bury your gifts and tell the Master when He comes that you were afraid of being wrong? Power and character are so closely aligned in Scripture that you cannot be weak in one without undermining the other.

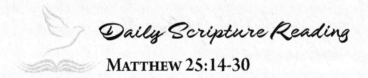

Daily Scripture Reading
MATTHEW 25:14-30

Prayer

I will not bury my gifts out of fear that I might do it wrong. I want to hear You say to me, "Well done, good and faithful servant." I will run after Your presence, pursuing an encounter with Your power-filled love.

Do not grieve the Holy Spirit (Ephesians 4:30).

AROUND TWENTY-FIVE YEARS AGO I heard someone mention that if we would learn what it meant to "not grieve" and "not quench" the Holy Spirit, we would know the secret to being full of the Spirit. While that may be overly simplistic, this individual tapped into two very important truths that deal directly with the "character vs. power" trap.

The command, *"Do not grieve the Holy Spirit"* (Ephesians 4:30), explains how our sin affects God. It causes Him grief. This command is character centered. Sin is defined in two ways: doing wrong things, and a failure to do right things: *"To him who knows to do good and does not do it, to him it is sin"* (James 4:17). Departing from the character of Christ in either of these ways brings grief to the Holy Spirit.

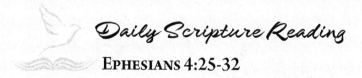

Daily Scripture Reading

EPHESIANS 4:25-32

Prayer

I never want to bring You grief, Holy Spirit. Show me if there is any action or any inaction of mine that has brought You sorrow. I want the choices of my life to bring You joy.

Do not quench the Holy Spirit (1 Thessalonians 5:19).

WHILE WE ARE CALLED not to sin against the Holy Spirit, bringing grief, we also have this command: *"Do not quench the Spirit"* (1 Thessalonians 5:19). This mandate is focused on our need to follow His leading. To quench means to "stop the flow" of something. As the Holy Spirit is ready to bring salvation, healing, and deliverance, we are to flow with Him. Failure to do so hinders His efforts to bring us into the supernatural.

If He is to be free to move in our lives, we will constantly be involved in impossibilities. The supernatural is His natural realm. The more important the Holy Spirit becomes to us, the more these issues will be paramount in our hearts.

Daily Scripture Reading
1 THESSALONIANS 5:14-22

Prayer

I let go of control and say "no" to fear. I give up my right to stop the flow of Your presence in my life, Holy Spirit. Have Your way in me. Lead me, and I will follow.

God will protect us in our pursuit of more of Him.

AT SOME POINT WE must believe in a God who is big enough to keep us safe in our quest for more of Him. Practically speaking, many Christian's devil is bigger than their God. How could a created, fallen being ever be compared with the infinite Lord of glory? It's an issue of trust.

If I focus on my need to protect myself from deception, I will always be overwhelmingly aware of the power of the devil. If my heart is completely turned to the One who is *"able to keep me from falling"* (Jude 24-25), He is the only One I become impressed with. My life reflects what I see with my heart.

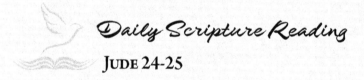

Daily Scripture Reading
JUDE 24-25

Prayer

I turn my heart completely to You, Lord. You are the One who is able to keep me from falling. You are the only One who inspires me with awe. I fill my heart with the knowledge of You.

We must cry out to God for specific, miraculous interventions.

HOW DO WE WALK in the power of God? First, we must pursue Him. The life of power is a life of abiding in Christ (staying plugged into our power source). The hunger for the demonstration of power must not be separated from our passion for Him. But realize this, our hunger for Him in part must be seen in our lustful pursuit of spiritual gifts (see 1 Corinthians 14:1). That is His command!

In this endeavor I must passionately desire life-changing encounters with God, over and over again. I must cry out day and night for them … and be specific. I must be willing to travel to get what I need. If God is moving somewhere else more than where I live, I must go! If He is using someone more than He is using me, I must humbly go to them and ask them to pray for me with the laying on of hands. The life of power is worth our pursuit.

Daily Scripture Reading
1 CORINTHIANS 14:1-12

Prayer

I humble myself before You, Lord. I will pursue You no matter where it takes me. I will run after the spiritual gifts with my whole heart. I will cry out for Your miraculous invasion into specific areas of my life and the lives of those around me. My hunger will look like something.

Wise men have always been willing to travel.

WHEN THE LORD IS moving powerfully somewhere else, it takes humility to leave home and pursue the more of God. Some may ask, "Why can't God touch me where I am?" He can. But He usually moves in ways that emphasize our need for others, rather than adding to our independence. Wise men have always been willing to travel.

In my personal quest for increased power and anointing in my ministry, I have traveled to many cities, including Toronto. Throughout Scripture, God invited men and women of God to leave their comfort zones to follow Him. When I have traveled, He has used my experiences in such places to set me up for life-changing encounters at home.

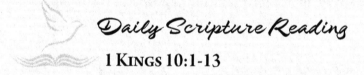

Daily Scripture Reading

1 KINGS 10:1-13

Prayer

When I say I will follow You anywhere, God, I mean it. If there is somewhere You would have me go, some way I can meet You by stepping outside of my comfort zone, show me. I will go if You ask me.

God, we want more of You at any cost!

ONCE IN THE MIDDLE of the night, God came in answer to my prayer for more of Him, yet not in a way I had expected. I went from a dead sleep to being wide-awake in a moment. Unexplainable power began to pulsate through my body, seemingly just shy of electrocution.

It was as though I had been plugged into a wall socket with a thousand volts of electricity flowing through my body. My arms and legs shot out in silent explosions as if something was released through my hands and feet. The more I tried to stop it, the worse it got.

I soon discovered that this was not a wrestling match I was going to win. I heard no voice, nor did I have any visions. This was simply the most overwhelming experience of my life. It was raw power…it was God. He came in response to a prayer I had been praying for months: "God, I must have more of you at any cost!"

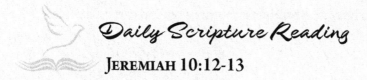

Daily Scripture Reading
JEREMIAH 10:12-13

Prayer

I want more of You at any cost, God. You are the living God, the everlasting King, and I invite You to invade my life in any and every way.

The favor of God doesn't always look like the favor of man.

WHEN I EXPERIENCED THAT powerful encounter with the Lord, it was glorious, but not pleasant. At first, I was embarrassed, even though I was alone in my room. As I lay there, I had a mental picture of me standing before my congregation, preaching the Word as I loved to do. But I saw myself with my arms and legs flailing about as though I had serious physical problems. The scene changed—I was walking down the main street of our town, in front of my favorite restaurant, again arms and legs moving about without control.

I didn't know of anyone who would believe that this was from God. I recalled Jacob and his encounter with the angel of the Lord. He limped for the rest of his life. And then there was Mary, the mother of Jesus. As a result of her experience with God, she bore the Christ-child … and then bore a stigma for the remainder of her days as the mother of the illegitimate child. It was becoming clear: The favor of God sometimes looks different from the perspective of earth than from heaven. My request for more of God carried a price.

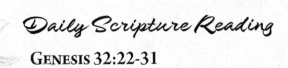

Daily Scripture Reading

GENESIS 32:22-31

Prayer

Your presence is worth it all, God. I don't want to think that more of You means an easier life. My eyes are fixed on You; pour out Your presence, even if it comes at a cost.

Great is the Lord and most worthy of praise; his greatness no one can fathom (Psalm 145:3).

IN THE MIDDLE OF that encounter, I cried, remembering my prayers for more of God's presence, but also feeling my own fear of the cost. I realized that God wanted to make an exchange: His increased presence for my dignity. It's difficult to explain how you know the purpose of such an encounter. All I can say is you just know. You know His purpose so clearly that every other reality fades into the shadows, as God puts His finger on the one thing that matters to Him.

In the midst of the tears came a point of no return. I gladly yielded, crying, "More, God. More! I must have more of You at any cost! If I lose respectability and get You in the exchange, I'll gladly make that trade. Just give me more of You!" The power surges didn't stop. They continued throughout the night, with me weeping and praying. It all stopped at 6:38 a.m., at which time I got out of bed completely refreshed. This experience continued the following two nights, beginning moments after getting into bed.

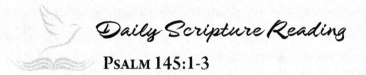

Daily Scripture Reading
PSALM 145:1-3

Prayer

I will not cherish my own image, the idea of my dignity, more than I cherish You. Lord, I open my arms to more of Your presence. If I lose respectability and get You in exchange, I gladly make that trade.

Lethargy will not be found in me.

BIBLICAL PASSION IS A mysterious mixture of humility, supernatural hunger, and faith. I pursue because I have been pursued. Lethargy must not be found in me. And if the average Christian life around me falls short of the biblical standard, I must pursue against the grain.

If people are not being healed, I will not supply a rationale so that all those around me remain comfortable with the void. Instead, I will pursue the healing until it comes or the individual goes to be with the Lord. I will not lower the standard of the Bible to my level of experience.

Jesus healed everyone who came to Him. To accept any other standard is to bring the Bible down to our level of experience and deny the nature of the One who changes not.

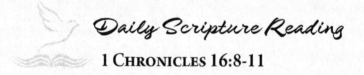

Daily Scripture Reading

1 CHRONICLES 16:8-11

Prayer

Shake me out of my comfort zone, Holy Spirit. Brush off any spiritual sleepiness and ignite my hunger to see all of Your promises fulfilled on the earth.

You only get to keep what you give away.

WHEN IT COMES TO the ministry of power, it's important to remember that whatever I receive from God I must give away. You only get to keep what you give away. If you want to see people healed, look for those who are sick and offer to pray for them. While I am not the healer, I do have control over my willingness to serve those in need.

If I minister to the needy, I give Him an opportunity to show His extravagant love for people. The ministry of signs and wonders will go nowhere if we are afraid of failure. As Randy Clark puts it, "I must be willing to fail to succeed."

Daily Scripture Reading
2 CORINTHIANS 9:6-9

Prayer

I refuse to let fear limit my engagement with Your presence. I want to receive from You openly, Lord, and give freely to others all that You've given me.

*Our childlike wonder and
curiosity are precious to the Lord.*

JESUS SAID THAT WE must receive the Kingdom like a child. The life of power is at home in the heart of a child. A child has an insatiable appetite to learn. Be childlike and read the works of those who have succeeded in the healing ministry. Stay away from the books and tapes of those who say it shouldn't or can't be done.

If the author doesn't walk in power, don't listen, no matter how proficient they may be in another field. An expert in biblical finances is not necessarily proficient in signs and wonders. Maintain respect for that individual's place in God and his or her area of expertise, but never waste precious time reading the stuff of those who do not do what they teach. We have grown fat on the theories of classroom Christians. We must learn from those who just do it!

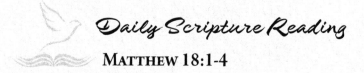

Daily Scripture Reading
MATTHEW 18:1-4

Prayer

Take me back to the beginning, Jesus. Refresh my heart and return me to the wonder-filled early days with You. I never want to lose my amazement at who You are. I refuse to grow out of my appetite for more of You.

Our challenge with faith is not an inability to hear God's voice, it's our willingness to listen to other voices.

CONSIDERING THE CRITICISMS OF this revival would be the same as giving audience to someone trying to prove I should have married another woman. First of all, I love my wife and have no interest in anyone else. Second, I refuse to entertain the thoughts of any person who desires to undermine my love for her. Only those who will add to my commitment to her are allowed such an audience with me. Anything less would be foolishness on my part.

The critics of this revival are unknowingly attempting to separate me from my first love. I will not give them place. I have many friends who are able to read the books of the critics with no ill effect. I respect them for their ability to stick their hands in the mire without getting their hearts dirty. I don't care to do it. It's just not my gift. Learn how you function best, then function!

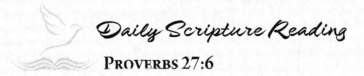

Daily Scripture Reading
PROVERBS 27:6

Prayer

> I have no obligation to listen to people who are speaking against
> Your presence and power, Father. I choose to be an audience only
> for those who are running after You.

Don't make excuses for powerlessness.

IF WE TEACH, PREACH, or witness and nothing happens, we must go back to the drawing board— our knees. Do not make excuses for powerlessness. For decades the Church has been guilty of creating doctrine to justify their lack of power, instead of crying out to God until He changed them. The lie they came to believe has given rise to an entire branch of theology that has infected the Body of Christ with a fear of the Holy Spirit. It deceives under the guise of staying undeceived.

The Word must go forth with power. Power is the realm of the Spirit. A powerless Word is the letter not the Spirit. And we all know, *"The letter kills, but the Spirit gives life"* (2 Corinthians 3:6). Lives must be changed in our ministry of the Word. Keep in mind that conversion is the greatest and most precious miracle of all. If the gospel is powerless, it is because human wisdom has had its influence.

Daily Scripture Reading
1 CORINTHIANS 1:17-19

Prayer

I must move in power as You did, Jesus. You never gave us a polite, powerless gospel. I refuse to be satisfied with anything but the full expression of the gospel.

Knock and keep knocking.

WHENEVER I HAVE TAKEN time to seek God about the need for power to back up His message, He always comes through with an increase. Miracles increase. I learned something very helpful along these lines from Randy Clark. When Randy notices there are certain kinds of healings that are not taking place in his meetings, he cries out to God mentioning specific diseases in his prayers.

He was having very few miracles having to do with the brain—such as dyslexia. After crying out for these kinds of miracle manifestations, he started to experience a breakthrough. I have followed his lead and have never seen God fail. Specific requests are good because they are measurable. Some of our prayers are too general. God could answer them and we would never know it.

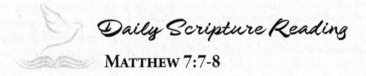

Daily Scripture Reading
MATTHEW 7:7-8

Prayer

I don't want to avoid praying specific prayers because of fear, God. Show me, right now, if there are any specific prayers I've been avoiding. I want to pray bold, measurable prayers!

It's possible to starve with millions of dollars in the bank.

WE HEAR A LOT about what the anointing costs. Without question, walking with God in power will cost all who give themselves to this mandate. But the absence of power is even more costly. Revival is the atmosphere in which Christ's power is most likely to be manifested. It touches every part of human life, breaking into society with sparks of revolution.

Such glory is costly, and it is not to be taken lightly. Nevertheless, a powerless Church is far more costly in terms of human suffering and lost souls. During revival, hell is plundered and heaven is populated. Without revival, hell is populated … period. Signs and wonders are necessary in our quest to see our cities transformed and the glory of God fill the earth.

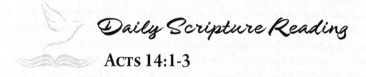

Daily Scripture Reading
ACTS 14:1-3

Prayer

Without the miraculous, the world cannot experience the fullness of Your redemption and hope, Father. Stir up my hunger for the specific signs and wonders You want to release over my city.

Signs and wonders reveal the nature of God.

A PRIMARY PURPOSE OF the miracle realm is to reveal the nature of God. The lack of miracles works like a thief, stealing precious revelation that is within the grasp of every man, woman, and child. Our debt to mankind is to give them answers for the impossible and a personal encounter with God. And that encounter must include great power.

We are to be a witness for God. To give witness is to "represent." This actually means to re-present Him. Therefore, to re-present Him without power is a major shortcoming. It is impossible to give an adequate witness of God without demonstrating His supernatural power. The supernatural is His natural realm. Jesus was an exact representation of the Father's nature. His re-presentation of the Father is to be a model for us as we learn how to re-present Him.

Daily Scripture Reading
HEBREWS 1:1-3

Prayer

I owe the world around me an encounter with You, God, and I cannot show them Your heart without showing them Your supernatural interventions. Let my life be a true witness for You.

When Jesus speaks, reality get redefined and what's possible changes.

THE MIRACLE REALM OF God is always with purpose. He doesn't come upon people with power to show off or entertain. Demonstrations of power are redemptive in nature. Even the cataclysmic activities of the Old Testament were designed to bring people to repentance.

Healing is never only one-dimensional. While a miracle may change one's physical health, it also sparks a revolution deep within the human heart. Both reveal the nature of God, which must never be compromised through powerless Christianity.

Daily Scripture Reading

LUKE 8:43:48

Prayer

You came to save, heal, and set us free in our spirits, souls, and bodies! Thank You, Jesus, that You care about every part of me. And You won't be satisfied until I receive all that You have for me.

Signs and wonders expose sin and bring people to a decision.

"WHEN SIMON PETER SAW *it* [the miraculous catch of fish], *he fell down at Jesus' knees, saying, "Depart from me, for I am a sinful man, O Lord!"* (Luke 5:8).

Peter had been fishing all night with no success. Jesus told him to cast the nets to the other side of the boat, which doubtless he had already done many times. When he did it at the bidding of the Master, the catch of fish was so great it nearly sank the boat. Peter called for help from the other boats. His response to this miracle was, "I am a sinful man."

Who told him that he was a sinner? There is no record of sermons, rebukes, or any such thing in the boat that day—just good fishing. So, how did he come under such conviction for sin? It was in the miracle. Power exposes. It draws a line in the sand and forces people to a decision.

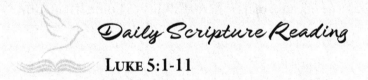

Daily Scripture Reading

LUKE 5:1-11

Prayer

Draw near with Your presence, Lord. Sift through every area of my heart, and draw any place that has strayed away back to You. Expose me in the light of Your glory.

When the Kingdom comes, the middle ground disappears.

DEMONSTRATIONS OF POWER ARE no guarantee that people will repent. One only needs to look at Moses to realize that sometimes the miraculous only causes our Pharaohs to become more resolved to destroy us when they see power. Without acts of power, the Pharisees might have forgotten about the Church that was born from the blood of Jesus poured out at the cross. Power stirred up the zeal of opposition in them. We must be sober-minded about this: power often causes people to decide what they're for or against. Power removes the middle ground.

Mercy ministries are absolutely essential in the ministry of the gospel. They are one of the ways the love of God can and must be seen. Yet they are not complete without demonstrations of power. Why? The reality is this: the world will usually applaud such efforts because they know we should be doing them. We must realize the sad truth—it is common for people to acknowledge the kindness of the Church and still not be brought to repentance. But power forces the issue because of its inherent ability to humble mankind.

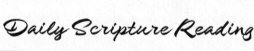

Daily Scripture Reading

EXODUS 8:1-14

Prayer

I want to stay humble and hungry in Your presence, God. Only You can change hearts. Come in Your mercy, Your glory, and in all of Your power. Reveal our hearts, God.

Power illuminates.

JESUS SAID, *"IF I had not done among them the works which no one else did, they would have no sin"* (John 15:24). Is He saying that sin didn't exist in the hearts of the Jews until He performed miracles? I doubt it very much. He is explaining the principle revealed in Peter's repentance.

Power exposes sin and brings people to a decision. When power is missing, we are not using the weapons that were in Jesus' arsenal when He ministered to the lost. The outcome? Most remain lost. Power forces people to be aware of God on a personal level, and it is demanding in nature.

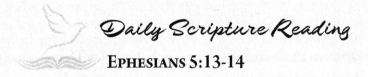

Daily Scripture Reading
EPHESIANS 5:13-14

Prayer

I cherish Your miracles throughout Scripture, Jesus. Teach me and renew my mind through Your Word. I am hungry to see Your miracles in and through my life.

The power of testimonies never depreciates.

A VERY PROFOUND PART of the Jewish culture was shaped by the command to keep the testimonies of the Lord. The family itself was driven by the ongoing revelation of God contained in His commandments and testimonies. They were to talk about the Law of God and what God had done when they went to bed at night, rose up in the morning, walked along, etc. Just about any time of the day was a perfect time to talk about God's wondrous works.

To insure they didn't forget, they were to build monuments that would help them to remember the invasion of God into their lives. For example: They piled stones to mark the place where Israel crossed the Jordan River. That was so that when their young ones would ask, "Hey Dad...why is that pile of stones there?" They could respond with the story of how God worked among them.

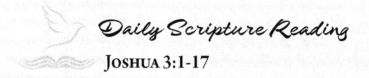

Daily Scripture Reading
JOSHUA 3:1-17

Prayer

It's so easy for me to forget all of the ways—both small and large—that You have intervened miraculously in my life. Forgive me, Father. I never want to stop meditating on Your wondrous works.

Signs and wonders bring courage.

THE TESTIMONY OF GOD creates an appetite for more of the activities of God. Expectation grows wherever people are mindful of His supernatural nature and covenant. When the expectation grows, miracles increase. When the miracles increase, testimonies increase as well. You can see the cycle. The simple act of sharing a testimony about God can stir up others until they expect and see God work in their day.

The reverse is also true. Where they decrease, miracles are expected less. If there is less expectation for miracles, they happen even less. As you can see, there is also a possible downward spiral. Forgetting what God has done by removing the testimony from our lips ultimately causes us to become fearful in the day of battle. The story of the children of Ephraim is tragic because they were thoroughly equipped to win. They just lacked courage. Their courage was to come from their memory of who God had been to them.

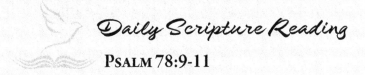

Daily Scripture Reading
PSALM 78:9-11

Prayer

I want to keep the testimonies from Scripture and from my own life at the forefront of my awareness. Holy Spirit, help me to think of a practical tool for remembering the miraculous. I want to feed on God's goodness and increase my expectation.

The supernatural is the key to the sin cities of the world.

Then He began to rebuke the cities in which most of His mighty works had been done, because they did not repent: Woe to you, Chorazin! Woe to you Bethsaida! For if the mighty works which were done in you had been done in Tyre and Sidon, they would have repented long ago in sackcloth and ashes.

But I say to you, it will be more tolerable for Tyre and Sidon in the day of judgment than for you. And you Capernaum, who are exalted to heaven, will be brought down to Hades; for if the mighty works which were done in you had been done in Sodom, it would have remained until this day.

But I say to you that it shall be more tolerable for the land of Sodom in the day of judgment than for you (Matthew 11:20-24).

This passage of Scripture makes a distinction between religious cities and those known for sin. The religious city had a numbed awareness of its need for God, while the sinful city was conscious that something was missing. Religion is even more cruel than sin.

The cities that Jesus addresses here saw more signs and wonders than all the rest combined. The miracles Jesus performed were so great in number that apostle John said recording them could fill up all of the books in the world. This gives us perspective on the rebuke of Jesus upon the hard-hearted cities.

Daily Scripture Reading

JOHN 21:25

Prayer

Holy Spirit, give me eyes to see all of the potential in those places that seem so dark to me. Darkness is not dark to You; You're not intimidated by evil. These cities are just one, powerful God encounter away from transformation.

The revelation that comes from the miraculous increases responsibility.

JESUS WAS LIMITED IN what He could do in Nazareth because of their unbelief. Yet in Chorazin and Bethsaida, His miracles appear to be limitless, which suggests these cities had a measure of faith. His stern rebuke didn't appear to come because they didn't appreciate His working of miracles. They must have. Their problem was that they added such a move to what they were already doing, instead of making Him the focal point of their lives. That's what religion does. Like Jesus said, they failed to repent and change their way of thinking (alter their perspective on life itself).

Many enjoy the move of God, but don't genuinely repent (change their life's perspective, making His activities the focus and ambition of their lives). The revelation that came to them through the miraculous increased their responsibility, thus requiring change. It never came.

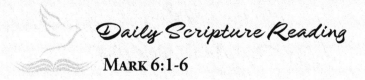

Daily Scripture Reading
MARK 6:1-6

Prayer

I never want to become lethargic about Your involvement in my life, Lord. All that I am is Yours. Your activities—not mine—are the focus and ambition of my life.

*The world is waiting for those
with the message of the Kingdom.*

TYRE, SIDON, AND SODOM would have repented had they been exposed to the same dimension of outpouring that was seen in Chorazin and Bethsaida (see Matthew 11:20-24). Did you hear it? They would have repented! It's a prophetic promise for today. Miracles on the streets of the "sin cities" of the world will cause them to repent! It is this secret that gives us access to the heart of these great cities!

The San Franciscos and the Amsterdams, the New Orleans and the Rio de Janeiros of this world will repent...if there is an army of saints, full of the Holy Ghost, walking their streets, caring for the broken, bringing the God of power into their impossible circumstances. They will repent! That's a promise. They simply await those with the message of the Kingdom to come. Powerlessness cancels that possibility, and in its place comes God's judgment.

Daily Scripture Reading

2 CHRONICLES 7:14

Prayer

Thank You, Father, that there is so much hope for the great cities of the world. Show me any place where I have lost hope. Give me Your perspective, and help me to partner with You to bring transformation.

AUGUST

Miracles Reveal God's Heart

Miracles reveal His glory.

"THIS BEGINNING OF SIGNS *Jesus did in Cana of Galilee, and manifested His glory, and His disciples believed in Him*" (John 2:11).

Jesus attended a wedding where they ran out of wine. As yet He hadn't performed any of the wonders for which He would later become known. Mary knew who her son was and what was possible. So in this time of need His mother, Mary, turned to Him and said, *"They have no wine."* Jesus responded to her saying, *'Woman, what does your concern have to do with Me? My hour has not yet come.'*

But then Mary did something amazing—she turned to the servants and said, *"Whatever He says to you, do it!"* (John 2:4-5). Her faith just made room for the extravagance of God! Jesus followed this with the miracle of turning the water into wine.

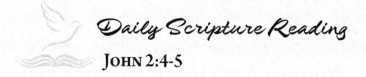

Daily Scripture Reading
JOHN 2:4-5

Prayer

Whenever I try to put You in a box, Jesus, I remember this miracle. Your first miracle was one of extravagance and celebration. Will You show me the joy You felt in this moment?

Faith moves heaven, so that heaven will move earth.

IT'S IMPORTANT TO REMEMBER that Jesus only did what He saw His Father do, and He only said what He heard His Father say. When Mary first mentioned the need for wine to Jesus, it is safe to say He noticed that the Father was not involved in doing any miracles for that wedding. Besides, He knew that this wasn't His hour… the time to be revealed as the miracle worker. That's what brought the response, *"Woman, what does your concern have to do with me. My hour has not yet come."* Mary, however, responded with faith and had the servants ready to do *"…whatever He says to you."*

Jesus again looked to see what the Father was doing and now noticed that He was turning water into wine. So Jesus followed His lead and did the miracle. Her faith so touched the heart of the Father that He apparently changed the chosen time to unveil Jesus as the miracle worker. Faith moves heaven, so that heaven will move earth.

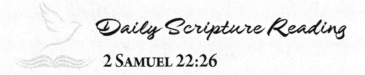

Daily Scripture Reading
2 SAMUEL 22:26

Prayer

> *I want to have faith like Mary. I want to know Your heart so well that my faith moves the heart of the Father. Help me, Jesus, to see things like You do.*

There will be a generation that reveals the living testimony of Jesus to the world.

SIGNS AND WONDERS RELEASE the glory of God into our cities. The need—be it physical sickness, poverty, oppression, etc.—represents the impact of darkness. The miracle displaces darkness and replaces it with light—glory. When miracles are absent, so is the glory of God, which is the manifested presence of Jesus.

As glory is released, it displaces the powers of darkness and replaces it with the actually ruling presence of God. The house is clean and swept and becomes filled with the furnishings of heaven. As the powers of darkness are removed they must be replaced with right things, or the enemy has legal access to return, making the last state of the man worse than the first. Miracles do both—they remove the ruling influence of hell while establishing the ruling presence of God. How will the glory of God cover the earth? I believe that, at least in part, it will be through a people who walk in power, bringing the testimony of Jesus to the nations of the world.

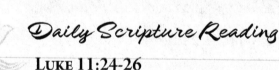

Daily Scripture Reading

LUKE 11:24-26

Prayer

I don't want to stop at destroying the works of the enemy. I want to reveal the glory of heaven to all areas of the world. God, show me how You would have me partner with You today.

Now when the multitudes saw it, they marveled and glorified God, who had given such power to men (Matthew 9:8).

I TALK ABOUT THE miracle-working power of God in almost every meeting I lead, whether it be a traditional church service, a conference, even a board or staff meeting. When I'm speaking away from home, I will often do this to stir up faith and help listeners to direct their hearts to God.

When I'm through sharing stories of God's miraculous interventions, I ask them this question: How many of you gave praise and glory to God when I shared those testimonies? Most every hand goes up. Then I remind them of this one important thing—If there were no power and corresponding testimony, God would have never received that glory. Without power, we rob God of the glory He is due! Signs direct people to give glory to God.

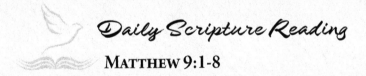

Daily Scripture Reading
MATTHEW 9:1-8

Prayer

You have been so consistently good, so wonderfully faithful in my life, God. I don't want to keep that a secret. I want to share with everyone around me how Your love and power has changed me forever.

Signs themselves give Him glory!

"ALL YOUR WORKS SHALL praise You, O Lord, And Your saints shall bless You" (Psalm 145:10).

Not only do miracles stir the hearts of men to give glory to God, miracles give Him glory on their own. I'm not sure how this works, but somehow an act of God has a life of its own and contains the ability to actually give God glory without the assistance of mankind. The absence of miracles robs God of the glory that He is to receive from the life released in His own works. *"Bless the Lord, all His works, in all places of His dominion. Bless the Lord, O my soul!"* (Psalm 103:22).

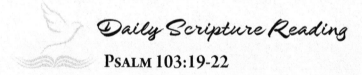

Daily Scripture Reading

PSALM 103:19-22

Prayer

The wonder, the beauty, the sudden restoration of the miraculous all show me aspects of who You are, God. More and more, I am captivated by You. I stand in awe of Your heart for mankind.

Miracles are a unifying force for the generations.

"ONE GENERATION SHALL PRAISE *Your works to another, And shall declare Your mighty acts*" (Psalm 145:4). Israel was to build monuments in memory of the activities of God. The reason? So that in their everyday existence there would be a reminder to coming generations of who God is and what His covenant with His people looks like.

The testimony was to be both a record of God's activity with His people and an invitation for others to know Him in that way. One generation would speak of God's testimony to another. It doesn't say that the older generation would speak to the younger. While that is what is most often thought of in this verse, it is equally true that a younger generation would experience God, and the older could benefit. Encounters with the almighty God become a unifying factor for generations!

Daily Scripture Reading

PSALM 78:4-8

Prayer

I won't keep Your goodness a secret. I will share the stories of Your mercy generously. I will steward them faithfully for the generations to come.

Signs and Wonders affirm who Jesus is.

"*IF I DO NOT do the works of My Father, do not believe Me; but if I do, though you do not believe Me, believe the works, that you may know and believe that the Father is in Me, and I in Him*" (John 10:37-38). If the Jews struggled with believing in Jesus as their Messiah, He simply told them to look at the miracles and believe them. Why? A sign always leads you somewhere.

Jesus was not afraid of where His signs would lead them. Somehow that simple step of believing in what they saw eventually could enable them to believe in Jesus Himself—as in the case of Nicodemus. Every miracle testified of Jesus' identity. Without miracles, there can never be a full revelation of Jesus.

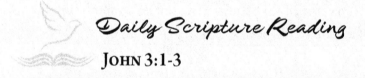

Daily Scripture Reading
JOHN 3:1-3

Prayer

Jesus, You were so confident in the faithfulness of the Father that You staked Your entire identity on the miraculous. I want that kind of faith, Lord. I want to move in signs that point people to who You are.

Miracles help people hear from God.

PHILIP WAS THE MESSENGER of God for the city of Samaria. They were able to hear his words as being from God because of the miracles. Acts of power help people to tune their hearts to the things of God. It helps to break them loose from the rationale that this material world is the ultimate reality. Such a shift in perspective is essential to the most basic response to God. In essence, that is what the word *repentance* means. Miracles provide the grace for repentance.

The desperation that miracles cause is in part responsible for this phenomenon. As our interests turn from all that is natural, we direct our attention to Him. This change of heart opens both the eyes and ears of the hearts. As a result, we see what has been right in front of us all this time, and we hear what God has been saying throughout our lives. Miracles cause a shift in priorities. They are an important aid in helping us to hear more clearly. Without them we are more inclined to be directed by our own minds and call it spirituality.

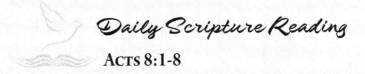

Daily Scripture Reading

ACTS 8:1-8

Prayer

Open my eyes, God. Shake me out of my limited perspective. My home is in heaven—show me what that means. Speak to me, today.

Miracles help people obey God.

IN ROMANS, THE APOSTLE Paul demonstrates how the Gentiles were brought into obedience through the power of the Spirit of God, expressed in signs and wonders. This was what he considered as fully preaching the gospel. It wasn't a complete message without a demonstration of the power of God. It's how God says amen to His own declared word!

The Bible is filled with the stories of heroes who gained the courage to obey God in the most difficult of circumstances through a personal encounter with the miraculous. Nothing thrills the heart more than knowing God. He is limitless in power. He is for us and not against us, and is big enough to make up for our smallness. Conversely, being raised in a home where there is little or no evidence of the things in which we believe disillusions a generation created for great exploits.

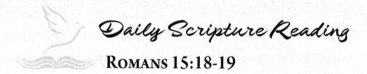

Daily Scripture Reading

ROMANS 15:18-19

Prayer

I have been created for great exploits, to face impossible situations and see breakthrough, to see Your limitless power to expand the limits of my perspective. Help me to live out the fullness of the gospel, Jesus.

Miracles validate the identity of both the Son of God and His Church

THE PROMISE, *"I WILL be with you,"* was given many times through-out the Scriptures. It was always given to one who would be brought into impossible circumstances—circumstances that would need a miracle. While His presence is comforting, while His sweet fellowship is what draws me into an intimate relationship with Him, His presence also is a provision from heaven designed to bring me into a place of great courage for signs and wonders.

It was understood by the Jews that if God is with you there should be miracles—*"... for no one can do these signs that You do unless God is with him"* (John 3:2). In the Great Commission of Matthew 28:18-20, we find this phrase—*"I am with you always, even to the end of the age."* His presence is the assurance of His intent to use us in the miraculous. His moving into the life of all believers is a prophetic act that declares His supernatural purpose for His people.

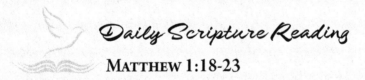

Daily Scripture Reading
MATTHEW 1:18-23

Prayer

You are Immanuel. You are God, with me. You came to earth to reveal the Father, changing the world forever. Your presence never leaves me. And, because of this, I can do great things through You.

His power sustains us.

JESUS COMMANDED THE MOST highly trained individuals in the super-natural to ever walk the earth to *"wait in Jerusalem for what the Father has promised"* (see Acts 1:4). Luke states it this way, *"Tarry in the city of Jerusalem until you are endued with power from on high"* (Luke 24:49). Even though they had been with Him, even though they had experienced His power through their own ministry, they were to wait for *Dunamis*—the ability to perform miracles.

It is as if they had been working under the umbrella of His anointing. The time had come for them to get an anointing of their own through an encounter with God. The baptism of fire would give them their own ongoing encounter that would help to keep them at the center of God's will when persecution came.

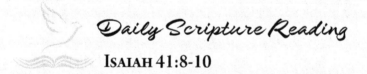

Daily Scripture Reading

ISAIAH 41:8-10

Prayer

Things haven't always been easy, God. The challenges I'm facing can feel like they're going to knock me off of my feet. I need You. I need Your sustaining dunamis power. Keep me at the center of Your will.

Fullness can only be measured by overflow.

THE BAPTISM OF THE Holy Spirit is an immersion into the dunamis of heaven. The ability to pray in tongues is a wonderful gift given through this baptism. I pray in tongues constantly and am grateful for such a gift from God. But to think that speaking in tongues is the purpose for such a holy invasion is embarrassingly simplistic. It would be the same as saying that when Israel crossed the Jordan River it was the same as possessing the Promise Land.

Yes, they were in it, they could see it, but they did not possess it! Their river crossing gave them the legal access to the possession. This wonderful Spirit baptism has given us such an access. But to stand on the banks proclaiming it's all mine, is foolishness at best. Such ignorance has caused great numbers of people to halt their pursuit once they've received their spiritual language. They have been taught they are now full of the Holy Spirit. A glass is only full when it overflows. Fullness can only be measured by overflow.

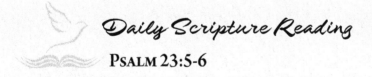

Daily Scripture Reading
PSALM 23:5-6

Prayer

You have brought me into the Promised Land, Lord. Fill me, guide me, and teach me what it looks like to now inhabit the land. Anoint me with Your oil; fill my cup until it overflows.

We are co-laborers with Christ.

GOD'S PURPOSE FOR THE miraculous is to bring us into a divine partnership in which we become co-laborers with Christ. Power came to make us witnesses. When the Spirit of God came upon the people in the Scriptures, all of nature bowed before them. Power was displayed, and impossibilities gave way to the full expression of God's presence.

Many fear signs and wonders because of the possibility of deception. So, in order to prevent any opportunity of being deceived they replace displays of power with religious traditions, Christian activities, or even Bible study. They often become satisfied with knowledge. But, when this happens who is deceived? We were designed to represent the fullness of God to the earth, and that is impossible to do without miracles.

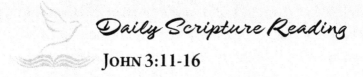

Daily Scripture Reading
JOHN 3:11-16

Prayer

I will not slide back into the safety of known religious traditions. I will move forward with You, God. I will pursue the fullest expression of Your love on the earth.

Signs point us to the Person of Jesus.

SIGNS HAVE A PURPOSE. They are not an end in themselves. They point to a greater reality. When we exit a building, we don't go out through the exit sign. When we need to put out a fire, we don't beat it out with the sign pointing to the fire hose. The sign is real. But it points to a reality greater than itself.

A sign along a highway can confirm we are on the right road. Without signs we have no way of knowing we are where we think we are. Signs aren't needed when I travel familiar roads. But I do need them when I'm going where I've never been. So it is in this present move of God.

We've gone as far as we can with our present understanding of Scripture. It's time to let signs have their place. They illustrate Scripture, all the while pointing to Jesus, the Son of God. Yet they also confirm to a people who have embraced an authentic gospel that they are going in the right direction.

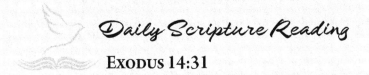

Daily Scripture Reading
EXODUS 14:31

Prayer

I will review Your miraculous works, God. I will meditate on Your signs and wonders in order to learn more of who You are. I will draw close to You as You fill the earth with wonder-working power and presence.

The anointing of the Holy Spirit is His actual presence upon us for ministry.

THE PURPOSE OF THE anointing is to make the supernatural natural.

God's covenant promise, *"I will be with you,"* has always been linked to mankind's need for courage to face the impossible. There is no question that the presence of God is what brings us great comfort and peace. But the presence of God was always promised to His chosen ones to give them assurance in the face of less than favorable circumstances.

He is the great treasure of mankind. He always will be. It is this revelation that enabled the revolutionary exploits of the apostle Paul. It's what strengthened a king named David to risk his life in order to transform the system of sacrifice and worship. Moses needed this assurance as the man who was sent to face Pharaoh and his demon-possessed magicians. They all needed incredible confidence to fulfill their callings.

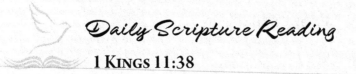

Daily Scripture Reading

1 KINGS 11:38

Prayer

Scriptures are filled with strong, powerful leaders who were dependent on Your presence, God. I need Your presence in the same way. I do not want to move forward without You.

God will be with us.

JOSHUA WAS FACED WITH filling the big shoes of Moses, who was the man with whom God talked face-to-face. And now, Joshua was to lead Israel to where Moses was unable to go himself. God's word to him was one of great encouragement and exhortation. It ends with the ultimate promise, *"I will be with you."*

Gideon was also given an impossible task. He was the least of his family, which was the least of his tribe, which was the least in Israel. Yet God had chosen him to lead Israel into victory against the Midianites. His encounter is one of the most interesting recorded in Scripture. Many a fearful person has taken comfort in Gideon's turnaround experience. God initiated his transformation with the promise, *"I will be with you."*

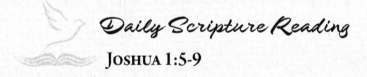

Daily Scripture Reading

JOSHUA 1:5-9

Prayer

You have spoken destiny over me that I cannot accomplish without Your grace and power. So often, I feel like Gideon—hiding in fear—but You have promised to be with me. I can take a step forward in confidence.

His presence is our greatest treasure.

THE GREAT COMMISSION PROVIDES more interesting reading for those who remember what kind of men God was giving His charge to—greedy, prideful, angry, and self-centered. Yet Jesus called them to change the world. What was the one word of assurance that He gave them before departing from sight? *"I will be with you always...."* (See Matthew 28:19-21.)

We know that such a promise is given to everyone who calls on the name of the Lord for salvation. But why do some walk with a greater sense of God's presence than others? Some people place high value on the presence of God, and others don't. The ones who do enjoy fellowship throughout their day with the Holy Spirit are extremely conscious of how He feels about their words, attitudes, and activities. The thought of grieving Him brings great sorrow. It's their passion to give Him preeminence in everything. That passion brings that believer into a supernatural life—one with the constant activity of the Holy Spirit working through them.

Daily Scripture Reading
1 CORINTHIANS 6:19

Prayer

Heighten my consciousness of Your presence, Holy Spirit. I never want to become dull to Your voice, Your comfort, or Your correction. You are precious to me.

*The anointing empowers
us to go into all the world.*

THE PRESENCE OF GOD is to be realized in the anointing. Remember, *anointing* means "smeared"—it is God covering us with His power-filled presence. Supernatural things happen when we walk in the anointing!

For the most part, the anointing has been hoarded by the Church for the Church. Many have misunderstood why God has covered us with Himself, thinking it is for our enjoyment only. But we must remember, in the Kingdom of God we only get to keep what we give away.

This wonderful presence of God is to be taken to the world. If it isn't, our effectiveness decreases. Does He leave us? No. But perhaps this phrase will help to clarify this point: He is in me for my sake, but He's upon me for yours!

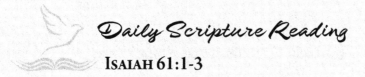

Daily Scripture Reading
ISAIAH 61:1-3

Prayer

You have a plan for the world, Lord, to bring good news and to heal the brokenhearted. I get to be a part of transforming the world with Your presence to bring You glory.

Every believer should cry out for a greater anointing!

NOT ONLY IS ALL ministry to be Spirit empowered, it is to have a gathering element to it. Jesus said, *"He who does not gather with me scatters"* (Luke 11:23). If our ministries do not gather, they will divide. Either we take what God has given us and give it to the world, or what we have received will bring division. It's our perspective on the world that keeps us in the center of His purposes.

The anointing equips us to bring the world into an encounter with God. That encounter is what we owe them. For that reason, every caring evangelist should cry out for a greater anointing; every believer should cry for the same. When we are smeared with God, it rubs off on all we come into contact with—and it's that anointing that breaks the yokes of darkness (Isaiah 10:27).

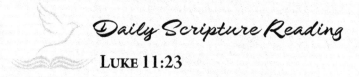

Daily Scripture Reading
LUKE 11:23

Prayer

> *I need more of You, God! I am running after You, my eyes fixed on Your face. Every encounter with You gives me something I can give away. Help me know what that looks like for me today.*

The anointing equips us to serve others.

THE MOST COMMON UNDERSTANDING of our need for the anointing is in the preaching of the Word or praying for the sick. These are just two of the very common ways of bringing this encounter to people. While these are true, it's the person with the continual anointing that opens up many more opportunities for ministry.

I used to frequent a local health-food store. It was the kind that had strange music and many books by various gurus and cultic spiritual guides. I did business there because of a commitment I made to bring the light of God to the darkest places in town. I wanted them to see a contrast between what they thought was light and what is actually Light.

Before entering, I would pray specifically that the anointing of God would rest upon me and flow through me. I would walk up and down the aisles praying quietly in the Spirit, wanting God to fill the store. One day the owner came to me and said, "Something is different when you come into the store." A door opened that day that gave me many opportunities for future ministry. The anointing upon me equipped me for service.

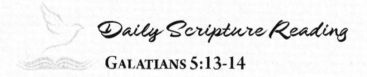

Daily Scripture Reading
GALATIANS 5:13-14

Prayer

Your presence carries the answer to every need. I want to serve my community, God, but I need Your anointing to do so effectively. How would You have me release Your presence today?

The anointing breaks the yoke.

JESUS WAS WALKING DOWN a crowded road with people from all sides trying to get close to Him. A woman reached out and touched His garment. He stopped and asked, *"Who touched Me?"* The disciples were startled by such a question because to them, it had such an obvious answer—everyone! But Jesus went on to say that He felt virtue *(dunamis)* flow from Him.

Jesus was anointed by the Holy Spirit. The actual power of the Spirit of God left His being and flowed into that woman and healed her. The anointing was resident in Jesus' physical body the same as with every believer. The faith of that woman put a demand on that anointing in Jesus. She was healed, because the anointing breaks the yoke (see Isaiah 10:27).

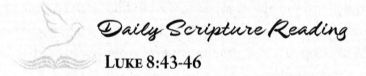

Daily Scripture Reading
LUKE 8:43-46

Prayer

I want to be so aware of You, Holy Spirit, that I can tell when someone's faith is pulling on Your presence. Build in me that unquenchable faith the woman with the issue of blood had.

Our greatest gift is meant to be given away.

A VERY POPULAR VERSE for receiving an offering is, *"Freely you have received, freely give"* (Matthew 10:8). But the context of the verse is often forgotten. Jesus was referring to the ministry of the supernatural. Listen to the implication: "I have received something that I am to give away!" What? The Holy Spirit. He is the greatest gift anyone could ever receive. And He is living in me.

When we minister in the anointing, we actually give away the presence of God—we impart Him to others. Jesus went on to teach His disciples what it meant to give it away. It included the obvious things, such as: healing the sick, casting out demons, etc. But it also included one often forgotten aspect: "When you go into a house…let your peace come upon it." There is an actual impartation of His presence that we are able to make in these situations. This is how we bring the lost into an encounter with God. We learn to recognize His presence, cooperate with His passion for people, and invite them to receive salvation.

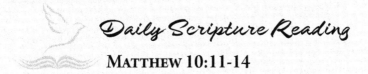

Daily Scripture Reading
MATTHEW 10:11-14

Prayer

I want to follow Your presence, Lord. I want to see where You are moving, who You are highlighting, and hear what You are saying. Thank You for trusting me with Your presence.

*Give God a chance to
do what only He can do.*

HE HAS MADE US stewards of the presence of God. It is not as though we can manipulate and use His presence for our own religious purposes. We are moved upon by the Holy Spirit, thereby becoming co-laborers with Christ. In that position we invite Him to invade the circumstances that arise before us. He looks for those who are willing to be smeared with Him, allowing His presence to affect others for good.

The more obvious ways are in preaching or praying for people's specific needs. Don't underestimate this important tool. By looking for chances to serve, we give the Holy Spirit the opportunity to do what only He can do—miracles. I don't see everyone I pray for healed. I'm not batting even close to a thousand. But there are many more healed than would be had I not prayed for anyone! If you don't see the miracle, keep going. Pray again. Don't quit.

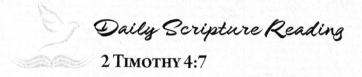

Daily Scripture Reading
2 TIMOTHY 4:7

Prayer

Thank You, God, that miracles are not my responsibility. Pursuing You, praying for people, following Your voice—this is what I will do. You will do what only You can do.

The spiritual gifts are worth our intense pursuit.

JESUS SAID, *"IF I do not do the works of My Father, do not believe Me"* (John 10:37). The works of the Father are miracles. Even the Son of God stated it was the miraculous that validated His ministry on earth. In that context He said, *"... he who believes in Me... greater works than these he will do, because I go to My Father"* (John 14:12). The miraculous is a large part of the plan of God for this world. And it is to come through the Church.

I look forward to the day when the Church stands up and says, "Don't believe us unless we are doing the works that Jesus did!" The Bible says that we are to pursue earnestly (lustfully!) spiritual gifts (see 1 Corinthians 14:1) and that those gifts make us established (see Romans 1:11). Which ones? All of them.

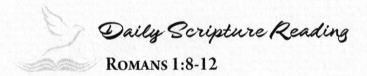

Daily Scripture Reading
ROMANS 1:8-12

Prayer

God, I need Your gifts in my life. I want to move with such confidence. I want to be naturally supernatural. Give me wisdom for how to practically increase my pursuit of Your gifts.

*Getting us to heaven is not as great
a challenge as getting heaven into us.*

I OWE THE WORLD a Spirit-filled life, for I owe them an encounter with God. Without the fullness of the Holy Spirit in and upon me, I do not give God a surrendered vessel to flow through.

The fullness of the Spirit was the goal of God throughout the law and prophets. Salvation was the immediate goal, but the ultimate goal on earth was the fullness of the Spirit in the believer. Getting us to heaven is not near as great a challenge as it is to get heaven into us. This is accomplished through the fullness of the Spirit in us.

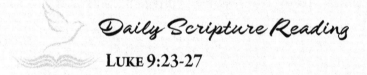

Daily Scripture Reading
LUKE 9:23-27

Prayer

I want to share Your ultimate goal for my life, Father. I long to be filled with heaven, to be filled with the fullness of Your Spirit. I surrender to You fully, unashamedly.

*Surely the Lord is in this place,
and I did not know it (Genesis 28:16).*

JACOB, AN OLD TESTAMENT patriarch, was sleeping in the great outdoors when he had a dream that contained one of the more startling revelations ever received by man. He saw an open heaven with a ladder coming down to earth. On the ladder were angels ascending and descending. He was frightened and said, "God is here and I didn't even know it" (see Genesis 28:16). That statement describes much of what we've been witnessing in this revival for the past several years—God is present, yet many remain unaware of His presence.

I have witnessed God's touch upon thousands of people in this present outpouring—conversions, healings, restored marriages, addictions broken, and the demonized set free. The list of how lives have been changed is gloriously long and increasing daily. Yet as these have been changed, there have always been those in the same meeting who can hardly wait for the service to end and get out the door. One person recognizes God's presence and is forever changed, the other never realized what could have been.

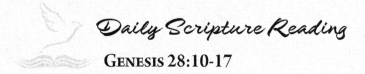

Daily Scripture Reading

GENESIS 28:10-17

Prayer

Keep my senses sharpened to Your Spirit, God. I want to follow how You move in the room. I want to see what You are doing and partner with it to bring heaven to earth.

The house of God is the person of Jesus.

JACOB'S DREAM PROVIDES US with the first mention of the house of God in Scripture. This house contained His presence, a gate into heaven, a ladder, and angels ascending and descending between heaven and earth. Jesus affirms Jacob's revelation about the house of God on planet Earth, but in a way that is completely unexpected.

John 1:14 says, *"The Word was made flesh, and dwelt among us."* The word *dwelt* means "tabernacled." Jesus is introduced here as the Tabernacle of God on earth. Later in the same chapter, Jesus says that His followers would see *"angels ascending and descending upon the Son of Man"* (John 1:51). The details of the Genesis 28 revelation of the house of God are seen in the person of Jesus. He is an illustration of Jacob's revelation.

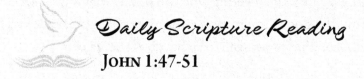

Daily Scripture Reading
JOHN 1:47-51

Prayer

I'm so grateful that You would send Your Son, the manifestation of Your heart and Your will upon the earth. Thank You, Father, that You want to be known by me.

We are to be the light of the world, the tabernacle of God on the earth.

FOR US TO BECOME all that God intended, we must remember that Jesus' life was a model of what mankind could become if it were in right relationship with the Father. Through the shedding of His blood, it would be possible for everyone who believed on His name to do as He did and become as He was. This meant then that every true believer would have access to the realm of life that Jesus lived in.

Jesus came as the light of the world. He then passed the baton to us announcing that we are the light of the world. Jesus came as the miracle worker. He said that we would do "greater works" than He did (see John 14:12). He then pulled the greatest surprise of all, saying, "right now the Holy Spirit is with you, but He's going to be in you." Jesus, who illustrates to us what is possible for those who are right with God, now says that His people are to be the tabernacle of God on planet Earth.

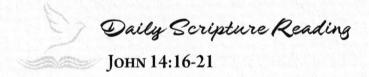

Daily Scripture Reading
JOHN 14:16-21

Prayer

You came to show me the way, Jesus. You showed me what a fully surrendered life could look like. You revealed the intimacy of Your relationship with the Father and the fruit of that communion. I will live with Your example in every way.

We are a dwelling place of God in the Spirit.

PAUL AFFIRMS TO US that we are meant to be a tabernacle of God's presence on the earth with statements such as, *"Do you not know that you are the temple of God?"* (1 Corinthians 3:16), *"you are a dwelling place of God"* (Ephesians 2:22).

Jacob's initial revelation of the house of God consisted of the presence of God, a gate to heaven, and a ladder with angels ascending and descending upon it. Why is this important to understand? This revelation shows the resources that are at our disposal to carry out the Master's plan.

Frank DaMazio, of City Bible Church in Portland, Oregon, has a great teaching regarding this principle and the local church. He calls them Gate Churches. This principle of being the stewards of the heavenly realm then becomes more than the assignment of the individual; it becomes the privilege of an entire church for the sake of their entire city.

Daily Scripture Reading
EPHESIANS 2:19-22

Prayer

Show me, God, how You would have me partner with my church to release Your presence in our city. You have intentionally placed me in community for such a time as this.

The angelic will assist us in our heavenly assignment.

ANGELS ARE IMPRESSIVE BEINGS. They are glorious and powerful. So much so that when they showed up in Scripture, people often fell to worship them. While it is foolish to worship them, it is equally foolish to ignore them. Angels are assigned to serve wherever we serve, if the supernatural element is needed. *"Are not all angels ministering spirits sent to serve those who will inherit salvation?"* (Hebrews 1:14).

I believe angels have been bored because we live the kind of lifestyle that doesn't require much of their help. Their assignment is to assist us in supernatural endeavors. If we are not people of risk, then there is little room for the supernatural. Risks must be taken to pursue solutions to impossible situations. When the Church regains its appetite for the impossible, the angels will increase their activities among men.

Daily Scripture Reading
PSALM 91:11-16

Prayer

There is not one part of our commission that You expect us to do on our own, God. You surround me, Your Spirit is within me, and Your angel armies will come alongside of me.

Faith is spelled R-I-S-K.

AS THE FIRES OF revival intensify, so do the supernatural activities around us. If angels are assigned to assist us in supernatural endeavors, then there must be need for the supernatural. Risk must be taken to pursue solutions to impossible situations. The gospel of power is the answer to the tragic condition of humankind. John Wimber said, "Faith is spelled R-I-S-K." If we really want more of God then we must change our lifestyle so that His manifested presence will increase upon us.

This is not an act on our part to somehow manipulate God. Instead it is the bold attempt to take Him at His Word, so that as we radically obey His charge, He says Amen (see Mark 16:20) with the miraculous. I challenge you to pursue God passionately! And in your pursuit, insist on a supernatural lifestyle—one that keeps the hosts of heaven busy, ushering in the King and His Kingdom!

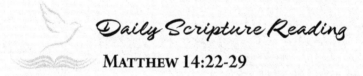

Daily Scripture Reading
MATTHEW 14:22-29

Prayer

Risking for You, Lord, is wisdom. You surround me, You go before me, and You know my path. I will pursue You no matter where You lead. My comfort zone is not worth missing out on what You're doing.

SEPTEMBER

Co-Laboring with God

Angels come in response to the prayers of the saints.

WHILE GOD HAS PROVIDED angels to assist us in our commission, I don't take the posture that we are to command angels. Some feel they have that liberty. However, I believe it is a dangerous proposition. There is reason to believe that they are to be commissioned by God Himself in response to our prayers.

Daniel needed an answer from God. After praying for 21 days, an angel finally showed up with his answer. When Daniel started praying, God had responded by sending an angel, but that angel ran into interference. Daniel continued to pray, though, which appears to have helped to release the archangel Michael to fight and release the first angel to deliver the message. There are many other times angels came in response to the prayers of the saints. Each time they were sent out for service by the Father.

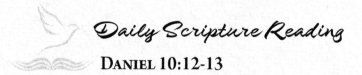

Daily Scripture Reading
DANIEL 10:12-13

Prayer

> My prayers are powerful. You do not turn a deaf ear to my cries, Lord. You hear my prayers and You answer them. If I haven't received an answer yet, I will just keep praying.

We are not impressed by the devil.

I TRAVEL TO MANY cities that are spiritually very dark. When you enter such cities you can feel the oppression. Considering what I represent to that city, it would be wrong for me to focus on the darkness. I don't ever want to be impressed with the devil's work. I come as a house of God. As such I contain a gate to heaven, with a ladder providing angelic activities according to the need of the moment. Simply put, I am an open heaven!

This does not apply to a select few. On the contrary, this revelation is about the house of God, and the principles of the house apply to all believers. But few realize or implement this potential blessing. With an open heaven I become a vehicle in the hand of God to release the resources of heaven into the calamities of mankind. Angels are commissioned to carry out the will of God. He is more eager to invade this world than we are to receive the invasion. And angels play an integral part. They respond to His command and enforce His Word.

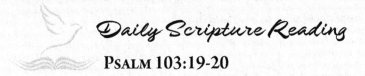

Daily Scripture Reading
PSALM 103:19-20

Prayer

You are more eager to invade every situation in my life than I am to have You here, God. Your love is unfathomable. I refuse to walk in any identity other than as a house of God, an open heaven.

*We can release the voice
of His word on the earth.*

BUT THE VOICE OF His word is heard when the Father speaks to the hearts of His people. Angels await the people of God speaking His word. I believe angels pick up the fragrance of the throne room through the word spoken by people. They can tell when a word has its origins in the heart of the Father. And, in turn, they recognize that word as their assignment.

I recently saw this happen at a meeting in Germany. Before the meeting, I was praying with some of the leaders. As we were praying, I saw a woman sitting to my right with an arthritic spine. It was a brief picture of the mind, which is the visual equivalent of the still small voice—as easy to miss as it is to get. In this picture I had her stand and declared over her, "The Lord Jesus heals you!"

When it came time for the meeting, I asked if there was anyone there with arthritis in the spine. A woman to my right waved her hand. I had her stand and declared over her, "The Lord Jesus heals you!" I then asked her where her pain was. She wept saying, "It is impossible, but it is gone!" Angels enforced a word that originated in the heart of the Father. But for that moment, I was the voice of His word.

Daily Scripture Reading

ACTS 10:1-8

Prayer

I want to be the voice of Your word to my family, to my friends, and to my community. I will sit quietly, God, to hear Your still, small voice today.

Service with purpose affirms identity.

WHEN GOD CHOSE TO bring the Messiah through the Virgin Mary, He sent Gabriel the angel to bring the message. When the apostle Paul was about to suffer shipwreck, an angel of the Lord told him what would happen. On numerous occasions throughout Scripture angels did what God could have done easily Himself.

But why didn't God do those things Himself? For the same reason He doesn't preach the gospel: He has chosen to let His creation enjoy the privilege of service in His Kingdom. Service with purpose affirms identity. A godly self-esteem is derived from doing "as He pleases." And true service is an overflow of worship.

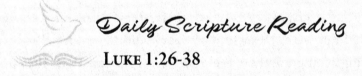

Daily Scripture Reading
LUKE 1:26-38

Prayer

I am Your creation, God. I have been designed for a purpose—to worship and adore my creator, to overflow with love onto the world around me. I want to say, like Mary, let it be unto me according to Your word.

When His world breaks into ours, humility and hunger keep us open.

HIS WORLD HAS BEEN breaking into ours with regularity in salvations, healings, and deliverances. The manifestations of that invasion vary. They are quite fascinating and too numerous to catalog. While some are difficult to understand at first glance, we know that God always works redemptively.

On many occasions, laughter has filled a room, bringing healing to broken hearts. Gold dust sometimes covers people's faces, hands, or clothing during worship or ministry time. Oil sometimes appears on the hands of His people; and it especially happens among children. A wind has come into a room with no open windows, doors, vents, etc. At some locations, believers have seen an actual cloud of His presence appearing over the heads of worshiping people. We've also had the fragrance of heaven fill a room.

I have seen the small gems that suddenly appeared in people's hands as they worshiped God. Since early in 1998 we have had feathers fall in our meetings. At first I thought birds were getting into our air conditioning ducts. But then they started falling in other rooms of the church not connected with the same ductwork. They now fall most anywhere we go—airports, homes, restaurants, offices, and the like. God loves to confound our understanding of Him.

Daily Scripture Reading
JEREMIAH 9:23-24

Prayer

Why do I expect You to come in the ways that my limited, human imagination can anticipate? You are the Creator of the universe and everything in it. I will stay humble and hungry. However You choose to invade our world, I will celebrate.

God will not be limited by the understanding of His creation.

THE UNUSUAL PHENOMENA OF God's manifestations seem to offend many that fully embrace this move of God. It's easy once we've made some adjustments in our belief system about what God can and will do to think that we have stretched far enough. "Our beliefs now encompass the move of God." Nothing could be further from the truth. Like the generations before us, those who judge His manifestations are dangerously close to regulating God's work by a new and revised list of acceptable manifestations.

No longer is it just tears during a special song or a time of repentance following a moving sermon. Our new list includes falling, shaking, laughter, etc. The problem is—it is still a list. And God will violate it. He must. We must learn to recognize His move by recognizing His presence. Our lists are only good for revealing our present understanding or experience. While I don't seek to promote strange manifestations, or go after novelty, I do refuse to be embarrassed over what God is doing. The list that keeps us from certain types of errors also keeps us from certain types of victories.

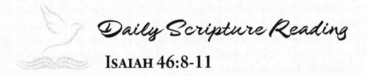

Daily Scripture Reading

ISAIAH 46:8-11

Prayer

I tear up any list I've had in my mind, God. I give You full rein over my life, over my church services, over my understanding of You. You are taking us somewhere, and I want to be led into more and more of You.

Signs and wonders are a natural part of the Kingdom of God.

HIS MANIFESTATIONS, WHILE OFFENSIVE to the minds of many, are limitless in number, and are simple indicators of God's presence and purpose. Why are they necessary? Because He wants to take us farther, and we can only get there by following signs. Our present understanding of Scripture can only take us so far.

Remember, signs are realities that point to a greater reality. If He is giving us signs, who are we to say they are unimportant? Many react to this position because they fear sign worship. While their reasoning may be noble in intent, it is foolish to think I can carry out my assignment from God and ignore God's personal notes along the way.

Had the wise men not followed the star they would have had to be content reading about the experiences of others. I am not. There's a difference between worshiping signs and following signs; the first is forbidden, the latter is essential. When we follow His signs to the greater depths in God, His signs follow us in greater measure for the sake of mankind.

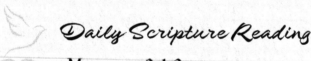

Daily Scripture Reading
MATTHEW 2:1-2

Prayer

I do not long for signs and wonders as an end to themselves. I long for them as a signpost to Your hand moving on the earth. I want to be one who says, "I saw the sign, and I've come to worship Him."

We are in pursuit of an authentic gospel.

WHENEVER I TEACH ON pursuing a gospel of power, someone occasionally follows my message with an affirmation of our need for power but reminds everyone of the priority of knowing the God of power. True words indeed. Power has little pleasure if there is no intimate relationship with God. But that comment is often religious in nature. Someone who has a passion for the power and glory of God intimidates those who don't.

My hunger for His power is only surpassed by my desire for Him. It's been my pursuit of Him that has led me to this passion for an authentic gospel. Something happened in me that won't let me accept a gospel that isn't backed with signs and wonders. Is it because I have caught a revelation of miracles on the earth? No! It caught me. I have discovered there isn't any lasting satisfaction in life apart from expressions of faith.

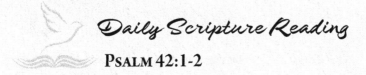

Daily Scripture Reading

PSALM 42:1-2

Prayer

I am running after Your presence, God. I want to know You, I want to see You move in my life, and I want to receive all that You have for me. My soul longs for You.

As He is, so are we in this world (1 John 4:17).

WHILE MOST OF THE Church is still trying to become as Jesus was, the Bible tells us that we are to be "as He is." Jesus was the suffering servant, headed for the cross. But Jesus is triumphantly resurrected, ascended, and glorified. In the Revelation of Jesus Christ, John described Him in this way: *"His head and hair were white like wool, as white as snow, and His eyes like a flame of fire; His feet were like fine brass, as if refined in a furnace, and His voice as the sound of many waters"* (Revelation 1:14-15).

The "as He is, so are we" declaration is far beyond what any of us could have imagined; especially in light of the glorified description of Jesus in Revelation, chapter 1. Yet, the Holy Spirit was sent specifically for this purpose that we might attain... *"to the measure of the stature of the fullness of Christ"* (Ephesians 4:13).

Daily Scripture Reading

REVELATION 1:12-18

Prayer

You are alive forevermore, Jesus, holding the keys of death and Hades in Your victorious hand. I stand in Your victory, releasing all of who You are onto the earth.

Jesus, glorified, is our model.

THE HOLY SPIRIT CAME with the ultimate assignment at the perfect time. During Jesus' ministry, it was said, *"The Holy Spirit was not yet given, because Jesus was not yet glorified"* (John 7:39). The Holy Spirit comforts us, gives us gifts, reminds us of what Jesus has said, and clothes us with power. But He does all this to make us like Jesus. That is His primary mission.

So why didn't the Father send Him until Jesus was glorified? Because without Jesus in His glorified state there was no heavenly model of what we were to become! As a sculptor looks at a model and fashions the clay into its likeness, so the Holy Spirit looks to the glorified Son and shapes us into His image. As He is, so are we in this world.

Daily Scripture Reading
JOHN 7:37-39

Prayer

Jesus, You've modeled the way to live fully surrendered to the Father, as You were on earth. You now model what it means to live in Your fully glorified state. Holy Spirit, shape me and fashion me into the image of Jesus as He is now.

The Cross is the beginning.

THE CHRISTIAN LIFE IS not found on the Cross. It is found because of the Cross. It is His resurrection power that energizes the believer. Does this diminish the value of the Cross? No! The shed blood of the spotless Lamb wiped out the power and presence of sin in our lives. We have nothing without the Cross!

Yet, the Cross is not the end—it is the beginning, the entrance to the Christian Life. Even for Jesus the cross was something to be endured in order to obtain the joy on the other side! (See Hebrews 12:2.) The great majority of the Christian world is still weeping at the foot of the cross. The consciousness of mankind remains fixed on the Christ who died, not on the Christ who lives. People are looking back to the Redeemer who was, not the Redeemer who is.[1]

Daily Scripture Reading
HEBREWS 12:1-3

Prayer

I am forever grateful for what You did on the Cross, Jesus. But I do not want to bring You sorrow by thinking that that was the final goal! You died so that I might live freely, united with the Father, bringing the Kingdom to reign on earth with Him.

---

1   John G. Lake—*His Life, His Sermons, His Boldness of Faith*, 57.

The resurrection redefined everything.

SUPPOSE I HAD BEEN forgiven a financial debt. It could be said I have been brought out of the red. Yet, after my debts are forgiven, I still am not in the black. I have nothing unless the one who forgave my debt gives me money to call my own, and that's what Christ did for you and me. His blood wiped out my debt of sin. But it was His resurrection that brought me into the black (see John 10:10).

Why is this important? Because it profoundly changes our sense of identity and purpose.

Jesus became poor so that I could become rich. He suffered with stripes to free me from affliction, and He became sin so I might become the righteousness of God (see 2 Corinthians 5:21). Why then should I try to become as He was, when He suffered so I could become as He is? At some point, the reality of the resurrection must come into play in our lives—we must discover the power of the resurrection for all who believe (see Ephesians 1:21 and 3:20).

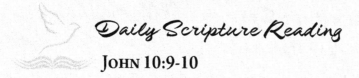

Daily Scripture Reading
JOHN 10:9-10

Prayer

I am dead to sin, free from judgment because of Your sacrifice, and now I get to live in the reality of Your resurrection. Show me if there is any place where I am living on the Cross rather than participating in the abundant life You have for me.

We were designed to live in joy!

JESUS SAID, "IF ANYONE *desires to come after Me, let him deny himself, and take up his cross, and follow Me*" (Matthew 16:24). A misunderstanding of this call has led many to follow His life of self-denial but to stop short of His life of power. For them the cross-walk involves trying to crucify their sin nature by embracing joyless brokenness as an evidence of the cross. But, we must follow Him all the way—to a lifestyle empowered by the resurrection!

Most every religion has a copy of the cross-walk. Self-denial, self-abasement, and the like are all easily copied by the sects of this world. People admire those who have religious disciplines. They applaud fasting and respect those who embrace poverty or endure disease for the sake of personal spirituality. But show them a life filled with joy because of the transforming power of God, and they will not only applaud but will want to be like you. Religion is unable to mimic the life of resurrection with its victory over sin and hell.

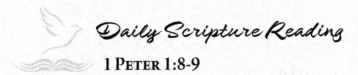

Daily Scripture Reading
1 PETER 1:8-9

Prayer

God, give me a fresh revelation of Your joy! Sometimes it's so much easier to focus on myself, on all of the areas of life where I still feel weak, but I want my gaze to be on You.

We die to ourselves so that we might live in Him.

ONE WHO EMBRACES AN inferior cross is constantly filled with introspection and self-induced suffering. But the cross is not self-applied—Jesus did not nail Himself to the cross. Christians who are trapped by this counterfeit are constantly talking about their weaknesses.

If the devil finds us uninterested in evil, then he'll try to get us to focus on our unworthiness and inability. This is especially noticeable in prayer meetings where people try to project great brokenness before God, hoping to earn revival. They will often re-confess old sins searching for real humility. But all of this merely takes our focus off of the main thing—His presence.

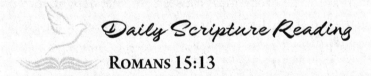

Daily Scripture Reading
ROMANS 15:13

Prayer

I will stay close to Your correction, Father, and humble to the guidance of those around me. But I will focus on running after You. I trust in Your redemption and in the process of Your sanctification. I am Yours!

*Self-condemnation is the
most subtle form of pride.*

IN MY OWN PURSUIT of God, I often became preoccupied with ME! It was easy to think that being constantly aware of my faults and weakness was humility. It's not! If I'm the main subject, talking incessantly about my weaknesses, I have entered into the most subtle form of pride.

Repeated phrases such as, "I'm so unworthy," become a nauseating replacement for the declarations of the worthiness of God. By being sold on my own unrighteousness, the enemy has disengaged me from effective service.

It's a perversion of true holiness when introspection causes my spiritual self-esteem to increase, but my effectiveness in demonstrating the power of the gospel to decrease. True brokenness causes complete dependency on God, moving us to radical obedience that releases the power of the gospel to the world around us.

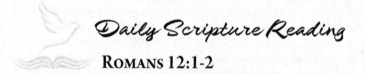

Daily Scripture Reading
ROMANS 12:1-2

Prayer

You are worthy, God. I present myself as a living sacrifice to You and I trust that You will transform me—spirit, soul, and body. I will look on Your holiness and move in radical obedience to You.

We cannot convict and deliver ourselves from sin.

I STRUGGLED FOR MANY years with self-evaluation. The main problem was that I never found anything good in me. It always led to discouragement, which led to doubt, and eventually took me to unbelief. Somehow I had developed the notion that this was how I could become holy—by showing tremendous concern for my own motives.

It may sound strange, but I don't examine my motives anymore. That's not my job. I work hard to obey God in everything that I am and do. If I am out to lunch on a matter, it is His job to point that out to me. After many years of trying to do what only He could do, I discovered I was not the Holy Spirit. I cannot convict and deliver myself of sin. Does that mean that I never deal with impure motives? No. He has shown Himself to be very eager to point out my constant need for repentance and change. But He's the one with the spotlight, and He alone can give the grace to change.

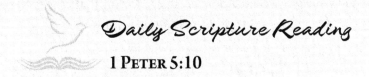

Daily Scripture Reading

1 PETER 5:10

Prayer

I am not the Holy Spirit. I invite Your correction and redirection, Lord. I open myself to Your conviction and deliverance. I need Your grace to go where You've called me to go.

By His grace, we are a new creation.

THERE IS A MAJOR difference between the believer who is being dealt with by God, and the one who has become introspective. When God searches the heart, He finds things in us that He wants to change. He brings conviction because of His commitment to deliver us. Such a revelation brought me to pray in the following manner:

Father, you know that I don't do so well when I look inward, so I'm going to stop. I am relying on You to point out to me the things that I need to see. I promise to stay in Your Word. You said that your Word was a sword—so please use it to cut me deeply. Expose those things in me that are not pleasing to You. But in doing so, please give me the grace to forsake them. I also promise to come before You daily. Your presence is like a fire. Please burn from me those things that are unpleasing to You. Melt my heart until it becomes like the heart of Jesus. Be merciful to me in these things. I also promise to stay in fellowship with Your people. You said that iron sharpens iron. I expect You to anoint the "wounds of a friend" to bring me to my senses when I'm being resistant toward You. Please use these tools to shape my life until Jesus alone is seen in me. I believe that You have given me Your heart and mind. By Your grace I am a new creation. I want that reality to be seen that the name of Jesus would be held in highest honor.

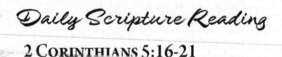

Daily Scripture Reading

2 CORINTHIANS 5:16-21

Prayer

Use every tool You've given me to shape my life until Jesus alone is seen in me. I believe that You have given me Your heart and mind. By Your grace I am a new creation. I want that reality to be seen in me, Holy Spirit, so the name of Jesus would be held in highest honor.

Seeing the dirt in ourselves, or in others, does not require faith.

I BELIEVE THAT FOR the most part this counterfeit cross-walk is embraced because it requires no faith. It's easy to see my weakness, my propensity toward sin, and my inability to be like Jesus. Confessing this truth requires no faith at all. On the contrary, to do as Paul commanded in Romans 6:13, to consider myself dead to sin, I must believe God!

Therefore, in your weakest state declare, "I AM STRONG!" Agree with God regardless of how you feel and discover the power of resurrection. Without faith it is impossible to please Him. The first place that faith must be exercised is in our own standing with God.

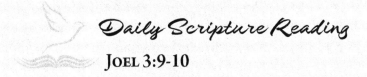

Daily Scripture Reading
JOEL 3:9-10

Prayer

It's so easy for me to get bogged down in the awareness of my own weakness, God. But You have called me Strong, Chosen, Beloved. I choose to see myself like You see me. I choose to agree with the names You have called me.

He is the God of abundance;
He equips us as He calls us.

WHEN GOD GAVE MOSES a noble task, he responded "Who am I?" God changed the subject saying, "Certainly I will be with you." When we are focused on our lack, the Father tries to change the subject to something that will lead us to the source and foundation of faith: Himself. The noble call always reveals the nobility of the Caller.

Apart from Christ, we are unworthy. And it's true that without Him we are nothing. But I'm not without Him, and I never will be again! At what point do we start thinking of our worth through His eyes? If it's true that the value of something is measured by what someone else will pay, then we need to rethink our worth. Do we ever acknowledge who we are before Him? Please don't misunderstand, I'm not encouraging arrogance or cockiness. But wouldn't it honor Him more if we believed that He actually did a good enough job in saving us, and that we really are saved?

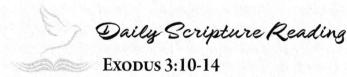

Daily Scripture Reading

EXODUS 3:10-14

Prayer

You believed that I was worth dying for, Jesus. You would have done the same if I had been the only human on the planet. Help me to see myself the way that You see me.

*Our confidence rests
in His faithfulness.*

JESUS PAID THE ULTIMATE price to make it possible for us to have a change in our identity. Isn't it time we believe it and receive the benefits? If we don't, we'll break down in our confidence as we stand before the world in these final days.

The boldness we need is not self-confidence, but the confidence that the Father has in the work of His Son in us. It's no longer a question of heaven or hell. It's only a question of how much of hell's thinking I will allow into this heavenly mind of mine.

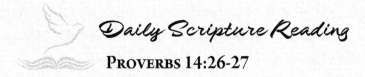

Daily Scripture Reading

PROVERBS 14:26-27

Prayer

Whenever I'm feeling insecure about my own worthiness, God, I will shift my gaze back to You. Your faithfulness is my firm foundation. It is in Your grace that I find my refuge.

We are no longer just sinners saved by grace; we are sons and daughters of the Most High.

DOESN'T IT HONOR HIM more when His children no longer see themselves only as sinners saved by grace, but now as heirs of God? Isn't it a greater form of humility to believe Him when He says we are precious in His sight when we don't feel very precious? Doesn't it honor Him more when we think of ourselves as free from sin because He said we are?

At some point we must rise up to the high call of God and stop saying things about ourselves that are no longer true. If we're going to fully come in to what God has for us in this last days' revival, we will have to come to grips with the issue of being more than sinners saved by grace. Maturity comes from faith in the sufficiency of God's redemptive work that establishes us as sons and daughters of the Most High.

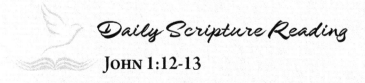

Daily Scripture Reading
JOHN 1:12-13

Prayer

I am no longer merely a sinner saved by grace. I am not making it into heaven by the skin of my teeth. I am an heir of God. I have been redeemed and made whole by the Creator of the universe.

He is returning for a glorious Bride.

"As He is, so *are we in this world*" (1 John 4:17). The revelation of Jesus in His glorified state has overwhelming characteristics that directly affect the coming transformation of the Church; these must be embraced as a part of God's plan in these final hours.

To be as He is involves revealing His glory to the world. This is the manifested presence of Jesus. Revival history is filled with stories of His manifest presence resting upon His people. He lives in all believers, but the glory of His presence comes to rest on only a few. It is sometimes seen and frequently felt. He is returning for a glorious Church. It is not an option.

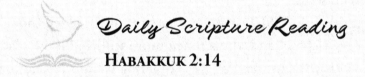

Daily Scripture Reading
HABAKKUK 2:14

Prayer

Father, I lift up the Church today. I cry out for more of Your glory to become visible through Your Bride. I honor the Body of Christ, and pray for more!

Let Your fire come!

FIRE HAS BEEN SEEN blazing from the top of church buildings when the people of God are gathered together in His name. At the Azuza Street revival, the fire department was called to extinguish a blaze, only to discover that the people inside were worshiping Jesus. Water couldn't put it out as it was not a natural fire. All the powers of hell cannot put it out. The only ones capable of such a thing are those to whom that fire has been entrusted.

Well-meaning believers will often use control as a means to bring this fire into order, thinking they are serving God. On the other hand, some will turn to hype to fan an emotional flame when the fire is no longer there. Both are expressions of the carnal man—and when the carnal man is in charge, the glory of God must lift.

If the Father filled the Old Testament houses with His glory, though they were built by human hands, how much more will He fill the place that He builds with His own hands! He is building us into His eternal dwelling place.

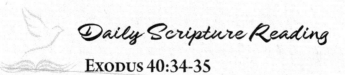

Daily Scripture Reading
EXODUS 40:34-35

Prayer

Your presence does not need my hype, and I refuse to quench Your fire through my control. Let Your fire fall, Lord; let Your glory fill this place! We worship You!

We are to be a continuous expression of His power.

THE BAPTISM IN THE Holy Spirit clothes us with this heavenly element. As clothing is on the outside of the body, so that power is to be the most visible part of the believing Church. It is the power of salvation—for the body, soul, and spirit.

Many in the world around us seek for help from the psychic and cultist before coming to the Church. They also reach for medical help, legitimate and otherwise, before they ask for our prayers. Why? For the most part we are not clothed with heaven's power. If we had it, they would see it. If they saw it, they would come.

The power vacuum in the Church allows cults and false prophetic gifts to flourish. But there will be no contest when such counterfeits go up against this Elijah generation that becomes clothed with heaven's power on the Mount Carmel of human reasoning.

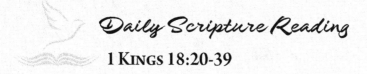

Daily Scripture Reading

1 KINGS 18:20-39

Prayer

> *I want to walk in the faith of Elijah, Holy Spirit. I want to have such confidence in God's desire to reveal Himself that I would be a continuous expression of His power until all the world says, "The Lord, He is God!"*

Jesus walked in triumph; so must we.

JESUS CONQUERED ALL THINGS: the power of hell, the grave, sin, and the devil. He was raised from the dead, ascended to the right hand of the Father, and was glorified above all. Every name and power has been placed under His feet.

He calls us His body—and this body has feet. Figuratively speaking, He is saying the lowest part of His body has authority over the highest part of everything else. This victory doesn't mean we live without battles; it simply means our victory is secured.

Daily Scripture Reading
ROMANS 8:37-39

Prayer

Jesus, You defeated death and were resurrected to sit at the right hand of the Father. You have brought me into Your victory so that I might live in triumph in every area of my life.

Jesus' blood paid for everything.

THE ATTITUDE OF THOSE who live from the triumph of Christ is different than those who live under the influence of their past. The only part of the past that we have legal access to is the testimony of the Lord. The rest is dead, buried, forgotten, and covered under the blood.

The past should have no negative effect on the way we live, as the blood of Jesus is more than sufficient. Living from the victory of Christ is the privilege for every believer. This realization is at the foundation of a Church that will triumph even as He has triumphed.

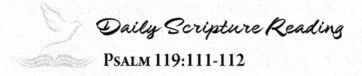

Daily Scripture Reading
PSALM 119:111-112

Prayer

Thank You, Jesus, that I no longer need to live in bondage to the shame of my past mistakes. Your blood paid for everything. I stand on Your testimony and walk forward in victory with You.

We must become captivated by His holiness.

JESUS IS PERFECTLY HOLY—SEPARATE from all that is evil, unto all that is good. Holiness is the language through which the nature of God is revealed. The psalmist penned the phrase, "in the beauty of holiness." Holiness in the Church reveals the beauty of God.

Our understanding of holiness, even in certain seasons of revival, has often been centered around our behavior—what we can and cannot do. However, what in the past incorrectly has been reduced to a list of "do's and don't's" will soon become the greatest revelation of God the world has ever seen. Whereas power demonstrates the heart of God, holiness reveals the beauty of His nature. This is the hour of the great unveiling of the beauty of holiness.

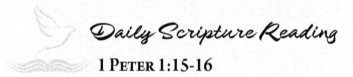

Daily Scripture Reading

1 PETER 1:15-16

Prayer

Lord, let my life reveal Your nature. I want to become captivated by Your beauty and enamored with who You are. Give me a fresh revelation of Your holiness.

How will I know for certain? (Luke 1:18).

ZACHARIAS WAS GIVEN A promise from God that was beyond his comprehension: he was to have a son in his old age. It was hard to believe, so he asked God to give him confirmation. Apparently an angel speaking to him wasn't a big enough sign! God silenced him for nine months. When God silences the voices of unbelief, it is usually because their words could affect the outcome of a promise.

When Zacharias saw God's promise fulfilled and he chose to name his son according to the command, against the wishes of his relatives, God loosed his tongue. Obedience against popular opinion will often reintroduce someone to personal faith. And that's a faith that goes against understanding.

Daily Scripture Reading
LUKE 1:5-20

Prayer

God, I want to answer Your invitations with trust first and foremost. I know Your plans for me are good and fulfilling. I will choose obedience no matter what.

Ignorance asks for understanding;
unbelief asks for proof.

MARY WAS ALSO GIVEN a promise beyond comprehension: she was to give birth to the Son of God. When she couldn't understand, she asked how it was possible since she was a virgin. Understanding a promise from God has never been the prerequisite to its fulfillment.

Ignorance asks for understanding; unbelief asks for proof. She stands apart from Zacharias because while being ignorant she surrendered to the promise. Her cry remains one of the most important expressions the Church can learn in this day—"Be it unto me according to your word."

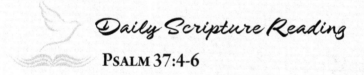

Daily Scripture Reading

PSALM 37:4-6

Prayer

Father, I want to respond to You like Mary did. I release my need to understand exactly how You will fulfill the promises over my life. I release control. I say "yes" to whatever You have for me.

We get to choose how we respond to a promise that feels hard to imagine.

THIS PROMISE, AS HE is so are we in this world, is of paramount importance for the Church. But there are few things further from our grasp than the statement. Hearing that we will be as Jesus is—as He is described in all of His glory at the right hand of the Father—sometimes feels incomprehensible to us.

And so, we have the choice: to stand in the shoes of Zacharias and lose our voice, or walk in the ways of Mary and invite God to restore to us the promises we cannot control. This identity establishes a security in character as we engage in spiritual warfare.

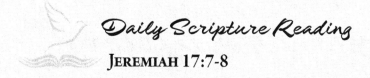

Daily Scripture Reading
JEREMIAH 17:7-8

Prayer

There are so many promises in the Bible that feel out of my grasp, God, but this is probably the hardest to fully comprehend. I trust in You, though, and I invite You to restore me to all of the promises You've made over my life.

OCTOBER

Created for Victory

We are called to be royal fighters.

JOHN G. LAKE ONCE said, "The real Christian is a royal fighter. He is the one who loves to enter into the contest with his whole soul and take the situation captive for the Lord Jesus Christ." For too long the Church has played defense in the battle for souls. We hear of what some cult or political party is planning to do, and we react by creating strategies to counter the enemies' plans. Committees are formed, boards discuss, and pastors preach against whatever it is the devil is doing or about to do.

This may come as a surprise, but I don't care what the devil plans to do. The Great Commission puts me on the offensive. I've got the ball. And if I carry the ball effectively, his plans won't matter.

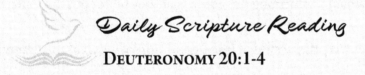

Daily Scripture Reading
DEUTERONOMY 20:1-4

Prayer

> *You are with me in every battle, Lord. You fight for me, so I never need to be afraid. You have made me victorious, so I keep my eyes on You as I take new territory for Your Kingdom.*

The weapons of our warfare are not of the flesh, but divinely powerful for the destruction of fortresses (2 Corinthians 10:4 NASB).

PICTURE A FOOTBALL TEAM in a huddle on the playing field. The coach sends in the play, and the quarterback communicates with his offensive teammates. On the sidelines is the opposing team's offense. Their quarterback lines up out-of-bounds with his offensive team, but they don't have the game ball, nor are they on the actual playing field.

Now imagine the real offense getting distracted by the intimidating actions of the other offense. Caught up in their antics, the quarterback runs off the field in a panic, informing the coach that they better put the defense on the field because the other team is about to use a surprise play.

As foolish as that may sound, it is the condition of much of the Church in this hour.

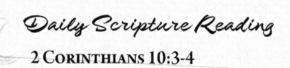

Daily Scripture Reading

2 CORINTHIANS 10:3-4

Prayer

I am not entering the battle with my own strength, but rather fully equipped by Your divinely powerful weapons to defeat darkness. I am on the winning team!

We are the devil's worst nightmare.

SATAN REVEALS HIS PLANS to put us on the defensive. The devil roars, and we act as if we got bit. But he can only make noise and intimidate us if we let him. Let's stop this foolishness and quit praising the devil with endless discussions of what's wrong in the world because of him. We have the ball.

The alumni from the ages past watch with excitement as the two-minute offense has been put on the field. The superior potential of this generation has nothing to do with our goodness, but it does have everything to do with the Master's plan of placing us at this point in history. We are to be the devil's worst nightmare.

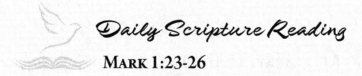

Daily Scripture Reading
MARK 1:23-26

Prayer

I will not be intimidated by the devil's attempts. I will not be distracted from the call on my life. I will run my race, confident that I am on the winning team!

We are responders, not reactors.

I HONESTLY BELIEVE THAT satan allows his strategies to become known so that we will react accordingly. Satan likes being in control. And he is whenever we're not. Reactions come from fear.

We are not holding on till Jesus comes! We are an overcoming body of people that has been blood bought, is Spirit-filled and commissioned by God Himself, in order that all He has spoken should come to pass. When we plan according to the devil's plans, we automatically clothe ourselves with the wrong mentality. Such incorrect attitudes can become the very stronghold in our thinking that invites a legal assault from hell. As such, our fears become self-fulfilling prophecies.

Daily Scripture Reading

REVELATION 12:10-11

Prayer

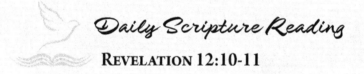

Reacting out of fear to the enemy's exploits leaves me feeling unbalanced, disoriented, and anxious. I give myself permission to turn off the news, to turn down the constant bad reports, and to keep my eyes fixed on You, Jesus.

*God leads us into the battles
He has prepared us to win.*

SPIRITUAL WARFARE IS UNAVOIDABLE, and ignoring this subject won't make it go away. Therefore, we must learn to battle with supernatural authority! God is mindful of what we can handle in our present state. He leads us away from any war that might cause us to turn and abandon our call. The implication is He leads us only into a battle we are prepared to win.

The safest place in this war is obedience. In the center of His will, we face only the situations we are equipped to win. Outside of the center is where many Christians fall, facing undue pressures that are self-inflicted. His will is the only safe place to be.

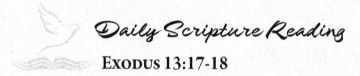

Daily Scripture Reading

EXODUS 13:17-18

Prayer

You have equipped me for the present battle I'm facing, God. I trust Your timing. I want to stand in the center of Your will—adjust me if I am off course.

Intimacy with God is our life source.

GOD IS IN NO way intimidated by the devil's antics. In fact, God wants fellowship with us right before the devil's eyes. Intimacy with God is our strong suit and our source of life. Never allow anything to distract you from this point of strength.

Many become too "warfare intense" for their own good. Such intensity often involves displays of human strength—not grace. Choosing this warfare intense mentality causes us to depart from joy and intimacy with God. It's an indication that we have strayed from our first love (see Revelation 2:4). Paul's intimacy with God enabled him to say from a demon-infested Roman prison, *"Rejoice always; again I say, rejoice!"* (Philippians 4:4).

Daily Scripture Reading
PSALM 23:4-6

Prayer

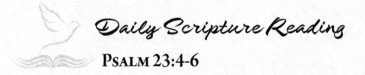

Sometimes I find myself wanting to hide from the devil—as if I could be small enough for him to ignore. But that is not how You think, Lord. You put our relationship on display, revealing the source of my victory to a defeated enemy.

What you fear will influence what you worship; what you worship will be proven by what you trust.

WHEN WE REFUSE FEAR, the enemy becomes terrified. A confident heart is a sure sign of his ultimate destruction and our present victory! Do not fear—ever. Return to the promises of God, spend time with people of faith, and encourage one another with the testimonies of the Lord. Praise God for who He is until fear no longer knocks at the door. This is not an option, for fear actually invites the enemy to come to kill, steal, and destroy.

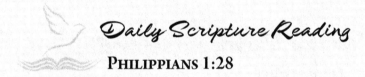

Daily Scripture Reading
PHILIPPIANS 1:28

Prayer

Give me a confident heart, God. I will review Your promises over my life again and again. I will hold fast to who You are in times of struggle. I will remember all that You have done for me.

Submit therefore to God (James 4:7 NASB).

WE HAVE BEEN DRAFTED into a heavenly army. We were never made to face the battle with darkness on our own, but rather as one aligned with the Kingdom. Our authority comes from positioning ourselves in submission to the mission of God.

Submission is the key to personal triumph. Our main battle in spiritual warfare is not against the devil. It is against the flesh. Coming into subjection puts the resources of heaven at our disposal for enduring victory—enforcing what has already been obtained at Calvary.

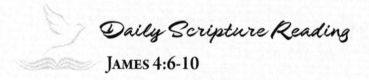

Daily Scripture Reading

JAMES 4:6-10

Prayer

The word "submission" sometimes feels scary, Father. But I know that it is in the place of surrender that I find my greatest peace, joy, and authority. I submit myself to You completely.

*Even the very gates of hell
will not prevail against us.*

IT'S EASY TO SLIP into a defensive posture when we think about the demonic. We can so quickly forget our own authority and assume that our job is simply to "shelter in place" until Jesus returns. But that would miss so much of God's design for our lives.

I was not left on planet Earth to be in hiding waiting for Jesus' return. I am here as a military representative of heaven. The Church is on the attack. The Kingdom is perpetually advancing across the face of the earth. That's why the gates of hell, the place of demonic government and strength, will not prevail against the Church.

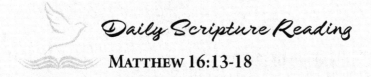

Daily Scripture Reading
MATTHEW 16:13-18

Prayer

You have prepared the way for me, God, setting Your Church up for increasing victory. I am a part of this victory, and I will not sit back on my heels. I will advance Your Kingdom daily.

The devil has to suffer continuous defeat at the hand of God's children.

PSALM 105:24-25 GIVES US insight into God's perspective on spiritual warfare. First God makes us strong, and then He stirs up the devil's hatred toward us. Why? It's not because He wants to create problems for His Church. It's because He likes to see the devil defeated by those who are made in His image, who have a relationship of love with Him by choice.

He is so confident in our victory that He isn't worried about pitting His sons and daughters against the enemy. We are His delegated authority. It is His delight to have us enforce the triumph of Jesus. *"To execute on them the written judgment—this honor have all His saints"* (Psalm 149:9).

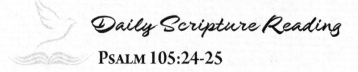

Daily Scripture Reading

PSALM 105:24-25

Prayer

God, You have strengthened me in Your Word, in the truth of my identity, and in my increasing intimacy with You. I step out in Your confidence, ready to defeat the enemy at His own game. It is my honor to represent You.

We become like the One we worship.

OUR MINISTRY TO GOD is one of life's most important privileges. It is the highest calling of our life. Praise honors God. But it also edifies us and destroys the powers of hell! God doesn't need our worship; He tells us to worship because of how it changes us. We become like the One we worship.

It's amazing to think that I can praise Him, have His peace fill my soul, and have Him call me a mighty man of valor. The Lord is the one going forth "like a warrior." All I did was worship Him. He destroyed the powers of hell on my behalf and gave me the "points" for the victory.

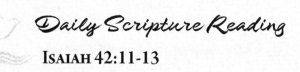

Daily Scripture Reading
ISAIAH 42:11-13

Prayer

You've set me up for success, Lord. You know what my spirit, soul, and body need in order to see victory. I will worship You. I will praise Your name and watch You prevail against Your enemies.

We were born into a war.

OUR PERSPECTIVE OF SPIRITUAL warfare must shift from one that is religious and carnal, to one of a Kingdom mindset. Repent, change your way of thinking, and you'll be able to see how "at hand" His Kingdom really is.

We were born in a war. There are no time-outs, no vacations, no leaves of absence. The safest place is in the center of God's will, which is the place of deep intimacy. There He allows only the battles to come our way that we are equipped to win. Not only is this the safest place, it is the most joyful place for each believer.

Daily Scripture Reading

HEBREWS 13:20-21

Prayer

I want to live in the center of Your will, Father. Keep me close—correct me quickly any time I begin to wander down my own path. I want to walk in step with You, aligning my thoughts with Yours.

God rarely shows up exactly as we expect Him to.

REVIVAL IS CENTRAL TO the message of the Kingdom, for it is in revival that we more clearly see what His dominion looks like and how it is to affect society. Revival at its best is, Thy Kingdom come. In a way, revival illustrates the normal Christian life, but a move of God is not always recognizable even by those who have been crying out for more.

Before the Messiah came, the religious leaders prayed for and taught about His coming. There was a worldwide stirring, even in a secular society, about something wonderful that was about to happen. And then in a manger in Bethlehem, Jesus was born. A baby in a manger wasn't exactly what they had been expecting, but then again God rarely shows up exactly as we are expecting.

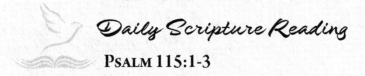

Daily Scripture Reading

PSALM 115:1-3

Prayer

Keep my heart tender to You, Holy Spirit. I want to recognize Your presence no matter how surprising it is to my natural senses. You are God; I welcome You to come in any way You see fit.

Open the eyes of our hearts, God.

GOD DID NOT ESCAPE the notice of the demon-possessed. Such was the man at the Gadarenes. When he saw Jesus, he fell down before Him in worship and was soon set free from his life of torment. Yet the religious leaders that prayed for His coming didn't recognize Him when He came.

Paul and Silas preached the gospel throughout Asia Minor. The religious leaders said they were of the devil. But a demon-possessed fortune-teller girl said they were of God. How is it that those who are thought to be spiritually blind are able to see, and those who were known for their insight didn't recognize what God was doing?

History is filled with people—some even with strong relationships with God—who prayed for a visitation of God and missed it when it came.

Daily Scripture Reading

EPHESIANS 1:18-21

Prayer

Humble my heart, Jesus, keep me close to You that I might recognize You when You come. I want to stay teachable, stay flexible, and remain an observant student of Your presence.

Hunger for God keeps our senses keen.

MANY BELIEVERS HAVE A blindness that the world doesn't have. The world knows its need. But for many Christians, once they are born again they gradually stop recognizing their need. There is something about desperation for God that enables a person to recognize whether or not something is from God.

Jesus spoke of this phenomenon saying, *"For judgment I have come into this world, that those who do not see may see, and that those who see may be made blind"* (John 9:39). The testimony of history and the record of Scripture warn us of the possibility of this error. *"Therefore let him who thinks he stands take heed lest he fall"* (1 Corinthians 10:12).

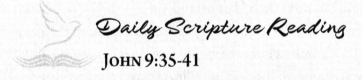

Daily Scripture Reading
JOHN 9:35-41

Prayer

Keep me hungry, Holy Spirit. I don't want to become satiated and stuck in my own limited perspective of who You are and how You will show up. I need You more than anything.

For the heart of this people has become dull, with their ears they scarcely hear, and they have closed their eyes... (Matthew 13:15 NASB).

MATTHEW SAYS IT'S THE dull of heart who can't see. (See Matthew 13:15.) A dull knife is one that has been used. The implication is that the dull of heart had a history in God, but did not keep current in what God was doing. We maintain our sharp edge as we recognize our need and passionately pursue Jesus. This first love somehow keeps us safely in the center of God's activities on earth.

The church of Ephesus received a letter from God. In it, Jesus addressed the fact that they had left their first love. First love is passionate by nature and dominates all other issues in one's life. If they didn't correct this problem, God said He would remove their "lampstand." While theologians don't all agree on what that lampstand is, one thing is for certain: a lamp enables us to see. Without it the church in Ephesus would lose their perceptive abilities.

The above-mentioned blindness or dullness is not always the kind that leads to hell. It just doesn't lead us to the fullness of what God has intended for us while here on earth. When passion dies, the lamp of perception is eventually removed.

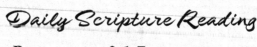

Daily Scripture Reading
REVELATION 2:1-7

Prayer

I am so grateful for my history with You, God. I never want that history to equate to a dulling familiarity, though. I will return to my first love; I will stoke the fires of my heart for You.

Now to Him who is able to keep you from stumbling, and to make you stand in the presence of His glory blameless with great joy (Jude 24 NASB).

CHURCH HISTORY SHOWS US that those who reject a move of God are generally those who were the last to experience one. This is not true of everyone, as there are always those whose hunger for God only increases throughout their years. But many form the attitude that they have arrived, not to perfection, but to where God intended. They paid a price to experience the move of God.

They wonder, "Why would God do something new, without showing it to us first?" God is a God of new things. Hungering for Him requires us to embrace the change brought on by His new things. Passion for God keeps us fresh and equips us to recognize the hand of God, even when others reject it. This present move requires that of us. The fear of deception gets swallowed up by confidence that God is able to keep us from falling.

Daily Scripture Reading

DEUTERONOMY 8:2-3

Prayer

God, thank You that You have never stopped moving. You are not a stagnant God. Your Kingdom is constantly advancing, You are always speaking, and You will always be on the move. Help me keep my passion fresh, my curiousity and wonder at the forefront.

Revival looks like freedom for the captives and restoration for the lost.

I'M THANKFUL FOR THE many seasoned saints who consider this present move a gift from heaven. Many Church historians have declared this revival to be genuine. They have seen that it bears the same fruit, and it causes the same stirrings in the Church as previous revivals in history. It's been encouraging to hear various theologians affirming this revival as a true move of God. Yet, it's not their seal of approval I look for.

Whenever the great leaders of the Church stand up and declare that this is a revival, I'm encouraged. It has happened in my own denomination. But even that does not interest me as much as God's true mark of a revival. In His wisdom, He created things in such a way that when He is on the move the world often takes notice first. I look for the response of the demonized. It's the drug addict, the ex-con, and the prostitute that I want to hear from.

Daily Scripture Reading

LUKE 4:16-21

Prayer

God, thank You that it's not hard to see when You're on the move. There will always be freedom, healing, and abundance in the wake of Your revivals. Open the eyes of my heart that I might see where You're moving today.

Let us maintain our desperate hearts for God.

WHEN GOD MOVES IN revival power, the people who have been the recipients of God's redeeming love look on, not as critics, but as people aware of their great need. And we are hearing from them in great numbers. They are being transformed, saying, "Only God could make this change in my life. This is God!"

Being in a place of great need enables a person to detect when God is doing something new. That place of great need doesn't have to be drug addiction or prostitution. Every Christian is supposed to maintain a desperate heart for God. We are in great need! Jesus addressed that fact with these words: *"Blessed are the poor in spirit, for theirs is the kingdom of heaven"* (Matthew 5:3). Remaining poor in spirit, combined with a first-ove passion for Jesus are the keys God created to anchor us to the center of His work.

Daily Scripture Reading
PSALM 84:1-7

Prayer

Keep me aware of my constant need of You, Holy Spirit. I feel my spiritual poverty, and I long for Your spiritual abundance.

If a more of God is pleasing to everyone,
it's probably not a more of God.

ANDREW MURRAY IS ONE of the great saints of God from the early part of the 20th century. He was known as a great teacher, with a passion for prayer. His cries for revival are legendary. When he visited Wales to examine the revival of 1904, he was moved by the awesome presence of God. But he left Wales thinking that if he stayed he could unintentionally contaminate the purity of God's work. He didn't press into the revival he had been praying for.

Moves of God usually come with a stigma—something that is unappealing and considered repulsive by some. Tongues became the 20th-century stigma that many were unwilling to bear. G. Campbell Morgan, the great man of God and Bible expositor, rejected the Pentecostal Revival, calling it the last vomit of hell! Bearing reproach is often a requirement to walk in revival.

Once a person is born again there seems to be little incentive to the natural mind to pursue more of what brings disgrace. It's that absence of desperation that causes believers to miss God.

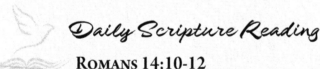

Daily Scripture Reading
ROMANS 14:10-12

Prayer

Forgive me, Father, for any time I've let a judgmental thought about another revival take residence in my mind. I will keep my eyes on You. Give me the strength to follow You despite the judgment of others.

The favor of God sometimes comes with challenges.

MARY RECEIVED THE MOST shocking announcement ever given to a person. She was to give birth to the Christ child. She was chosen by God, being called *"highly favored of the Lord."* This favor started with a visitation from an angel. That experience was quite frightening! Then she was given news that was incomprehensible and impossible to explain. The initial shock was followed by the duty of having to tell Joseph, her husband to be.

His response was to "put her away secretly" (see Matthew 1:19). In other words, he didn't believe it was God, and didn't want to go through with their wedding plans. After all, where is the chapter and verse for this manifestation of how God works with His people? It's never happened before. There was no biblical precedent of a virgin giving birth to a child. On top of this obvious conflict with Joseph, Mary would have to bear the stigma of being the mother of an illegitimate child all the days of her life. Favor from heaven's perspective is not always so pleasant from ours.

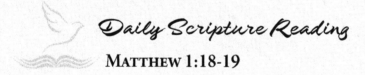

Daily Scripture Reading
MATTHEW 1:18-19

Prayer

> *God, fill me with grace for the leaders in my church and my Christian community. I have no idea what challenges they are walking through personally as a result of Your favor on their lives. Fill me with mercy for the trials of others.*

If you don't live by the praises of man, you won't die by their criticisms.

THOSE WHO EXPERIENCE REVIVAL have spiritual encounters that are beyond reason. We seldom have immediate understanding of what God is doing and why. Sometimes our dearest friends want to put us away, like Joseph initially planned to do with his pregnant fiancé. It's easy to imagine that things we don't understand must be from the devil.

And then there's the fact that we are looked at as a fringe element by the rest of the Body of Christ. The willingness to bear reproach from our brothers and sisters is part of the cost we pay for the move of the Spirit. But we will not change the subject: We will pursue sustained revival no matter what the cost.

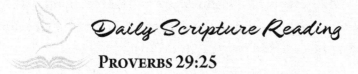

Daily Scripture Reading
PROVERBS 29:25

Prayer

Jesus, show me where there is any fear of man hiding in my heart. I don't want to be snared by it in the future. I open my heart to You; I will follow You wherever You lead, no matter what the cost.

Stigma is not a guarantee of revival.

"THEREFORE JESUS ... SUFFERED OUTSIDE THE gate. *Therefore let us go forth to Him, outside the camp, bearing His reproach*" (Hebrew 13:12-13). Revival usually takes us outside the camp—the religious community. That is often where He is—outside the camp!

Stigma by itself is no guarantee what we're experiencing is a true move of God. Some people earn reproach through heresy, impurity, and legalism. The embarrassing tension of being numbered with these is what makes the true stigma that much harder to bear. Daniel knew this inner conflict. He remained true to his call despite being considered just another magician by the king and his court (see Daniel 2).

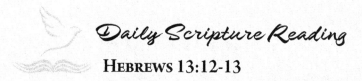

Daily Scripture Reading
HEBREWS 13:12-13

Prayer

It's hard and sometimes embarrassing to be lumped in with the outcasts of the faith. It's not a comfortable place for me to be, Holy Spirit. Keep my heart clean of judgment or resentment, and show me how I might continue to follow You in all humility and love.

*No revival ends because of
excess; it ends because of control.*

AS HAS BEEN STATED, quenching the Spirit is probably responsible for the end of more revivals than any other single cause. There hasn't been a revival that has ended because of excess. This doesn't mean that we don't concern ourselves with excess, or that moves of God don't need to be pastored. But it does mean that God won't be controlled.

Often, even those who previously embraced the move of God come to a place where their comfort zone is stretched about as far as they are willing to go. They then begin to look for a place to settle—a place of understanding and control.

Daily Scripture Reading

PROVERBS 19:21

Prayer

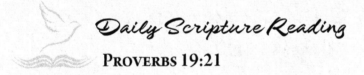

I want to be a lifelong learner of Your presence, God. Let me never think that I have arrived in the journey of knowing You. You are the Lord over my life, and I will spend my days searching after You.

The fields are white for harvest.

THE SECOND GREATEST REASON for a revival's end is when the Church begins to look for the return of the Lord instead of pursuing a greater breakthrough in the Great Commission. That kind of hunger for heaven is not encouraged in Scripture. It turns the blessed hope into the blessed escape.

To want Jesus to come back now is to sentence billions of people to hell forever. It's not that we shouldn't long for heaven. Paul said that longing was to be a comfort for the Christian. But to seek for the end of all things is to pronounce judgment on all of mankind outside of Christ. Even Paul didn't want to return to Corinth until their obedience was complete. Is Jesus, the One who paid for all sin, eager to return without that final great harvest? I think not.

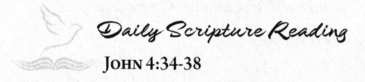

Daily Scripture Reading

JOHN 4:34-38

Prayer

I never want to become so focused on myself, Lord, that I forget what You have called me to do. I can be filled with extreme hope for that final great harvest, because I know the One who made it possible.

Our cry is heaven, come!

I BELIEVE THE DESIRE for the Church to be in heaven now is actually the counterfeit of seeking first the Kingdom. There's a difference between crying for heaven now and crying for heaven here! If a revival has brought us to the end of our dreams, does that mean we have reached the end of His? A revival must go beyond all we could imagine. Anything less falls short.

Many revivalists had such significant breakthroughs that they viewed the Lord's return to be at hand. They failed to equip the Church to do what they were gifted to do. As a result, they touched multitudes instead of nations and generations. We must plan as though we have a lifetime to live, but work and pray as though we have very little time left.

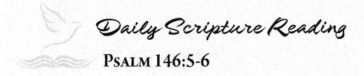

Daily Scripture Reading

PSALM 146:5-6

Prayer

I long to see Your plan of redemption unfold on the earth, Lord. I am filled with hope because of Your goodness and Your faithfulness. Show me what You would have me do to advance Your vision for wholeness on the earth.

These all with one mind were continually devoting themselves to prayer... (Acts 1:14 NASB).

THE DISCIPLES, WHO WERE accustomed to Jesus surprising them at every turn in the road, found themselves in yet another unusual situation: waiting for the promise of the Father—whatever that was. The ten days spent together no doubt provided opportunity to express sorrow over their stupid conversations about who was the greatest among them and who would never forsake the Lord. Something of that nature must have happened, because they were still together without Jesus being there keeping the peace.

They were about to have an encounter that would dwarf every previous experience. God was about to saturate their beings with Himself, taking the power they saw flowing through Jesus and causing it to explode within them. This would be the culmination of God's restorative and commissioning efforts since man abandoned the call to subdue the earth back in Genesis. This would become the high-water mark for all of mankind—ever.

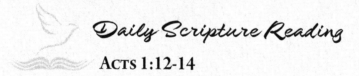

Daily Scripture Reading
ACTS 1:12-14

Prayer

When I'm in that agonizing space of waiting on the fulfillment of Your word, God, give me the wisdom to follow the disciples' lead. I will stand with my brother and sister in faith, devoting myself to prayer and communion with You.

The Church in Acts hadn't learned enough to try and control God.

TEN DAYS HAD PASSED, Pentecost had come, and they were still praying as they did the other nine days. *"And suddenly…"* (Acts 2:2). A room with one hundred and twenty people was now filled with the sound of wind, fire, and ecstatic expressions of praise uttered through known and unknown languages.

No matter how people interpret Paul's instruction on the use of spiritual gifts, one thing must be agreed upon: this meeting was entirely directed by the Holy Spirit. This infant Church hadn't learned enough to try and control God. They hadn't developed biases over acceptable and unacceptable practices. They had no biblical or experiential grid for what was happening.

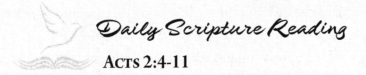

Daily Scripture Reading
ACTS 2:4-11

Prayer

Take me back to a place of ~~childlike wonder,~~ Holy Spirit. I don't want to ever think I know too much to be astounded by Your ways. I want You to direct every meeting we have.

The Bible does not confine God.

CONSIDER THE ACTS 2 company's predicament: they just had an encounter with God without a chapter and verse to explain what just happened. Peter, under the direction of the Holy Spirit, chose to use Joel 2 as the proof-text to give the needed backbone to their experience. Joel 2 declares there would be an outpouring of the Holy Spirit involving prophecy, dreams, and visions. The outpouring happened as promised in Acts 2, but it had none of the things mentioned by Joel. Instead it had the sound of wind, fire, and tongues. It was God who used this passage to support this new experience.

The very fact that this seems like an improper interpretation of Scripture should reveal to us that it is we who often approach His book incorrectly. The Bible is not a book of lists that confine or corral God. The Word does not contain God—it reveals Him. Joel 2 revealed the nature of God's work among man. Acts 2 was an illustration of what God intended by that prophecy.

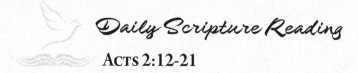

Daily Scripture Reading
ACTS 2:12-21

Prayer

Thank You, Father, that You are doing a new thing on the earth that is beyond my awareness or comprehension. I want to encounter the wildness of Your presence as I read Your Word.

For I am not ashamed of the gospel, for it is the power of God for salvation... (Romans 1:16 NASB).

MANY CHURCH SERVICES ARE designed to be as inoffensive as possible. The idea is to make the services as palatable as possible. The assumption is any use of the gifts of the Spirit will send people running, turning them off to the gospel. Often those same people are already turned off from the idea of the gospel.

For the most part, expressive worship, ministry in spiritual gifts, and the like only turn off Christians who have had the unfortunate experience of being taught against them. And many of these same individuals warm up to such things when they face an impossible situation and need the help of someone experienced in the gospel of power.

Daily Scripture Reading

ROMANS 1:16

Prayer

You never offered a diluted version of Yourself, Jesus. You confronted peoples' beliefs with a whole different paradigm—the reality of Your Kingdom at hand. I want to walk in the same boldness and clarity of faith.

We can't be afraid of messes if we want increase.

THE CHURCH HAS AN unhealthy addiction to perfection: the kind that makes no allowances for messes. This standard can only be met by restricting or rejecting the use of the gifts of the Spirit. *"Let all things be done decently and in order"* (1 Corinthians 14:40). The "all things" of this verse refer to the manifestations of the Holy Spirit. Therefore, all things must be done before we have the right to discuss order.

Keeping things tidy has become our great commission. The gifts of the Spirit interfere with the drive for order, and order becomes valued above increase. So why should we value an occasional mess? *"Where no oxen are, the trough is clean; but much increase comes by the strength of an ox"* (Proverb 14:4). Messes are necessary for increase.

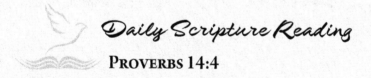

Daily Scripture Reading
PROVERBS 14:4

Prayer

> The idea of a messy revival feels scary sometimes, and it's so easy for me to subconsciously prefer the order and perceived safety of predictability. But I want more of You, Holy Spirit, and I trust that You will give me the wisdom to navigate the messes as they come.

NOVEMBER

The Leaven of Heaven

The purpose of order is to promote life.

HOW IMPORTANT IS INCREASE to God? Jesus once cursed a fig tree for not bearing fruit out of season! A man in one of His parables was cast into outer darkness for burying his money and not obtaining an increase for his master (see Matthew 25:24-30). There is a big difference between graveyards and nurseries. One has perfect order, and the other has life.

The childless person may walk into the church nursery with all the joyous activities of the children and mistakenly call the place out of order. Compared to their living room, it is. But when a parent walks in and sees her little one playing with other youngsters, she thinks it is perfect! It's all a matter of perspective. Order is for the purpose of promoting life. Beyond that it works against the things we say we value.

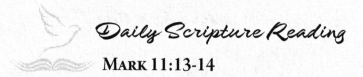

Daily Scripture Reading
MARK 11:13-14

Prayer

You love life, growth, and increase, God! Help me to see things like You do. I never want to inadvertently crush life with my desire for order. Give me Your wisdom to design order that promotes increase with You.

*We have to have mystery
in order to develop trust.*

WE MISS GOD WHEN we live as though we have Him figured out. We have the habit of making Him look like us. We imagine that He would probably think about things the way we do. In fact, if we think we understand Him we have probably conformed Him into our image.

There must remain mystery in our relationship with this One who has purposed to work beyond our capacity to imagine (see Ephesians 3:20). We must face things that offend us, embrace questions that we cannot answer, in order to live a life of trust in God. To endeavor to know Him is to embark on an adventure in which our questions increase.

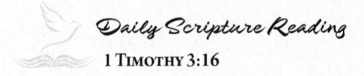

Daily Scripture Reading

1 TIMOTHY 3:16

Prayer

Mystery is uncomfortable, God. I'd much rather understand Your motives, Your timing, and Your plans. But my desire to live a life fully trusting in You is greater than my desire for control. I welcome Your mystery.

We are called to be salt and light to the world systems.

OUR GOD-BORN DESIRE FOR revival must keep us desperate enough to recognize Him when He comes. Without such desperation, we get satisfied with our present status and become our own worst enemies at changing history. God is not interested in us maintaining the status quo. His Kingdom is all about expansion, restoration, and reformation.

Change is at the very foundation of our salvation, and we are called to be world-changers and hope-bringers for His glory. But history cannot be changed effectively until we are willing to get our hands dirty. We do that when we embrace the call to become salt and light to the world.

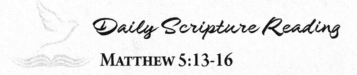

Daily Scripture Reading
MATTHEW 5:13-16

Prayer

Father, show me the ways I've hidden my light under a basket rather than sharing it with the world. Show me what You've placed in me to give. I want to change the course of history with You.

Leaven influences its surroundings in irreversible ways.

I ONCE TAUGHT AT a small pastor's conference in a European country. My subject was: The Infiltrating Power of the Kingdom of God. Much like light that exposes or salt that preserves, leaven influences its surroundings in a subtle but overpowering way. So it is with the Kingdom of God. I spoke about some of the practical strategies we had taken as a church to influence the social system in our area for the cause of Christ.

Following my message to the pastors, several leaders met together discussing the concepts I had presented. They broke from their huddle to inform me that I was in error. "Leaven always refers to sin" they said, "and this parable shows how the Church will be filled with sin and compromise in the last days." They saw it as a warning, not a promise.

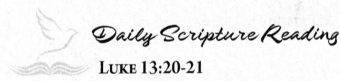

Daily Scripture Reading

LUKE 13:20-21

Prayer

Father, You placed me in my community for a reason. The government of my nation is not hopeless or overwhelming for You. Help me to see things as You do; show me how You would have me influence the social system in my area.

God always has a plan for redemption.

MANY YEARS AGO, WE had a young man in our church who was on trial. He had already spent time in prison and was looking at a possible 20-year sentence. He committed the crime before his recent conversion. Both the judge and the prosecuting attorney admitted this young man's life had been transformed by God. But they wanted some measure of justice for the crime. So, they sentenced him to six months in a short-term prison.

The Sunday before he left we laid our hands on him, sending him out as a missionary to a mission field that none of us could get into. As a result of this infiltration, over 60 of the approximate 110 prisoners confessed Christ within a year.

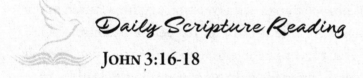

Daily Scripture Reading
JOHN 3:16-18

Prayer

God, thank You that nothing is wasted with You. Even my mistakes get folded into Your perfect plan for redemption. Will You reveal to me what arena You are calling me to influence today?

It is impossible to have faith where there is no hope.

THE CHURCH CAN FALL into a survivalist posture. The problem is, focusing on keeping ourselves safe actually disarms and distracts us from the true mind of Christ. His plan for us is one of great triumph. When we are more focused on sin "infecting" the Kingdom than we are on the Kingdom influencing the world, our mistake is twofold:

1. They mistake the Church for the Kingdom. They are not the same. The Church is to live in the realm of the King's domain, but it in itself is not the Kingdom. While sin does infect the Church, the Kingdom is the realm of God's rule. Sin cannot penetrate and influence that realm.

2. The predisposition to see a weak, struggling Church in the last days has made it difficult to see the promise of God for revival. It is impossible to have faith where you have no hope. Such approaches to understanding Scripture have crippled the Church.

Daily Scripture Reading

PSALM 27:13-14

Prayer

Holy Spirit, fill my heart with Your hope for my family, for my city, and for my nation. Sometimes my own well of hope seems to run dry, but I know that Yours never does. You have made me for victory in every area of my life.

*Jesus is returning
for a glorious Bride.*

WITHOUT A REVELATION OF what God intends to do with His Church, we cannot move in overcoming faith. When the main goal of our faith is keeping us safe from the devil, our faith becomes inferior to what God expects. Jesus had in mind more for us than survival. We are destined to overcome.

Every conversion plunders hell. Every miracle destroys the works of the devil. Every God encounter is an invasion of the Almighty into our desperate condition. This is our joy.

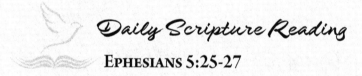

Daily Scripture Reading
EPHESIANS 5:25-27

Prayer

You have so much goodness planned for my life and for this world, God. Thank You that I can see Your goodness and mercy every day. It is my joy to partner with You to see heaven come on earth in my lifetime.

Arise, shine; for your light has come! And the glory of the Lord is risen upon you (Isaiah 60:1).

THE ORIGINAL FLAME OF Pentecost, the Holy Spirit Himself, burns within my soul. I have a promise from God. I am a part of a company of people destined to do greater works than Jesus did in His earthly ministry.

Why is it so hard to see the Church with significant influence in the last days? It was God who determined that the Bride should be spotless and without wrinkle. It was God who declared, *"Behold darkness will cover the earth, but His glory will appear upon you"* (Isaiah 60:2 NASB). It was God who calls us, His Church, overcomers (see Revelation 12:11).

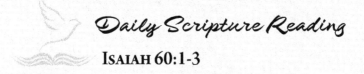

Daily Scripture Reading

ISAIAH 60:1-3

Prayer

Holy Spirit, inhabit me—spirit, soul, and body—as You cover the earth with the glory of God. I join the company of people who are destined to do even greater works than Jesus did in His life on earth. I will be a part of preparing the Bride for Your return.

God's Church is to shine brightly against the backdrop of the world.

THE PARABLE ABOUT LEAVEN illustrates the subtle but overwhelming influence of the Kingdom in any setting into which it is placed. In these days, God has planned to put us into the darkest of situations to demonstrate His dominion.

A jeweler often places a diamond on a piece of black velvet. The brilliance of the gem is clearer against that background. So it is with the Church. The dark condition of world's circumstances becomes the backdrop upon which He displays His glorious Church! *"Where sin abounded, grace abounded much more"* (Romans 5:20).

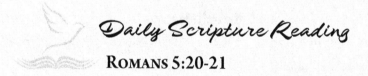

Daily Scripture Reading
ROMANS 5:20-21

Prayer

Yeast is so small, but it changes the nature of bread dough completely. I will never look to my own insignificance as an excuse for a lack of Your transformative power. You can do so much with so little, God. I give all that I have to You.

There is no system too demonic for God to infiltrate.

DANIEL WAS PROBABLY AROUND fifteen years old when we begin his story. He was taken away from his family, made a eunuch, and put into the king's service. He, along with Shadrach, Meshach, and Abednego, were chosen because they were: *"good looking, gifted in all wisdom, possessing knowledge and quick to understand, who had ability to serve in the king's palace, and whom they might teach the language and literature of the Chaldeans"* (Daniel 1:4).

Daniel started as a trainee in Nebuchadnezzar's court, but later was promoted to an advisor of foreign kings. He grew above all others in wisdom and became a counselor to the king. Because of his excellence in service and power, the king considered him ten times better than all the others (see Daniel 1:20). Daniel was a part of one of the most demonically inspired kingdoms to ever rule the earth. He was deeply embedded into that system, numbered alongside the magicians, astrologers, and sorcerers. He was perfectly placed by God.

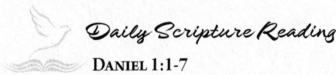

Daily Scripture Reading
DANIEL 1:1-7

Prayer

Thank You, Lord, that darkness is not dark to You. There is no system of the world that cannot be infiltrated by Your transformative love and power. I lift up those, like Daniel, who have been embedded deeply into broken systems. Give them strength, cover them with Your presence.

Greatness in God is often found on the other side of injustice and offense.

BABYLON WAS A SOPHISTICATED society, with enough distractions to keep any Hebrew in the constant tension between devotion to God and an unhealthy love for this world. When you add strong idolatrous worship and the demonic presence it brings, you have a deadly combination that would undermine the faith of any casual Christian.

Daniel, on the other hand, was absolute in His devotion to God, and uncompromising in his purpose. He sought for excellence in his position as leaven. If you want to find someone with a reason for bitterness, you've just found him—taken away from his family, made into a eunuch, and forced to serve among the cultists. Greatness in God is often on the other side of injustice and offense. Daniel made it over this hurdle, but not because he was great. He was victorious because of His devotion to the One who is great!

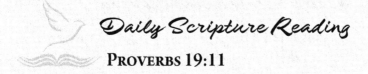

Daily Scripture Reading
PROVERBS 19:11

Prayer

Father, give me the faith of Daniel. I want to keep my eyes on You even in the midst of great offense and betrayal. I will not compromise my purpose. I am devoted to You.

*A Spirit-empowered life will
act as leaven to a dark world.*

DANIEL DISCOVERED EARLY ON, the power of holiness. He was unwilling to eat the king's delicacies. Separation to God is demonstrated in personal lifestyle, not associations. He could not control his surroundings. So often the Church gets this backward. Many in the Church live the same way as those in the world, but they will not associate with unbelievers so as not to be defiled.

Many Christians prefer to work in a Christian business, attend Christian meetings, and isolate themselves from the very people we are left on the planet to touch in His name. This is the logical product of survival theology. The Kingdom is the realm of the Spirit of God demonstrating the lordship of Jesus. And it's a Spirit-empowered life that has the effect of leaven in a dark world.

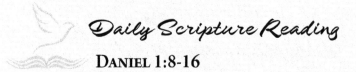

Daily Scripture Reading
DANIEL 1:8-16

Prayer

Father, I want to be set apart for You. I want my life to speak of Your goodness, Your compassion, and Your holiness. Help me be a living witness for the gospel.

False humility will keep you from your destiny; true humility will bring you toward it.

THE ULTIMATE CHALLENGE CAME to all the king's wise men when he asked them not only to interpret a dream he just had, but also tell him what the dream was! When they couldn't, he ordered all the wise men killed. In the process, they sought to kill Daniel and his friends. Daniel asked for an audience with the king. He believed God would enable him to bring the Word of the Lord.

Before he told the king the dream and its interpretation, he taught him a virtue of the Kingdom of God called humility. Daniel stated, *"This secret has not been revealed to me because I have more wisdom than anyone living, but for our sakes who make known the interpretation to the king, and that you may know the thoughts of your heart"* (Daniel 2:30). In other words, it's not because I am great or gifted; it's because God wants us to live, and He wants you to have this message. He then interprets the dream as a servant.

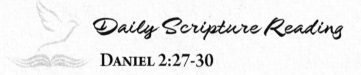

Daily Scripture Reading

DANIEL 2:27-30

Prayer

Do the work necessary in my heart now, Holy Spirit, that will prepare me to respond like Daniel. I want to be so focused on Your presence, Lord, that I can speak truth to power with love and in all humility.

When you know who you are, serving
is an opportunity to enable others.

SO MUCH OF TODAY'S Kingdom theology is focused on us ruling, in the sense of believers becoming the heads of corporations and governments. And, in measure, it is true. But our strong suit has been, and always will be, service.

If in serving we get promoted to positions of rulership, we must remember that what got us there will keep us useful. In the Kingdom, the greatest is the servant of all. We are most like Jesus when we—knowing the authority we have in Him—pick up a towel and wash the feed of others. Use every position to serve with more power.

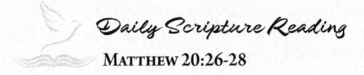

Daily Scripture Reading

MATTHEW 20:26-28

Prayer

Jesus, You knew that You carried all of the authority of heaven and yet You washed the feet of Your disciples. Help me to operate in the same sense of identity. I am called to serve others, just like You.

God positions us for dependence on Him.

THE BIBLE NEVER MENTIONS Daniel operating in the prophetic before he was in Nebuchadnezzar's court. Something similar happened to an evangelist friend of mine while still in his youth. He was invited to speak in a church in Canada. When he got off the plane, the pastor met him with a surprised look on his face, saying, "You're not Morris Cerullo!" The pastor had a great hunger for signs and wonders to be restored to his church and thought he had booked a week of meetings with Morris Cerullo.

The shocked pastor asked the young man if he had a signs and wonders ministry. He answered, "No." The pastor, looking at his watch said, "You've got four hours to get one" and then took him to the hotel. Out of desperation, the young evangelist cried out to God, and God honored his cry. That night was the beginning of the signs and wonders ministry that has marked his life to this day. God orchestrated these circumstances so that both Daniel and this young evangelist would earnestly pursue spiritual gifts.

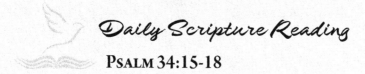

Daily Scripture Reading

PSALM 34:15-18

Prayer

God, thank You that I am never alone. Thank You that when it feels as though I have been backed into a corner, You are there to reveal to me new levels of Your goodness, Your faithfulness, and Your power. I depend entirely on You.

The spiritual gifts were never intended to be trapped inside the four walls of the Church.

WE ARE CALLED TO be salt, to add flavor to the world. But we can't do this by keep ourselves isolated, only connecting with other Christians. Infiltrating the system often involves our willingness to bring spiritual gifts into our world. It's the wisdom and creativity of God that allows us to influence society for the Kingdom.

The spiritual gifts actually work better in the world than in the confines of church meetings. When we practice the gifts only in the church, they lose their sharp edge. Invading the world system with His dominion keeps us sharp and brings hope and salvation to those who are lost.

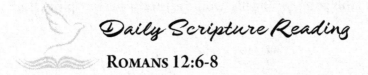

Daily Scripture Reading

ROMANS 12:6-8

Prayer

Father, You have designed every part of me with a unique purpose. Show me the particular gifts You have placed within me. How would You have me offer those gifts to the world?

Promotion will not go unchallenged.

THE WHOLE GROUP OF wise men, comprised of magicians, astrologers, etc., were spared because of Daniel's faith and courage. The presence of the Kingdom saves the lives of people who have not earned it through personal obedience. Such is the power of righteousness—it protects those around it.

Promotion does not go unchallenged. Just when you think you have been placed into a position of influence, something will happen to totally rock your boat. Nebuchadnezzar made a golden image that stood 90 feet tall. All in his kingdom were to worship this thing. But the Hebrew children would not. There is a distinction between submission and obedience. Sometimes we are to go against the command of our leaders—but even then, only with submissive hearts.

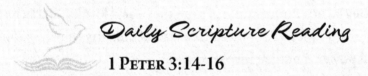

Daily Scripture Reading
1 PETER 3:14-16

Prayer

Holy Spirit, help me to discern the difference between submission and obedience. I want to obey You in all things, living righteously in a way that impacts those around me. Prepare my heart, if necessary, to act against the command of leadership with a submissive heart.

The Lord is faithful, and He is the source of our loyalty.

AN ADDITIONAL LESSON FROM Daniel's life as leaven is found in Chapter 4. He has been given the interpretation to another dream. It is about the judgment of God against Nebuchadnezzar. Remember, this is the leader of a demonically inspired kingdom—one that required idolatry! Men of lesser character would have rejoiced in God's judgment. Not Daniel. His response to his master was: *"My lord, may the dream concern those who hate you, and its interpretation concern your enemies"* (Daniel 4:19).

What loyalty! His devotion was not based on the character of his king. It was based on the character of the One who assigned him the position of service. Some would have had an "I told you so" response to their boss if God judged them in the same way. The world has seen our "holier than thou" attitude, and they're not impressed. It's time they see a loyalty that is not based on genuine goodness. Responses like Daniel's display the Kingdom in its purity and power. They are revolutionary.

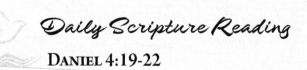

Daily Scripture Reading

DANIEL 4:19-22

Prayer

Convict me, Holy Spirit, of any place where I've determined my loyalty by the goodness of the individual rather than by the One who is always faithful. You have placed me strategically in relationship, and I want to reveal Your Kingdom through my revolutionary loyalty.

Revival must be taken out of the Church walls.

THE CLOSING VERSES OF Chapter 4 record what is possibly the greatest conversion of all time: that of Nebuchadnezzar. He was the darkest ruler ever to live. His final recorded words are: *"Now I, Nebuchadnezzar, praise and extol and honor the King of heaven, all of whose works are truth, and His ways justice. And those who walk in pride, He is able to put down"* (Daniel 4:37). He was saved from hell because of the leavening power of the Kingdom of God. The system was invaded, righteousness was established, power was displayed, and people were saved.

For massive worldwide revival to reach it's dominating potential, it must be taken out of the four walls of the Church and launched into the marketplace (see Mark 6:56). Quietly, powerfully, decisively invade through service; and when you run into a person with an impossibility, let him know the reality of heaven is within arm's reach! And "let your peace come upon it" (see Matthew 10:13).

Daily Scripture Reading
DANIEL 4: 34-37

Prayer

Open my eyes, Jesus, to any invitation to serve my community that You have placed before me. I want to take Your Kingdom into every area of the marketplace. I want to reveal Your heart for the world through my honor, loyalty, and service.

God will establish His Kingdom in our hearts, no matter the circumstance.

GOD HAD SPOKEN TO Joseph about his purpose in life through dreams. Sharing those dreams with his family, though, got him in trouble. His brothers were already jealous because he was his father's favorite. They later captured him and sold him into slavery.

God prospered him wherever he went because he was a man of promise. As a great servant, he obtained favor in Potiphar's house. When Potiphar's wife tried to seduce him, he said no. She then lied and had him put in prison, where he again prospered. While circumstances had gone from bad to worse, God was establishing the qualities of leaven in His man.

Daily Scripture Reading

DEUTERONOMY 7:7-11

Prayer

You have spoken promises over my life, God, but sometimes those promises feel so far from the reality I'm currently living. Thank You, Lord, that my circumstances do not dictate Your faithfulness. You are working the qualities of Your Kingdom leaven into me.

It is not in me; God will give Pharaoh a favorable answer (Genesis 41:16 NASB).

WHEN JOSEPH WAS SENT to prison, he met a butler and a baker who worked for the king. They each had a dream but were sad because they didn't understand them. Joseph responded, "Do not interpretations belong to God? Tell them to me please." Joseph had obviously not become bitter against God, and used his gift to interpret their dreams. For the butler it was good news, and he was freed. But the baker was executed.

Sometime later, Pharaoh had two troubling dreams. The butler remembered Joseph's gift, and he was brought before the king. When asked to interpret the king's dream, Joseph replied, "It is not in me." Such a humble heart keeps us useful to God. Joseph interpreted the dreams and then operated in the gift of wisdom by giving the king counsel as to what to do next. The king honored him by putting him second in command over the entire Egyptian Empire.

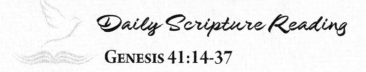

Daily Scripture Reading

GENESIS 41:14-37

Prayer

> *You are the source of all of my gifting and goodness, Lord. You are the one who touches the hearts of people and changes the world. You are the One I look to always.*

Forgiveness does not mean forgetting the pain of what happened.

JOSEPH GIVES US ONE of the best illustrations of forgiveness in the Bible. His brothers come to him (unknowingly) because of famine in their land. When he finally reveals who he is, and the obvious fulfillment of his dreams, he says, *"But now, do not therefore be grieved or angry with yourselves because you sold me here; for God sent me before you to preserve life"* (Genesis 45:5).

Notice that Joseph did not forget what happened to him. The notion that we are expected to forget what someone has done to us causes us more damage than good. Suppression simply hides a wound from view. Incubating the wound causes the infection to worsen.

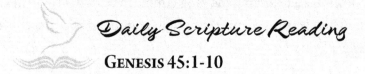

Daily Scripture Reading
GENESIS 45:1-10

Prayer

Open my heart to Your heavenly perspective, Lord. I don't want to get stuck harboring old offenses. I want to grieve fully, receive Your comfort, and live so aware of Your forgiveness of me that forgiving others comes easily.

*We are to walk in
both purity and power.*

INFILTRATING THE SYSTEM INVOLVES both purity and power. Purity is seen in the character of those—like Joseph and Daniel—who demonstrate loyalty and forgiveness, beyond reason. Power was released through the use of their gifts.

To be effective as leaven in the Babylonian system, we must rethink our understanding of these subjects. God's people must find a heart to see others succeed. Anyone can wish good upon someone who conforms to his or her beliefs and disciplines. But the ability to express loyalty and forgiveness before someone is saved may be the key to touching that individual's heart.

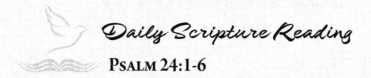

Daily Scripture Reading
PSALM 24:1-6

Prayer

Thank You, Father, that You are stretching me and growing me in both Your purity and Your power. I want to show Your love, loyalty, and forgiveness to a world hungry to know You.

Holiness is the nature of God.

PERSONAL INTEGRITY IS THE backbone of all life and ministry, and our credibility is founded on this one thing. We can be gifted beyond measure. But if we can't be trusted, the world will turn a deaf ear to our message.

Integrity is holiness, and holiness is the nature of God. Holiness is not some impossible standard we are constantly trying to achieve by our own merit. Holiness is found in the beauty of His presence. We do not work our way to holiness; we are transformed into His likeness as we surrender to God's transformative presence. Yieldedness to the Holy Spirit is at the heart of the integrity issue.

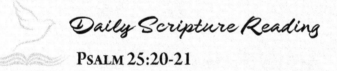

Daily Scripture Reading
PSALM 25:20-21

Prayer

I want to fall in love with Your holiness, God. I want to see the beauty of it when I look at You. I want to grow—every day— toward Your integrity manifest in my life.

Any gospel that doesn't work in the marketplace, doesn't work.

WE SEE BUSINESSMEN USE the gifts of the Spirit to identify the needs of their co-workers and customers. A young teammate laid hands on the star running back of his high school football team after he had been knocked out of the game with a serious leg injury. After the running back was healed, he returned to the game acknowledging God had healed him!

Any gospel that doesn't work in the marketplace, doesn't work. Jesus invaded every realm of society. He went where people gathered. They became His focus, and He became theirs.

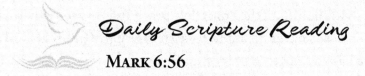

Daily Scripture Reading

MARK 6:56

Prayer

> *Thank You, Holy Spirit, that You have not confined the truth of the gospel to the Church. Thank You that even pre-believers know when the Kingdom has come near. Thank You that the wisdom of Your Kingdom is recognizable to everyone.*

Love looks like something.

A YOUNG GIRL WITH diabetes was suffering from insulin shock. Her Christian friend prayed for her on the way to the nurse's office. When the mother picked her up from school and took her to the doctor, they found she no longer had diabetes.

A ten-year-old asked her mom to take her to the mall so she could find sick people to pray for. Students set up a sign at their table at our local coffee shop. It says, "Free Prayer." People not only got prayer, they received a prophetic word that brought them to a greater awareness of God's love.

Teams of people bring hot meals to our local hotels to touch the needy. A hotel owner gave us a room for a season just so we would have a place to pray for the many sick patrons. Some invade the bars looking for people who need ministry. The gifts of the Spirit flow powerfully in these environments. The gospel was never meant to be kept inside the Church; God's miraculous love has an answer to every situation.

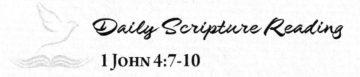

Daily Scripture Reading

1 JOHN 4:7-10

Prayer

> *I want to be Your hands and feet, Jesus. I want to spread Your love and transformative power over the earth. What does love look like for the people around me?*

We get to be God's love, practically manifested, within our communities.

YARDS IN THE POOREST communities are mowed and cleaned, while others clean the insides of the homes. Some go house to house looking to pray for the sick. Miracles are the norm. Skateboarders are touched by other skateboarders who look to bring them into an encounter with the God of all power. If people are there, we go there. Under the bridges, out in the vacant lots, we look for the homeless. They are fed, clothed, and ministered to for their most basic natural and spiritual needs.

Jesus doesn't only care for the down-and-outer, but He also loves the "up and outer." The wealthy are some of the most broken of our cities. But we must not serve them for their money! They are accustomed to people becoming friends to get something from them. We serve because we have the love of the Father flowing through us to address practical needs in our community.

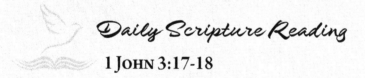

Daily Scripture Reading

1 JOHN 3:17-18

Prayer

Jesus, You were constantly filled with compassion as You walked the earth. Fill me with the same compassion for my community. Show me where You would have me love my neighbors today.

Your field of ministry is wherever your daily life takes you.

WHERE DO YOU FIND yourself spending your time? If it's your workplace, ask the Lord what love would look like to your coworkers. If it's your children's school, how could you bless their teachers. Where does life take you? Go there in the anointing and watch the impossibilities bow to the name of Jesus.

Parents become Little League coaches. Some lead after-school programs in our public schools. Others volunteer at a local hospital or become trained as chaplains for the police department or local high schools. People visit their sick neighbors seeing God do the impossible. God's love is ready to invade wherever we will carry the anointing.

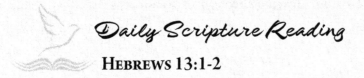

Daily Scripture Reading

HEBREWS 13:1-2

Prayer

God, I lift up my daily schedule to You. I invite You to interrupt it. Help me to see the divinely orchestrated opportunities You've prepared for me to be Your witness. You have set me up for ministry exactly where I am right now.

Pray much and take risks.

BEING INVOLVED IN THE supernatural through spiritual gifts is what makes our influence of the world systems possible and effective. The Kingdom of God is a Kingdom of power! We must be in pursuit of a fuller demonstration of the Spirit of God. Pray much and take risks.

The ultimate example of this is Jesus. In Him, the supernatural invaded the natural. The blind were given sight, the dead were raised, the captives were set free. He saw what the Father was doing and released it on the earth, and our world was never the same again. Vision, defined by the dreams of God, equip us with undying courage.

Daily Scripture Reading

1 CHRONICLES 28:20

Prayer

Give me vision, Father, to see things as You do. I want my hopes and dreams to be shaped by Yours. I want to walk in courage and boldness to see Your Kingdom come in power.

We do not know how to pray as we should, but the Spirit Himself intercedes for us with groanings too deep for words... (Romans 8:26 NASB).

WHAT GOD HAS PLANNED for the Church in this hour is greater than our ability to imagine and pray. We must have the help of the Holy Spirit to learn about these mysteries of the Church and God's Kingdom. Without Him we don't have enough insight even to know what to ask for in prayer.

Understanding what is about to come is important, but not to equip us to plan and strategize more effectively. On the contrary, it's important to understand God's promise and purpose for the Church so that we might become dissatisfied—so that we will become desperate. Intercession from insatiable hunger moves the heart of God as nothing else can.

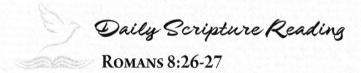

Daily Scripture Reading
ROMANS 8:26-27

Prayer

> Thank You, Holy Spirit, that I don't need to fully understand how You're moving over the earth to partner with You. You intercede for me. You teach me how and what to pray.

DECEMBER

God's Ever-Increasing Kingdom

Revival is not for the faint of heart.

REVIVAL BRINGS FEAR TO the complacent because of the risks it requires. The fearful often work against the move of God—sometimes to their death—all the while thinking they are working for Him. Deception says that the changes brought about by revival contradict the faith of their fathers. As a result, the God-given ability to create withers into the laborious task of preserving. The fearful become curators of museums, instead of builders of the Kingdom.

Others are ready to risk all. The faith of their fathers is considered a worthy foundation to build upon. They have caught a glimpse of what could be and will settle for nothing less. Change is not a threat, but an adventure. Revelation increases, ideas multiply, and the stretch begins.

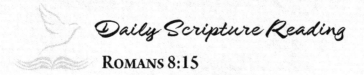

Daily Scripture Reading

ROMANS 8:15

Prayer

I will take the testimonies of the past, Lord, and learn from them. I will listen to Your wonderful works in anticipation of You doing them—and more—once again.

Christianity is life on the resurrection side of the Cross.

GOD'S ACTIVITIES ON EARTH begin with a revelation to mankind. The prophet hears and declares. Those with ears to hear respond and are equipped for change. In order to understand who we are and what we are to become, we must see Jesus as He is. We are about to see the difference between the Jesus who walked the streets healing the sick and raising the dead, and the Jesus who today reigns over all.

As glorious as His life was on earth, it was the before side of the Cross. Christianity is life on the resurrection side of the Cross. This shift in focus will come in these last days. It must happen if we are to become what He has purposed for us.

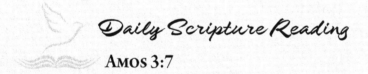

Daily Scripture Reading

AMOS 3:7

Prayer

You do not hide from Your people, God. You reveal Yourself to those who love You. Give me ears to hear and a heart to respond. Equip me for the change You are bringing to the world.

There is no economy Holy Spirit.

AS WE UNDERSTAND THE power and glory of the resurrected Christ, we begin to understand how we are to be in the world. As believers, we cannot settle for a diminished life with Him. Religion (which is "form without power") will be more and more despised in the hearts of those who truly belong to Jesus.

Revelation creates an appetite for Him. He doesn't come in a "no frills" model. There's no economy-class Holy Spirit. He only comes fully equipped. He is loaded, full of power and glory. And He wants to be seen as He is, in us.

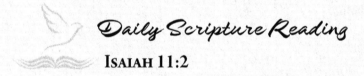

Daily Scripture Reading

ISAIAH 11:2

Prayer

You have promised to fill me with Your Spirit, Jesus, to take up residence inside of me. I want the evidence of Your presence to be obvious to anyone who encounters me. Show me how I can grow in my appetite for You.

The Kingdom of God is at hand!

THE POWER OF ONE word from the mouth of Jesus can create a galaxy. His promises for the Church are beyond all comprehension. Too many consider them to be God's promise either for the Millennium or heaven, claiming that to emphasize God's plan for now instead of eternity is to dishonor the fact that Jesus has gone to prepare a place for us.

Our predisposition toward a weak Church has blinded our eyes to the truths of God's Word about us. This problem is rooted in our unbelief, not in our hunger for heaven. Jesus taught us how to live by announcing, "The Kingdom of God is at hand!" It is a present reality, affecting the now.

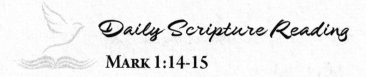

Daily Scripture Reading
MARK 1:14-15

Prayer

When You describe Your Church, Jesus, You never describe her as weak. You call her beautiful, Your spotless bride, Your united Body. Help me to see Her from Your perspective.

We are becoming like the resurrected Christ.

WE LACK UNDERSTANDING OF who we are because we have little revelation of who He is. We know a lot about His life on earth. The Gospels are filled with information about what He was like, how He lived, and what He did.

Yet that is not the example of what the Church is to become. Scripture tells us that we are to be *"as He is"* (1 John 4:17). What He is today, glorified, seated at the right hand of the Father, is the model for what we are becoming!

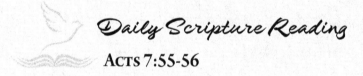

Daily Scripture Reading
ACTS 7:55-56

Prayer

Jesus, will You show me a picture right now of how it looks for You to be seated at the right hand of the Father? I need a great revelation of who You are as the resurrected Christ. I want to see Your glory and power.

We cannot let the fear of disappointment dictate our pursuit of more!

CONSIDER THE STATEMENT: WHAT God has planned for the Church in this hour is greater than our ability to imagine and pray. Such statements cause some to fear the Church will not be balanced. Many say that we must be careful over how much emphasis we put on what we are to become in the now. Why? For the most part it is a fear of disappointment that creates such caution.

Fear of disappointment has justified our unbelief. What is the worst that could happen if I pursued what is reserved for eternity? God could say, "No!" We make a big mistake to think we can figure out what has been reserved for heaven, from this side of heaven.

Daily Scripture Reading

DEUTERONOMY 29:29

Prayer

The fear of disappointment has tried to steal so much hope from me. I am breaking up with that fear; I am launching on a new, bold adventure with You, Lord.

We were not designed for lukewarm mediocrity.

BECAUSE MANY FEAR EXCESS, mediocrity is embraced as balance. Such fear makes complacency a virtue. And it's the fear of excess that has made those that are resistant to change appear noble-minded. Excess has never brought an end to revival.

William DeArteaga states, "The Great Awakening was not quenched because of its extremists. It was quenched because of the condemnation of its opponents." He also says, "Divisions occur whenever the intellect is enthroned as the measure of spirituality—not because spiritual gifts are exercised, as many charge." I pay no attention to the warnings of possible excess from those who are satisfied with lack.

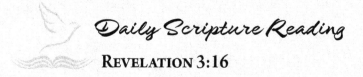

Daily Scripture Reading

REVELATION 3:16

Prayer

I don't want my fear of failure or fear of being too much to hold me back from a wholehearted pursuit of You, Holy Spirit. I give You permission to shake up my normal. I will not be satisfied with lack.

Our obsession with perfection has led to some of our greatest blemishes.

THIS GENERATION IS A generation of risk takers. And not all the risks taken will be seen as real faith. Some will come to light as steps of foolishness and presumption. But they must be taken just the same. How else can we learn? Make room for risk takers in your life that don't bat a thousand. They will inspire you to the greatness available in serving a Great God.

While I don't want to honor presumption or error, I do want to applaud passion and effort. When I taught my sons to ride a bike I took them to the park where there was lots of grass. Why? Because I wanted them not to get hurt when they fell. It was not a question of "if."

The addiction to perfection has given place to a religious spirit. People who refuse to step out and be used by God become the critics of those who do. Risk takers, the ones who thrill the heart of God, become the targets of those who never fail because they seldom try.

Daily Scripture Reading

2 CORINTHIANS 12:9-10

Prayer

You're not afraid of my mistakes, Father. You're not worried about me taking a wrong turn. You're right beside me, ready to correct my path or draw me close. I've been made to take risks in pursuit of more of You.

The Church is to be filled with His wisdom.

SCRIPTURE IS FILLED WITH the promises of God for His Church. There are so many that we have yet to see fulfilled. Jesus intends for us to become mature before He returns. We must run after these promises, because they provide a prophetic glimpse into the heart of God for us right now.

"That now the manifold wisdom of God might be made known by the church to the principalities and powers in the heavenly places, according to His eternal purpose..." (Ephesians 3:10-11).

Wisdom is to be displayed by us NOW! It is clear that God intends to teach the spirit realm about His wisdom through those made in His image—us.

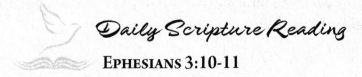

Daily Scripture Reading

EPHESIANS 3:10-11

Prayer

God, Your desire is that Your Church would display Your manifold wisdom to the world. Show me what that looks like in my life. Help me to press in for a further fulfillment of Your promises over Your Body.

*The Church will display
the excellence, creativity,
and integrity of God.*

SOLOMON WAS THE WISEST man ever to live, apart from Jesus who is wisdom personified (see 1 Corinthians 1:30). The queen of Sheba came to examine Solomon's wisdom. *"And when the queen of Sheba had seen the wisdom of Solomon, the house that he had built, the food on his table, the seating of his servants, the service of his waiters and their apparel, his cupbearers and their apparel, and his entryway by which he went up to the house of the Lord, there was no more spirit in her"* (2 Chronicles 9:3-4). She acknowledged that his wisdom was far greater than she ever imagined.

The depth of his wisdom was actually identified by these three attributes: excellence, creativity, and integrity. When she saw it in action, it took her breath away! The wisdom of God will again be seen in His people. The Church, which is presently despised, or at best ignored, will again be reverenced and admired. The Church will again be a praise in the earth.

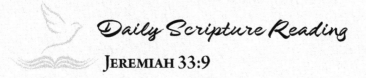

Daily Scripture Reading
JEREMIAH 33:9

Prayer

Holy Spirit, fill me with Your wisdom for my everyday activities. Thank You that I can display Your excellence, creativity, and integrity even with the food on my table or the layout of my home.

December 11

We are to carry a heart of excellence.

EXCELLENCE IS THE HIGH standard for what we do because of who we are. God is extravagant, but not wasteful. An excellent heart for God may appear to be wasteful to those on the outside. For example: In Matthew 26:8 we find Mary pouring out an ointment upon Jesus that cost a full year's income. The disciples thought it would be put to better use if it would have been sold and the money given to the poor.

In 2 Samuel, King David humbled himself before the people by taking off his kingly garments and dancing wildly before God. His wife, Michal, despised him for it. As a result she bore no children to the day of her death—either from barrenness or from the lack of intimacy between her and her husband, David. It was a tragic loss caused by pride. In both situations outsiders considered the extravagant actions of these worshipers to be wasteful. God is good. Excellence comes from viewing things from His perspective.

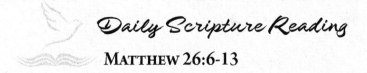

Daily Scripture Reading

MATTHEW 26:6-13

Prayer

I will pour myself out on Your feet, Jesus. I won't hold anything back. Extravagant worship of You is the only kind of worship that makes sense. You are worthy of it all!

Arise and create!

CREATIVITY IS NOT ONLY seen in a full restoration of the arts, but is the nature of His people in finding new and better ways to do things. It is a shame for the Church to fall into the rut of predictability and call it tradition. We must reveal who our Father is through creative expression.

The Church is often guilty of avoiding creativity because it requires change. Resistance to change is a resistance to the nature of God. Because the winds of change are blowing, it will be easy to distinguish between those who are satisfied and those who are hungry. Change brings to light the secrets of the heart.

This anointing will also bring about new inventions, breakthroughs in medicine and science, and novel ideas for business and education. New sounds of music will come from the Church, as will other forms of art. The list is endless. The sky is the limit. Arise and create!

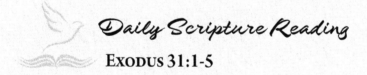

Daily Scripture Reading
EXODUS 31:1-5

Prayer

Thank You, Father, that Your creativity is not reserved for artists. You are creative, and I look just like You. Show me where I can lean into new solutions and breakthrough in my life.

True holiness is refreshingly good.

INTEGRITY IS THE EXPRESSION of God's character seen in us. And that character is His holiness. Holiness is the essence of His nature. It is not something He does or doesn't do. It is who He is. It is the same for us. We are holy because the nature of God is in us. It begins with a heart separated unto God, and it becomes evident in the Christ nature seen through us.

If we can keep the soiled hands of religion from the beautiful expression of God's holiness, people will be attracted to the Church as they were to Jesus. Religion is not only boring; it is cruel. It takes the breath out of every good thing. True holiness is refreshingly good.

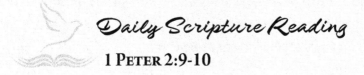

Daily Scripture Reading

1 PETER 2:9-10

Prayer

Every heart is hungry to see Your holiness expressed on the earth, Father. Help me, guide me, shape me into one who manifests Your nature in every area of my life. I want to show Your true love and goodness to the world.

...that He might present to Himself the church in all her glory... (Ephesians 5:27 NASB).

GOD'S ORIGINAL INTENT FOR mankind is seen in the passage, *"For all have sinned and fall short of the glory of God"* (Romans 3:23). We were to live in the glory of God. That was the target when God created mankind. Our sin caused the arrow of His purpose to fall short.

The glory of God is the manifested presence of Jesus. Imagine this: a people that are continually conscious of the presence of God, not in theory, but the actual presence of God upon them!

We will be a Church in which Jesus is seen in His glory! It is the Holy Spirit's presence and anointing that will dominate the Christian's life. The Church will be radiant. *"The latter glory of this house will be greater than the former"* (Haggai 2:9 NASB).

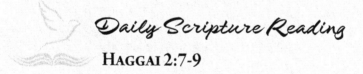

Daily Scripture Reading
HAGGAI 2:7-9

Prayer

I was designed to live in Your glory, Father. Every aspect of my being has been made to recognize Your presence. Let my life be a radiant manifestation of You.

...that He might present to Himself the church in all her glory, having no spot or wrinkle or any such thing; but that she would be holy and blameless (Ephesians 5:27 NASB).

IMAGINE A BEAUTIFUL YOUNG woman prepared for a wedding. She has taken care of herself by eating right and getting all the exercise she needs. Her mind is sharp and she is emotionally secure and free. By looking at her, you'd never know she had ever done anything wrong. Guilt and shame do not blemish her countenance. She understands and exudes grace.

According to Revelation 19:7, she made herself ready. Romance will do that to you. As Larry Randolph puts it, "It's a perversion to expect the groom to dress the bride for the wedding." The Church is to make herself ready. The tools are in place for such an event. The Church must now use them.

Daily Scripture Reading

REVELATION 19:7-8

Prayer

> *Holy Spirit, help me to do my part to not only prepare myself but also to prepare the Bride for Jesus. I want to be a part of equipping the Church to be her most beautiful, most radiant, and most effective for revealing Your glory.*

The Perfect One will return for the spotless one.

THE BIBLE DESCRIBES THE Church as glorious, as spotless and without blame. We are the Bride of Christ, but it doesn't take a prophet to see that we are not there yet. This is God's plan for us, though. And when we truly see how great God is, we'll not question His ability to pull this one off.

Paul makes a statement to the church at Corinth that he didn't want to return to them until their obedience was complete. That is the heart of God for the Church. And so, Jesus, the perfect One, will return for the spotless one when He views our obedience as complete.

Daily Scripture Reading

2 CORINTHIANS 10:5-6

Prayer

You are perfect in every way, Jesus, and You are in the process of transforming me to look just like You. I trust Your faithfulness in my process. I trust my transformation to You.

Love and faith are the two essentials of the Christian life.

THIS THAT IS CALLED the unity of faith is the faith that works through love mentioned in Galatians 5:6. Love and faith are the two essentials of the Christian life. Faith is what pleases God. It is active trust in Him as Abba Father. He alone is the source of such faith. It comes as the result of Him speaking to His people. Unity of faith means we will hear His voice together and demonstrate great exploits. It is a lifestyle, not just a concept.

The exploits of the present and coming revival will surpass all the accomplishments of the Church in all history combined. Over one billion souls will be saved. Stadiums will be filled with people 24 hours a day, for days on end, with miracles beyond number: healings, conversions, resurrections, and deliverances too many to count. No special speaker, no well-known miracle worker, just the Church being what God has called her to be. And all this will be the outgrowth of the unity of faith.

Daily Scripture Reading

EPHESIANS 4:11-13

Prayer

I stand with my brothers and sisters in faith, trusting in Your guiding voice, Father. Help us to protect our unity in You. Help me to love Your Body like You do.

The Church will receive fresh revelation of Jesus Christ as He is now.

THE APOSTLE JOHN ONCE laid his head on the chest of Jesus. He was called the one whom Jesus loved. Toward the end of his life, on the Isle of Patmos, he saw Jesus again. This time Jesus looked nothing like the one he shared that final meal with. His hair was white like wool, His eyes were a flame of fire, and His feet were like burnished bronze. God felt that this revelation was worthy of a book. It is called: The Revelation of Jesus Christ.

This revelation, seeing Jesus as He is in His resurrected state, will launch the Church into a transformation unlike any experienced in a previous age. Why? Because as we see Him, we become like Him! If the revelation of Jesus is the primary focus of the book of Revelation, then we'd also have to admit that worship is the central response. The coming increase in revelation of Jesus will be measurable through new dimensions of worship—corporate throne room experiences.

Daily Scripture Reading

HEBREWS 12:28-29

Prayer

I don't want to restrict my understanding of You, Jesus, to the gospel stories in Scripture. Those are precious and holy, but they are not the complete depiction of who You are. Give us a fresh revelation of Your glory, Lord.

*Till we all come to the unity of
the faith and of the knowledge
of the Son of God, to a
perfect man... (Ephesians 4:13)*

AN OLYMPIC ATHLETE WILL never get to the games by gifting alone. It's the powerful combination of a gift brought to its full potential through discipline. That is the picture of the Church becoming a mature man. It is singular, meaning we all function together as one. All its members will work in perfect coordination and harmony, complementing each other's function and gift, according to the directions given by the head.

This was not a promise to be fulfilled in eternity. While I don't believe that this is speaking of human perfection, I do believe there is a maturity of function, without jealousy, that will develop as His presence becomes more manifest. We need to embrace this as possible because He said it is.

Daily Scripture Reading

EPHESIANS 4:14-16

Prayer

God, thank You for the gifts that You have poured out on me and on my fellow believers. Help us to know how to steward those gifts faithfully unto Your glory. Show me how my gifts complement those who are so different from me. Mature me in every way.

...to know the love of Christ which passes knowledge; that you may be filled with all the fullness of God (Ephesians 3:19).

IMAGINE A HOUSE WITH many rooms. This house represents our life. Every room that we allow His love to touch becomes filled with His fullness. That is the picture of this verse. The Church will know the love of God by experience. This will go beyond our ability to comprehend. That intimate love relationship with God will help us to receive all that He has desired to release since the beginning of time.

"... till we all come to the unity of the faith and of the knowledge of the Son of God, to a perfect man, to the measure of the stature of the fullness of Christ" (Ephesians 4:13). The experiential love of God and the corresponding fullness of the Spirit is what is necessary to bring us to the full stature of Christ—Jesus will be accurately seen in the Church, just as the Father was accurately seen in Jesus.

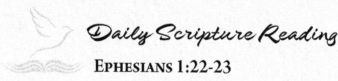

Daily Scripture Reading

EPHESIANS 1:22-23

Prayer

I fling open the rooms of my heart, Holy Spirit. I open every door of my life to Your transforming presence. Fill me with Your fullness. Let me experience Your goodness and love throughout my life.

There is a revival coming that will touch all flesh.

THIS PASSAGE QUOTED FROM Joel 2 has never been completely fulfilled. It had initial fulfillment in Acts 2, but its reach was far greater than that generation could fulfill:

> And it shall come to pass in the last days, says God, That I will pour out of My Spirit on all flesh; Your sons and your daughters shall prophesy, Your young men shall see visions, Your old men shall dream dreams. And on My menservants and on My maidservants I will pour out My Spirit in those days; And they shall prophesy (Acts 2:17-18).

First of all, all flesh was never touched by that revival. But it will happen. In the coming move of God, racial barriers will be broken, as will the economic, sexual, and age barriers. The outpouring of the Spirit in the last generation will touch every nation on the earth, releasing the gifts of the Spirit in full measure upon and through His people.

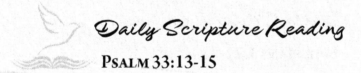

Daily Scripture Reading
PSALM 33:13-15

Prayer

> *I can sometimes feel like giving up on people, Father, but You never do. You have a vision that is so much greater than mine. You have promised a revival that will touch everyone, and I cry out, "Yes!"*

This generation will be a voice in the wilderness, preparing the way of the Lord.

FIRST CORINTHIANS 12-14 IS a wonderful teaching on the operation of the gifts of the Spirit. But it is so much more. It is a revelation of a body of believers who live in the realm of the Spirit that is essential for last days' ministry. These manifestations of the Holy Spirit will be taken to the streets where they belong. It is there that they reach their full potential.

This generation will fulfill the cry of Moses for all of God's people to be prophets. We will carry the Elijah anointing in preparing for the return of the Lord in the same way that John the Baptist carried the Elijah anointing and prepared the people for the coming of the Lord.

Daily Scripture Reading

1 CORINTHIANS 13:8-13

Prayer

I will run after Your gifts, Lord. I will pursue all that You have for me. Show me where I can share Your voice in the world. How can I hear Your word for those around me today?

He who believes in Me, the works that I do he will do also; and greater works than these he will do, because I go to My Father (John 14:12).

JESUS' PROPHECY OF US doing greater works than He did has stirred the Church to look for some abstract meaning to this very simple statement. Many theologians seek to honor the works of Jesus as unattainable, which is religion, fathered by unbelief. It does not impress God to ignore what He promised under the guise of honoring the work of Jesus on the earth. Jesus' statement is not that hard to understand. Greater means "greater." And the works He referred to are signs and wonders. It will not be a disservice to Him to have a generation obey Him and go beyond His own high-water mark. He showed us what one person could do who has the Spirit without measure. What could millions do? That was His point, and it became His prophecy.

This verse is often explained away by saying it refers to quantity of works, not quality. As you can see, millions of people should be able to surpass the sheer number of works that Jesus did simply because we are so many. But that waters down the intent of His statement. The word *greater* is *mizon* in the Greek. It is found 45 times in the New Testament. It is always used to describe "quality," not quantity.

Daily Scripture Reading

ACTS 19:11-12

Prayer

Doing greater works that You've done does feel like such a lofty goal, Jesus. I need Your perspective. I need to see the fulfillment of that promise as You do. You are true to Your Word, always.

Your kingdom come. Your will be done on earth as it is in heaven (Matthew 6:10).

HE'S NOT THE KIND of Father who gives us a command to ask for something without fully intending to answer our request. He directs us to pray this prayer because it is in His heart to fulfill it. The safest prayers in existence are the ones He tells us to pray. His answer will be beyond all we could ask or think. And it is *"according to the power that works in us"* (Ephesians 3:20).

Jesus said that He would be returning after the gospel of the Kingdom is preached in all the world—then the end would come (see Matthew 24:14). The present-day understanding of preaching the gospel of the Kingdom means to preach a message that will bring as many people to conversion as possible. But what did preaching the gospel of the Kingdom mean to Jesus? Every instance in which He either did it, or commanded it, miracles followed.

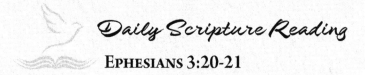

Daily Scripture Reading

EPHESIANS 3:20-21

Prayer

You have told us to pray for Your Kingdom to come, Jesus. You're the One who said that it was even possible for Your will to be done on earth in the same way as it is done in heaven. Let it be.

The lordship of Jesus will be seen in every nation of the world!

JESUS DECLARED THAT, BEFORE the end times, *"the gospel of the kingdom will be preached in all the world"* (Matthew 24:14). The message was to be a declaration of His lordship and dominion over all things, followed by demonstrations of power, illustrating that His world is invading ours through signs and wonders. Consider what is meant by this promise: there will be a generation of believers that will preach as He did, doing what He did, in every nation of the world before the end comes! That is quite a promise.

The present reality of the Kingdom will become manifest and realized in the everyday life of the believer. That world will break into this one at every point where the Christian prays in faith. The lordship of Jesus will be seen, and the bounty of His rule will be experienced. While the full expression of His Kingdom may be reserved for eternity, it has never entered our minds what God would like to do before then. It's time to explore that possibility.

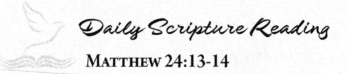

Daily Scripture Reading
MATTHEW 24:13-14

Prayer

God, I know that missions holds such a precious place in Your heart. Reaching every person with the full gospel of Jesus Christ—operating in truth, love, and power—will happen! Show me how You would have me partner with that vision.

Structure serves purpose, not the other way around.

WOULDN'T IT BE WONDERFUL to have churches so explosive in the supernatural that we would have to find ways to calm them down? That's what Paul had to do with the Corinthian church. The instructions about the gifts of the Spirit were given to a people who had so much that they needed to organize it. *"Let everything be done decently and in order"* (1 Corinthians 14:40).

You can't organize what you don't have. Everything has to be done before you can add a structure to make it more effective. Order is a poor substitute for power. But if you have much power, you'll need good order. Only in that case will order add a new dimension to the role of power in the Church.

Daily Scripture Reading
1 CORINTHIANS 14:39-40

Prayer

Holy Spirit, You are welcome here. I will not try to control Your out-pouring; I invite You to come even more in every situation. Thank You for the wisdom You give as we consider the structures that will best facilitate Your presence.

We must not create doctrine to justify our lack of power.

IN DISCUSSING THE PRESENT move of God with a cessationist, he told me that I was under deception because of my pursuit of a gospel of power. He informed me that all miracles ended with the death of the last of the twelve apostles. He further stated that the miracles of healing, the testimonies of restored families, the new zeal for the Scriptures, and the passion to give a witness of God's love to others was probably a work of the devil.

I told him that his devil was too big and His God was too small. In order to feel good about our present condition, the Church has created doctrines to justify weaknesses. Some have even made those deficiencies seem like strengths. These are doctrines of demons! While I love and honor people who believe such things, I feel no need to honor such nonsense. We are the most to be pitied if we think we've reached the fullness of what God intended for His Church here on earth.

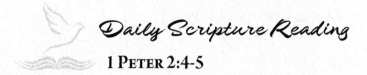

Daily Scripture Reading
1 PETER 2:4-5

Prayer

I will not make the devil bigger than he is, Lord. I will not give him more attention or more concern than he deserves. I have the Almighty God, the King of Kings, on my side. You have greater plans for me than I'll ever comprehend.

We need a new wineskin to hold what God will pour out in the coming years.

ALL CHURCH HISTORY IS built on partial revelation. Everything that has happened in the Church over the past 1900 years has fallen short of what the early Church had and lost. Each move of God has been followed by another, just to restore what was forfeited and forgotten. And we still haven't arrived to the standard that they attained, let alone surpassed it. Yet, not even the early Church fulfilled God's full intention for His people. That privilege was reserved for those in the last leg of the race. It is our destiny.

As wonderful as our spiritual roots are, they are insufficient. What was good for yesterday is deficient for today. To insist that we stay with what our fathers fought for is to insult our forefathers. They risked all to pursue something fresh and new in God. In reality, what we think of as the normal Christian life cannot hold the weight of what God is about to do. Our wineskins must change. There is very little of what we now know as Church life that will remain untouched in the next ten years.

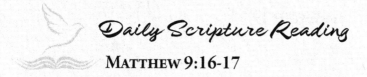

Daily Scripture Reading
MATTHEW 9:16-17

Prayer

> *Thank You for all that You have poured out on the Church throughout history, Holy Spirit. I honor the past, but I look to the future. You are not done with us; You have great plans for more!*

The greatest challenge to our
faith is found between our ears.

IT'S NOT THAT EVERYTHING must change for us to flow with what God is saying and doing. It's just that we make too many assumptions about the rightness of what presently exists. Those assumptions blind us to the revelations still contained in Scripture. It has never entered the mind what God has prepared for us while on this earth. His intent is grand.

Instead of limiting ourselves by our imagination and present experience, let's press on to a renewed hunger for things yet to be seen. As we pursue the Extravagant One with reckless abandon, we will discover that our greatest problem is the resistance that comes from between our ears. But faith is superior. And it's time for us to make Him unconcerned about whether or not He'll find faith on the earth. The Kingdom is in the now! Pray for it, seek it first, and receive it as a child. It is within reach.

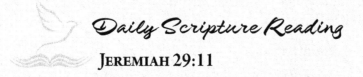

Daily Scripture Reading

JEREMIAH 29:11

Prayer

Show me, Lord, if there is any place where I have been blinded by my own assumptions of how You can and will move on the earth. You are so much bigger than my own understanding. I will not limit my anticipation of You.

The power of testimony never depreciates.

WHEN WE READ ABOUT a miraculous healing or a testimony of restoration, we are encountering the goodness of God. God's goodness is the testimony of Jesus. The book of Revelation reveals this principle, *"The testimony of Jesus is the spirit of prophecy"* (Revelation 19:10).

A testimony prophesies what is possible again. It declares another miracle is now available. It illustrates to all who will listen, the nature of God and His covenant with mankind. All He looks for is someone who will add his or her faith to the testimony given. Because He is no respecter of persons, He will do for you what He did for another. Because He is the same today as yesterday, He is willing to do again what He did long ago.

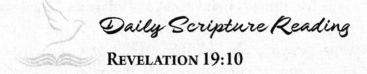

Daily Scripture Reading
REVELATION 19:10

Prayer

Thank You, Father, that my life is filled with evidence of Your goodness. I can search Your Word and find example after example of Your lovingkindness. I stand on these testimonies, looking toward my future with such confidence.

Of the increase of His government and peace there will be no end (Isaiah 9:7).

A THREE-YEAR-OLD BOY NAMED Chris, who had clubfeet, had sores on the tops of his feet where they would rub on the carpet in his effort to walk. When they were through praying, they put him down on the floor. For the first time in his life his feet were flat on the ground! He stared in amazement at his feet. One of his little friends whispered to him, "Run!" He suddenly took off and ran in a circle exclaiming, "I can run!"

Two weeks after Chris' miracle, I showed his video to our church. The next day two of our young men went to the mall and saw an elderly woman with a cane. When they asked to pray for her, she wasn't interested, until she heard Chris's story. His testimony prophesied God's goodness to her, and she became hungry for prayer. As they laid hands on her, the tumor on her knee disappeared and another tumor on her back—one she hadn't told them about—disappeared.

On another Sunday, I taught on the power of the testimony and used Chris' story as an illustration. There was a family visiting with a similar need; their little girl's feet turned inward at about 45 degrees. When her mother heard the testimony, she said in her heart, "I'll take that for my daughter!" Following the service, she picked up her child from our nursery and discovered that her daughter's feet were perfectly straight! The testimony prophesied, the mother believed, and the daughter was healed. His invasion continues and will continue without end!

Daily Scripture Reading
REVELATION 11:15

Prayer

You are indescribably good, Lord. You are better than I could even think or imagine, and You are at work in my life and in my world in so many ways. Your Kingdom is invading—bringing love, healing, and freedom—and it will continue without end!

BILL JOHNSON is a fifth-generation pastor with a rich heritage in the Holy Spirit. Bill is the senior leader of Bethel Church in Redding, California, and serves a growing number of churches that cross denominational lines, demonstrate power, and partner for revival. Bill's vision is for all believers to experience God's presence and operate in the miraculous—as expressed in his bestselling books *When Heaven Invades Earth* and *Hosting the Presence*. He has three children and eleven grandchildren.

From

BENI JOHNSON

365 Mornings and Evenings Encountering the Powerful Presence of God!

In our busy lives, it can be easy to forget to listen for God's ever-present whisper. But if you choose to turn toward Him, a life-changing encounter is only a moment away.

Pastors Bill and Beni Johnson, bestselling authors and senior leaders of the Bethel movement, deliver 365 inspiring morning and evening devotionals for every day of the year that will help you enjoy a more intimate walk with the Holy Spirit and a more victorious life empowered by the presence of God.

You will learn how to: bring Heaven to earth, live a miraculous lifestyle, host the Holy Spirit's presence, dream with God, experience the supernatural power of communion, renew your mind, strengthen yourself in the Lord, walk in divine health, discover the joy of intercession, and much more!

In your mornings and evenings, choose to spend a moment with the Lord. One encounter in His presence can set the course of your day and change your world!

Purchase your copy wherever books are sold.

Printed in the USA
CPSIA information can be obtained
at www.ICGtesting.com
LVHW011646271223
767218LV00007B/284